THE PELICAN CLASSICS

A NEW VIEW OF SOCIETY
AND REPORT TO THE COUNTY OF LANARK

ROBERT OWEN (1771–1858), reformer, philanthropist, and first socialist theorist, was born in Newtown, Montgomeryshire. In managing the New Lanark cotton mills from 1800 until his retirement in 1829, he became one of the greatest cotton manufacturers of his time. Encouraged by his partners, Jeremy Bentham and William Allen, he established a model factory village, reduced the hours of children's employment, and established for them an educational system whose principles he had outlined in *A New View of Society* (1813–14). Owen's conviction that man's character is wholly determined by his environment informed his agitation for factory reform and for the solution of the problem of pauperism by the establishment of 'Villages of Cooperation'. The cooperative and communitarian idea he amplified in the *Report to the County of Lanark* (1821), the earliest statement of 'socialist' principle to be published in Britain. The rest of Owen's life was devoted to the construction of a communitarian society – most ambitiously attempted at New Harmony in Indiana between 1824 and 1829. Back in England in the 1830s, he headed the general trade union movement and the cooperative retailing movement, and thereafter preached his own brands of secularism and socialism to an expanding working-class audience. He died in Newtown at the age of eighty-seven.

V. A. C. GATRELL was born in South Africa in 1941. He was educated at Rhodes University, and was awarded an Elsie Ballot Scholarship which took him to St John's College, Cambridge, where he read Part II of the Historical Tripos, graduating with a first in 1964. He was elected a Fellow of Gonville and Caius College, Cambridge, in 1967. His research is concerned mainly with the politics of class conflict in nineteenth-century England.

D1431969

A New View of Society

AND REPORT
TO THE COUNTY OF LANARK

———

ROBERT OWEN

EDITED WITH AN INTRODUCTION BY

V. A. C. GATRELL

PENGUIN BOOKS

Penguin Books Ltd, Harmondsworth, Middlesex, England
Penguin Books Inc., 7110 Ambassador Road, Baltimore, Maryland 21207, U.S.A.
Penguin Books Australia Ltd, Ringwood, Victoria, Australia

—

A New View of Society first published 1813/14
Report to the County of Lanark first published 1821
Published in Pelican Books 1970

—

Introduction Copyright © V. A. C. Gatrell, 1969

—

Made and printed in Great Britain by
Cox and Wyman Ltd, London, Reading and Fakenham
Set in Linotype Georgian

Contents

Introduction

POSTERITY has always thought well of Robert Owen, and his hold on the English imagination is a secure one. Properly speaking, however, he really came into his own only at the beginning of this century: the dozen or so biographies published in the forty years after his death in 1858 were certainly a respectable enough number, but in the first quarter of this century a book or a pamphlet about him was published on average almost once a year, most of of them with splendid titles ('Pioneer of Social Reforms', 'Idealist', 'Leader of Socialism' – even 'Hero of Wales') which would have flattered their subject enormously. This quite remarkable rate of publication shows little signs of subsiding even yet, though historians' attention has recently begun to turn from Owen to the movements which tried to put his ideas into practice.

Even allowing for the idiosyncrasies of his personality, so sustained an interest in Owen might seem curious. It has been rightly pointed out that he did not change history; he was one of its victims. In one sense he was a heroic failure: every one of his most ambitious experiments collapsed before his death. Nor was he a notable thinker: he usually substituted assertion for argument, and most of his assertions begged questions of which he was unaware. He was an even worse writer. His style was only occasionally lucid; consistently it lapsed into rhetoric. His books were repetitive and ill-planned – indeed hardly planned at all.

Nonetheless, the reason for the perennial fascination Owen has exerted upon later generations is no real conundrum, nor is it difficult to say who secured him the historical niche he now occupies. The titles above give a clue. Around 1900 the Fabian socialists and their circle discovered in him their forebear, germane to British soil, the proper father, in short, of English socialism. A careful chain of succession was implicit, sometimes explicit, in their writings, which traced from him a burgeoning socialist but non-Marxist tradition of which they appeared the most recent trustees. And such was the effect of their vigour that their interpretation of his significance has become something of a historical orthodoxy to which more than a few historians still subscribe.[1]

In important respects, we shall see, the orthodoxy does not do proper justice to its subject. At worst it has turned Owen into a text-book stereotype – a good if simple man, who so loathed capitalism and its works that he dedicated his life to the emancipation of the working class from its thrall. At best, it has made of Owen the prophet of political developments with which he would not have sympathized. Until his later and declining years at least, to have been saddled with the paternity of socialism would have disconcerted him utterly. But of this more later. It remains true that the Fabians had a substantial case for insisting on their interpretation: this, indeed, was not so much a caricature or a falsehood as a quite understandable simplification. Its basis will be apparent even in a brief review of Owen's career and leading ideas.

His career was probably one of the most diverse of his generation. He entered the public stage around 1812, already established as one of the greatest and wealthiest cotton

1. Among the more prominent of the Fabians who wrote about Owen were G. D. H. Cole, the Webbs, Frank Podmore, Graeme Wallas, C. E. M. Joad, Max Beer, B. L. Hutchins, Joseph Clayton. The fullest bibliography of works by and about Owen and his followers is contained in J. F. C. Harrison, *Robert Owen and the Owenites in Britain and America* (London, 1968).

spinners of his time. From 1800 until his retirement in 1829 he was partner-manager of the New Lanark Mills not far from Glasgow, and it was here that he made his name as the archetype of the benevolent entrepreneur. In educating the factory children, diminishing the hours of labour, and quite spectacularly improving conditions, his main concern, as he explained it, was to make the workpeople 'rational' – thus to bring 'harmony' to the community, to make it a place where social peace would reign, rather as he believed it had reigned in the rural community he had known as a boy in Wales. Success at New Lanark widened his horizons: for a man of Owen's temperament it was not a great step from the positions he had there taken up to work also, on similar principles, for the complete regeneration of society. To his achievement at New Lanark he was to refer again and again, in justification of his greater ambitions, for the remaining forty years of his life. It was this achievement, and the reputation which went with it, which gave him his huge self-righteousness, for a few years his access to the drawing-rooms of the great, and most notably the impetus to write his principles large upon the face of the nation and then of the world.

Henceforth his public commitments were innumerable. From 1813 onwards he ceaselessly urged his ideas first upon the government and ruling classes of Britain and then upon those of Europe and America. Publicly he agitated for a national system of education, for the reform of factory conditions, and then for the provision of state-aided unemployment relief in 'Villages of Cooperation'. These last, his greatest conception, became the vehicle for the implementation of his most deeply held beliefs. The cooperative village, and the communitarian way of life it engendered, became ends in themselves. His most ambitious experiment in this direction was at New Harmony in Indiana, and to support it, from 1824 until its collapse in 1828, he spent

£40,000, the bulk of his fortune.[2] Always his own best publicist, Owen became very widely known. When he returned to England from America, he found himself the nominal head of a series of popular movements, based in the great towns, sometimes millenarian in their expectations, almost always explicitly anti-capitalist, and all sheltering men who had more or less directly found their enlightenment in his writings. From 1829 until its disintegration in 1834 he was the figure-head of the general trade union movement. He founded a short-lived 'Equitable Labour Exchange' in London in 1832. Over the ensuing decade he supported the expanding cooperative retailing movement; he sponsored another short-lived community at Queenwood in Hampshire; he established a *Rational Quarterly* in 1853 (one of many of his periodicals); he preached secularism, rationalism, spiritualism. Then, senile, he published the unfinished autobiography which yet remains the most attractive of his works, and our major source for the first fifty years of his life. Had it been completed, its narrative would have encompassed almost every aspect of the history of British working men over nearly half a century. He died quite at peace with himself, certain that where he had failed it had been only because he was ahead of his time.

By any standard, this was a career calculated to impress posterity, and it is sufficient alone to account for Owen's stature in the history and mythology of the British labour movement. His status was doubly confirmed when his biographers came to consider the ideas which he developed and propagated in its course.

2. Owen's activities in America are most recently and succinctly discussed in Harrison, op. cit. Although New Harmony was his grandest venture, it was one of many such communities established either by Owen or by his followers. At least sixteen were formed on Owenite principles in America, and ten in Britain. (Harrison, pp. 163–92.) The fullest account of New Harmony itself is contained in A. E. Bestor, *Backwoods Utopias* (Philadelphia, 1950).

Introduction

Owen and his followers were prolific, not to say prolix, writers. The Owenite message was driven home in over 130 tracts written by Owen himself, in numerous articles in his own periodicals, and in the literature, many times as vast, of the movements owing him some debt. We do not have to concern ourselves with all this material. A lot of it is happily forgotten. Always, and especially after about 1820, Owen was much given to repetition – to what one of his disciples, G. J. Holyoake, charitably called a 'recurrency of anterior ideas'. Jeremy Bentham put it more bluntly: 'He is always the same – says the same thing over and over again.' And in later years, what Owen said was often very confused indeed. The substance of his thought was in fact contained in the several tracts he wrote between 1812 and 1820 while still the great 'social father' of New Lanark. Of these, the two most influential and comprehensive are those reprinted in this volume: the four essays of *A New View of Society*, published separately in 1813 and 1814; and the *Report* which he submitted on request to the magistrates of the County of Lanark, written in 1820 and published in the following year.[3]

It is clear why later socialists should have been attracted to these works. Admittedly there was little that was 'new' in the *New View*: most of it had been said before. And since the book was in no way concerned with economic in justice, still less was there anything in it which might have forecast Owen's future 'socialism'. The work did, however, announce one fundamental principle which, together with its corollaries, is usually assumed to have played

3. But the fullest restatement of his earlier ideas is contained in the *Book of the New Moral World*, published in seven parts between 1826 and 1844. Owen did develop some themes in his later works which are absent from the earlier (on the deficiencies of the institution of marriage, for example), but they were incidental to his more durable preoccupations.

a very important part in directing his preoccupations in later years. Man's character, he asserted, is moulded by his cultural and physical environment; hitherto his environment, and particularly his religious beliefs, have made him into a creature both irrational and selfish; once this is understood, he will be free so to engineer his environment as to make his fellow men and his children more rational, and therefore happier and less selfish, human beings. These principles, he went on to argue, should be spread abroad through a national and strictly non-denominational system of education comparable to that which he had himself instituted at New Lanark.

Had Owen written no more than this book, he would have filled a minor niche in the history of education. Although it was fashionable when it appeared, it had little more than a modest influence on educational thought in its day, and still less influence on practice. But the significance of the premises it elaborated lay in what they portended. Owen himself believed that the idea that man is formed by his environment would be 'be found to be, like the little grain of mustard seed [sic], competent to fill the mind with new and true ideas, and to overwhelm in its consequences all other ideas opposed to it'.[4] And it is true that within the half-dozen years which separated the publication of the *New View* and that of the *Report to the County of Lanark*, under particular pressures we shall discuss shortly, his perception of the effects of environment upon character widened in a most original direction. By 1820 he had come to see that religious error was not the only cause of human ills. There was another cause of more recent development: this was the machine. Its effects, he realized, were threefold. It degraded labour into a dispensable commodity; among the rich it encouraged competition for wealth; it divided men

4. Robert Owen, *The Life of Robert Owen* (London, 1920), p. 105. Henceforth referred to as *Life*.

when they should be united, and made them selfish. Thus, though deviously, the premises of the *New View* seemed to have led Owen in the *Report* to the first statement clearly in the socialist tradition. Here he asserted the moral values inherent in a life where men cooperated with each other instead of pursuing the 'principle of individual interest'. He explained how a communitarian way of life might at once solve poverty and unemployment by making the machine subordinate to men, and recreate in industrial conditions the imagined social harmony of pre-industrial Britain. And, as best he could, he challenged the structure of orthodox economic thought which justified the subsistence wage paid to labour, seemingly accepted its increasing misery, and thereby gave a doctrinal authority to an economic system devoid, he felt, of principle and moral value. Years later Owen looked back upon the *Report* as a 'full view of society in its whole extent, including every department of real life necessary for the happiness of our race. It was the first time that the outlines of a science of society were given to the world.'[5] A characteristic claim: but certainly the work was more comprehensive than its better-known predecessor, more relevant to the analysis of industrial society, and infinitely more influential upon small groups of working men who were seeking weapons with which to assail the morality and rationale of early capitalism.

So far, then, we can and must go along with the traditional interpretation of Owen's significance: there is no doubt that he really did stand at the beginning of a tradition of social criticism which later socialists were right to recognize as akin to their own. It is true that he was close to the Fabians in particular in his belief that to attain the end of community men need not exploit class conflict – that change would come about by the exercise of reason and good sense and by the growth of education. But it was after

5. *Life*, p. 328.

all natural that Owen should have agreed with Bernard
Shaw's denial of the inevitability of an opposition between
'the Virtuous Worker and the Brutal Capitalist': Owen was
actually a capitalist himself. Despite this, in his more important writings he initiated a theme upon which later socialists
were to build very effectively indeed. And not only did his
ideas, and to some extent his personal leadership, inspire the
intellectual and political history of working men for thirty
years. In the cooperative retailing movement, and more substantially in the judgements he taught men to pass upon a
competitive society, his influence survived his death. Thus
it was appropriate that the very word 'socialist' had been
first coined in the *Cooperative Magazine* in 1827 in a reference to Owenite 'Communionists or Socialists': even if he
was a utopian, even if his advocacy of cooperative colonies
did argue, as Sidney Webb said, 'a complete misconception
of the actual facts of industrial and social life', Owen was
altogether a rather attractive ancestor to look back to.

But despite such acknowledgement, the time for a re-
assessment of Owen's significance is overdue. The traditional emphases too clearly betray the purposes and the
assumptions of the historians who first established their
orthodoxy. Sooner or later every political movement must
seek in the past its own mythology, its own martyrs, its own
pantheon of heroes. To this search, in varying degrees, even
Owen's best biographers were dedicated: and in the pantheon he was duly established. Their search, moreover, was
justified by a curiously whiggish assumption about history.
The whig historians believed the British Constitution had
developed from dim origins to Victorian consummation by
a linear progression: they stressed events and institutions
which gave weight to their belief, and tended to ignore those
that did not. The Fabians too seemed to believe that the
labour 'movement' (the very word betrayed them) was pro-

gressing towards its own consummation – a stage of which was to be defined, presumably, in the Independent Labour Party or the Trade Union Congress. Preoccupied, therefore, in Shaw's words, with 'the necessity for mastering the history of our own movement and falling into our ordered place in it', they were deeply concerned with their origins. To matters which could not be so conceived they were rather indifferent. They found their origins in many disparate phenomena – in people like Owen, in social movements like Luddism, in dramas like Peterloo – phenomena whose most insistent common factor resided in the minds of men who looked back down a very particular perspective of subsequent history. What is at issue is not the structure of facts they uncovered, for they exhibited at best a scrupulous regard for historical accuracy. What is at issue is the degree of selectivity this perspective, and these purposes, imposed upon them.

Neither their perspective nor their purposes are ours any longer. The selectivity of their emphases begins to offend. In Owen's case, it caused them to ignore his relationship to a tradition rather wider than their own. They took both his 'socialism' and his contribution to the labour movement for granted. Failing with any comprehensive sympathy to examine his ideas and intentions in the context of his own age, they ignored the fact that by any critical standards his socialism was a very weak construct indeed. What they also ignored is that Owen was as much a 'conservative' as he was a 'socialist'. If he must be seen as the precursor of the socialist tradition, he has a good claim, perhaps a better, to be regarded as the father of a particular form of conservatism as well. His conservatism, in fact, was among the most insistent motifs of his career.

To ignore this is not only to distort his achievement, it is cruelly to limit it. As a socialist theorist Owen evokes scepticisms rather than respect: he is a very easy aunt sally to knock down. About the coherence of his socialism we can present a catalogue of reservations at once. His understanding of social mechanisms was primitive and his economic theory was crude and ill-formulated. He saw that the working classes were getting a rough deal out of the new productive system initiated by the machine, but he had no real conception of the strength of class antagonisms, and certainly no belief in their inevitability. Nor would he have understood people who might have argued that the existence of class conflict was a prerequisite of social change. As often as not he talked as if society were ordered still in a pyramid of estates; or alternatively as if the real dividing line was that which existed between 'productive' and 'unproductive' classes, the former encompassing both masters and men, the latter aristocracy and gentry. This was the common framework of the eighteenth century. There was no theory of class here which a socialist would recognize. He was as unsure, further, about the intimacy of the relationship between the economic and social orders, as he was muddled about the rights of property owners and the role of the capitalist. He firmly believed that the changes he advocated in the distribution of wealth would 'touch not one iota of the supposed advantages' enjoyed by the governing classes. Certainly he wanted their 'advantages' to be shared by all, but he abdicated entirely from any direct assault on the survival of their privileges. Not only had he no desire whatever to assail the established structure of status and political power: to the contrary, he declared that his measures were calculated to strengthen it. He merely thought the wealthy would surrender their advantages once they saw that it was intelligent and decent and to their moral benefit to do so. (Fanny Godwin was wiser: 'How he can expect the rich to give up their possessions, and live in a state of equality, is too romantic to be believed.') A comprehension of men's self-interest never entered his thinking, and therefore he

failed to see that change might be effected only by a form of
political coercion. Towards the Chartists his hostility was
as candid as that of the prime minister. Politically, he was
one of the naïvest men in Britain, and that is really why we
have to agree with Marx and Engels that he was the quint-
essential utopian. If Owen was a socialist, the connexion
between him and those who in an excess of piety later
thought of themselves as his descendants was tenuous. The
line of succession was so intermingled with bastard blood
that Owen might have disowned his paternity.

Now it is important that these attitudes were not mere
aberrations, peculiar to his age, in an otherwise right-
minded man. Nothing could be further from the truth.
They were fundamental to the whole structure of his
thought, and they can be understood only if we see at once
how remote he was, in thought and feeling, from his
nominal successors. In this context, two points are crucial.
First, in conscious belief, Owen was very much the
eighteenth-century rationalist, akin to nobody so much as to
Rousseau or to William Godwin. To this theme we shall
return shortly. It is more relevant to the present argument,
secondly, that in temperament, in prejudice, and in actual
policy, Owen was a tory.

This characteristic has been seldom remarked upon, for it
ill accords with the customary interpretation of his significance. But no just assessment of the man can ignore it. On
the one hand, it was the uneasy conjunction of his rationalist premises and his conservative feeling – and not, as is
usually implied, his rationalist premises alone – that constituted the real dynamism of his career. And on the other
hand, it is in his expression of certain conservative *values*
that much of the interest of Owen may be said to lie for us
today. His rationalism was unoriginal, indeed out-dated:
as 'philosopher' he was merely the last great popularizer
of Enlightenment thought. His conservativism, by con-

trast, was something new: it marked not an end but a beginning. In this sense: it prompted him to pass upon the new
industrial order judgements which foreshadowed those pro-
claimed, more strongly and certainly, by the great Victorian moralists. Of these perhaps the most representative
were Carlyle and Ruskin. Owen was as close to these men
as he was to any socialist; for his toryism embodied a particular structure of values which they would have shared,
and which Marx at the other extreme, for all his admiration
of Carlyle, would have thought merely self-indulgent.

Of course it is true that both traditions, socialist and conservative (as thus defined), had much in common. Both in-
insisted that the unchecked working of the free market destroyed the proper harmony which should exist between men.
Both at the same time proposed an interpretation of the
social good which stressed an 'organic', integrated ideal, the
value of which was defined by the interrelationship and in-
terdependence of man with man, and threatened by the
divisions between them.[6] In certain respects, of course, these
traditions were soon to differ: over their interpretation of the
character of that interrelationship (whether it should exist
between equals or otherwise), and also in their methods of
attaining it. But it is important that Owen wrote, in 1813–
20, in a period when the differences in question had not become overt. As a result, his reflections and judgements upon
industrial society, his condemnation of the competitive ethic,
and his assertion of an organic social ideal, were generalized
enough in expression to prefigure a quite new form of social
consciousness, of which later conservative and socialist
thought were two not so distantly related manifestations.
Thus Owen's judgements have passed into our cultural

6. No one has written to greater effect on this ideal and its amplification in nineteenth-century literature than Raymond Williams,
Culture and Society, 1780–1950 (London, 1963): for his definition of
the organic ideal see pp. 145–6, 256–7.

bloodstream, so to speak, through many channels, and those not exclusively socialist. It is this fact which makes Owen accessible and relevant to us today.

This fact, too, makes a comparison of Owen with Carlyle and Ruskin a meaningful one. Certainly both these men were more incisive and cultured intellects than Owen; and both were more lucid in their definition of the values to which they subscribed. But like Owen's their position turned on a denial that the good society was attainable through the premium placed by the new productive system upon self-interest and material self-advancement, and accordingly they too deplored what the *laissez-faire* doctrines of the Ricardian political economists and their successors had wrought upon the social order. In terms which Owen had anticipated, they condemned the 'degradation of the operative into a machine' (Ruskin), and accounted for it by the introduction of 'Cash Payment as the sole nexus between man and man': 'Men are grown mechanical in head and in heart, as well as in hand' (Carlyle). And when Ruskin asserted that 'Government and cooperation are in all things the Laws of Life; Anarchy and competition the Laws of Death,' Owen would have agreed emphatically: he had said much the same. (See pp. 48–9.)

The similarity can be extended a good deal further. For Owen would probably have agreed with Carlyle and Ruskin where Marx and even the Fabians would have contested them most bitterly: on precisely those issues, in fact, on which by the second half of the century conservative and socialist thought diverged – the conception of what the organic society should be, the means of attaining it, and the source from which their respective ideals derived. While socialists sought the organic society in the fulfilment of an abstract egalitarian ideal, Owen, Carlyle, and Ruskin, none of them egalitarians, sought their ideal in historical precedent. Carlyle looked back to the medieval past in his depic-

tion of the Abbot Samson and his community. Ruskin tried
to resurrect a medieval guild. Owen believed that the proper
relations between men had been attained in rural England,
and the mutual dependence and the reciprocal obligations
there exemplified he tried consciously to reconstitute within
the industrial village of New Lanark (see pp. 38–47, 50).
The good society thus defined in the microcosm of monastic,
guild, and village community, each respectively implied,
should be recreated as the ideal of the integrated society in
modern England. It followed from their allegiance to these
archetypes that none of these men was a democrat. They
sought order in a system of authority and obedience, in
which, as in the past, the relationships between men and
classes should be clearly delimited and made acceptable by
the reciprocity of obligations, rather than of economic and
material interest, which knit them together. And all three
of them, unlike the socialists, strove to attain that order not
in political or economic conflict, but, consonant with what
we may now feel to be the impossibility of their hopes, by
the power of their pens and the eloquence of their voices.

The idea of a society based on 'intrinsic' as against
economic values was hostile to economic liberalism. In its
retrospective vision, in its projection of a paternalist and
hierarchical social order, and in its refusal to countenance
conflict as a means to the totally incompatible end of social
harmony and peace, this tradition of thought was patently
hostile to militant socialism as well. To the extent that
Owen anticipated its characteristic themes he himself was
a very dubious socialist indeed. To be sure, his advocacy of
community and his attempted refutation of *laissez-faire*
economics came exclusively to dominate a working-class
audience. But this was because the ambiguities in his
thought, which were many, facilitated its quite inapt appropriation by the poor; and in any case there were some quite
straightforward historical explanations for this, as we shall

see. The fact remains that his thought derived from a
strictly paternalist, anti-democratic, and retrospective social
ideal which was ill-attuned to the part it was called upon to
play in the history of working men, and that is one reason
why 'Owenism' was an ideology which did not survive mid-
century. Much of what he first conceived, though of course
not all, was quite alien to the socialist tradition as it came to
be defined even by Owenites within his own lifetime.

Viewed from this perspective, the fact that after about
1820 circumstances obliged him and temperament inclined
him to turn to a working-class audience, was an important
but largely fortuitous twist in the career of a man who saw
himself initially as the spokesman of tory philanthropy. It
might be extreme, but it would not be unreasonable, to suggest that in so far as the epithet is meaningful Owen became
a 'socialist' by accident. He would rest more securely upon
his modest Olympus were he remembered, not as the first
socialist, but with a more just acknowledgement of his position in his own time, as the first to express an unease about
the values inherent in a capitalist society, as the first to
assert judgements and express an ideal which in their
amplification by later writers have exerted a lasting influence on the English imagination. In this sense, he was
the first critic of what is recognizably our own industrial
age.

The complexity of the influences working upon him, and
the increasing focus of his thought, will become clear when
we examine the experience and the writings of his most
fertile years, up to 1820. Particularly we must turn to the
structure of beliefs which he consciously held, and which
so far we have omitted to consider.

OWEN'S PREMISES: THE FORMATION OF CHARACTER

It has been implied in the above that many of the peculiari-

ties and much of the originality of Owen's thought derived
from the uneasy and not always reconciled conjunction of
two quite distinct ways of looking upon the world. The
underlying motif of his career was his concern to recon-
struct in an industrial and competitive age a harmonious and
integrated social order. But the professed rationale of his
career was quite different: it was to educate men into
rationality, and the *New View* was written to show how
this might be done. In this two-fold commitment lay the
source of his most radical plans. If the idea of harmony
provided him with a life-goal, the faith in rationality provided a means to attain it. Once men saw that their characters were formed by environment, they would be free to
alter their environment and build a harmonious society.
This proposition was the crux of Owen's message.

Acquired in adolescence, his faith in the eventual tri-
umph of reason never wavered throughout life. It gave him
immense confidence in the possibility of social reconstruction. It led him, sometimes unwittingly, into curious positions: he always pursued his premises to what seemed to him
their logical conclusions in practice. Hence his quite remarkable strength and single-mindedness of purpose. His simple
certainty, further, prevented him from understanding those
who were opposed to him. He believed that persuasion and
repetition would enable others to see the light he saw. Thus
he had no cause to believe in the usual panaceas proposed
in his time for the solution of human ills – parliamentary
reform, revolution, class conflict. He was certain that the
solvent of injustice was to be the power of reason. Therein,
we have suggested, lay the essence of his utopianism. And
thus, in turn, his rationalism came full circle to confirm his
political conservatism.

How he acquired his convictions is obscure: Owen never
once acknowledged another man's influence. (His occasional
association with the thinkers of the Scottish Enlightenment

does not help, because most of his ideas were set long before he went to Scotland.)

Born in 1771 in Newtown, Montgomeryshire, the son of a saddler and ironmonger, he had only an elementary education at the local day school before becoming a draper's assistant in Stamford and London. We know little of his reading in these years. Nonetheless, if his own account is to be trusted, even at the age of ten he had become convinced that there was something wrong with religions because of the contradictions between them. Then, one day in the shop at Stamford, it dawned on him that the contradictions 'emanated ... from the same false imaginations of our early ancestors'. Man, he decided, was responsible for his character neither to God nor to his fellows, for he was, despite himself, entirely 'the child of Nature and Society; ... Nature gave the qualities, and Society directed them.' In 1788, at the age of seventeen, therefore, he went to seek his fortune in Manchester,

relieved from religious prejudices and their obstructive influences to the attainment of common sense, my mind ... simple in its new arrangement of ideas. ... Knowing that they did not make themselves, or the circumstances or conditions in which they were involved, and that these conditions combined necessarily forced them to be that which they became, – I was obliged to consider my fellow-men as beings made by circumstances before and after their birth, not under their own control ... and therefore to have illimitable charity for their feelings, thoughts, and actions. ... My mind, in consequence, gradually became calm and serene, and anger and ill-will died within me.[7]

It is not too much to say that Owen adhered to the definition thus attained in youth until the day of his death. He did so because in Manchester he found his beliefs confirmed by experience. In Manchester too, forced to defend

7. *Life*, pp. 22, 41–2. See also text, p. 140.

them, he retreated into the intractable dogmatism which characterized his whole career.

Had he been at all sensitive to the fact, he would have found the town a fitting place in which to ponder these themes. Few other places could more starkly have given his ideas substance by illustrating the effects of technological change on environment and of environment on the character of men and the community. Within his lifetime, steam power had brought the cotton mills into Manchester and transformed it. In 1773 its population had been about 22,000; some fifteen years later it had risen to nearly 49,000; by the time Owen left in 1800 it was over 70,000. With this increase nearly every feature of that grim environment whose memory has passed into our folklore had asserted itself; bad housing and bad factory conditions, labour exploitation, cyclical unemployment, poverty. Yet after all their impact on Owen does not appear to have been very profound. It is true that he helped draw up the report of the Board of Health set up in Manchester in 1796, urging parliament to legislate for the 'wise, humane, and equal government' of all factories employing children: but no further than this did he anticipate his later campaigns. He was too busy establishing his reputation, and it was his success in this respect rather than the phenomenon of Manchester which confirmed him in his philosophy.

After an abortive partnership in machine-making and a period as an independent spinner, he was appointed in 1791, at the age of twenty, to manage a mill owned by one of the largest fine-spinners in the country. Quite inexperienced, and with a work force of 500 in his charge, he made the firm's reputation as the spinners of the finest yarn in Britain. Some four years later he became the managing partner of another very large concern, the Chorlton Twist Company. It was this position which opened the way to what was to become his little kingdom at New Lanark. In 1799

the company bought the New Lanark Mills from David
Dale; Owen took over their management in the next
year, and crowned his giddy rise by marrying Dale's
daughter.

Owen had no doubt that he owed his success to his unique
understanding of men. His knowledge of human nature,
he wrote of his first position,

produced such effects over the workpeople in the factory in the
first six months of my management, that I had the most complete influence over them, and their order and discipline exceeded
that of any other in or near Manchester; and for regularity and
sobriety they were an example which none could then imitate.

More generally he felt his understanding 'gave me for a
long period an unconscious advantage over others ... I had
the good will of all.'[8]
We can detect something too insistent in these years
in Owen's declarations of his own popularity and of the
rightness of his principles. It was a touch of hysteria in
his self-justifications which became more overt as he grew
older. His beliefs were not merely strong: they tended to the
obsessive. In a character as complex but as little self-critical
as Owen's, this curious twist to his mind is difficult to explain.
We can only guess that it was the consequence of profound
and lasting intellectual insecurity. He had to come to terms
with it in Manchester for the first time, and the experience
was in some form to stay with him throughout his life. In
one context this insecurity defined itself fairly clearly. In
his early twenties, known only as a factory manager, feeling
himself even in that fluid society something of a parvenu, he
became a member of the Manchester Literary and Philosophical Society. The Society encompassed the élite of the
town, doctors and lawyers, Unitarians and Quakers, religious
and political dissenters all of them, drawn from families

8. *Life*, p. 42.

long established in Lancashire and from a milieu whose manners had been acquired in great schools or famous academies. In their company Owen never forgot his origins, nor that he was all but self-taught:

> I was yet but an ill-educated awkward youth, strongly sensitive to my defects of education, speaking ungrammatically, a kind of Welsh English. . . . I felt the possession of ideas superior to my power of expressing them, and this always embarrassed me with strangers, and especially when in the company of those who had been systematically well educated, according to existing notions of education.[9]

It was perhaps to assert himself that quite deliberately he set out to become a 'philosopher'.

We do not know how far he succeeded. He debated religion with the poet Coleridge, and although the latter's references must have been almost meaningless to him, he claimed to have won.[10] He tells us that he came to be called 'the reasoning machine' – 'because they said I made man a mere reasoning machine, made to be so by nature and society': he does not tell us with what irony the epithet might have been applied. He read four papers to the Society, two of which seem to have anticipated his later preoccupations; but they were not thought worthy of publication. It is only in the light of his later work, in the light too of his later relationships with his intellectual betters, that we can suggest what really happened. Challenged, he closed his mind in his twenties, and he saw no reason to open it again

9. *Life*, p. 43.

10. Coleridge was preoccupied in 1794 with his Pantisocracy, a community of the virtuous (initially comprising himself and a less enthusiastic Southey) in which 'we should remove the *selfish* principle from ourselves . . . by an abolition of property'. If he mentioned the plan to Owen, Owen does not recall it in his account of their debate. If he did, it is conceivable that the idea, like many others obscurely embedded in Owen's mind, had some influence on him a dozen years later.

in maturity. Nothing else can account for his lasting hostility to the conventionally educated:

The learned ... have been taught to suppose that the book of knowledge has been exclusively opened to them [he told the assembled population of New Lanark in 1816]. ... They are totally ignorant of human nature. They are full of theories, and have not the most distant conception of what may or may not be accomplished in practice. It is true their minds have been well stored with language, which they can readily use to puzzle and confound the unlettered and inexperienced. ... [But] with a few exceptions, their profound investigations have been about words only.[11]

His son recalled that 'he usually glanced books over without mastering them, often dismissing them with some curt remark as that "the radical errors shared by all men made books of little value." ' This is all too credible.

Owen's excessive anti-intellectualism, and the insecurity it was meant to conceal, helped dictate the nature of his following throughout his life. If the urban masses were one day to take his arguments seriously, trained minds could not. They were offended both by his inconsistencies and by his profound ignorance of the new currents of thought which were then asserting themselves in the romantic movement, in early evolutionary theory, in men's growing apprehension of the workings of heredity on the human character. 'Never having read a metaphysical book, nor held a metaphysical conversation, nor ever having heard of the disputes respecting free will and necessity, he had no clear conception of his subject, and his views were obscure': thus Francis Place. For Jeremy Bentham (who according to Owen 'spent a long life in an endeavour to amend laws, all based on a fundamental error, without discovering this

11. *Address to the Inhabitants of New Lanark* ... (1816); reprinted in *A New View of Society and Other Writings*, ed. G. D. H. Cole, (London, 1927), p. 107.

error', and who 'had little knowledge of the world, except through books') – for Bentham, 'Robert Owen begins in vapour and ends in smoke. He is a great braggadocio. His mind is a maze of confusion, and he avoids coming to particulars.' For Hazlitt, he was the 'man of one idea', whose 'puff will not take with us: we are old birds, not to be caught with chaff'. None of these was unsympathetic to Owen. Place helped him revise the fourth essay of the *New View*. Bentham (at first tolerant of his aberrations: 'he is not mad *simpliciter,* but only *secundum quid*') joined the New Lanark partnership in 1813 to free him of the control of profit-minded partners who threatened to impede his educational experiments. But between them and Owen there could be little real communication. Owen was a lonely man who belonged to no defined intellectual or indeed social circle. His solitude and his insecurity found expression henceforth in his reiterated assertions of the truth which he believed had been revealed to him alone. In old age it was expressed in his communion with departed spirits. From the late 1820s, it led to an increasing dependence on and evocation of a mass working-class audience. Before them alone he could believe himself to be the harbinger of the millennium. The rest of the world stayed sceptical.[12]

In the light of Owen's intellectual inadequacies, it would be unrealistic to expect the *New View* to be other than an incoherent reformulation of eighteenth-century rationalist doctrine. Indeed if sense is to be made of its argument we have to be quite ruthless in imposing a logical sequence through its digressions and repetitions. More than this, the work had little to add to what over a century had become a

12. 'Circumstances train men into character; a truth which the world recognized for about two thousand years, and only began to doubt when it was propounded as a novelty by Robert Owen.' W. Cooke Taylor, *Notes of a Tour ... of Lancashire* (1842), p. 123.

set of received platitudes about the origin of ideas. The original theory had been Locke's: ideas are not innate but are conceived out of the mind's reflection upon its own sensory experience of the external environment. By 1813 this thesis had been worked over a hundred times. Owen trod a very well-worn path indeed. It was also inherently a dangerous path: the doctrine Owen was playing with was potentially subversive of the social and political hierarchy which at one level of consciousness he wished to preserve. If the mind at birth were a *tabula rasa*, all men at birth were to that extent equal: thus Rousseau and Helvetius. Since, secondly, 'the characters of men originate in their external circumstances', it followed that if those circumstances were good, the sensations the mind received and therefore its thoughts and motives would be good as well: reform the external environment, then, and you reform man: thus, among many others, William Godwin. From these propositions derived the egalitarian and the revolutionary motifs, not only of Enlightenment, but in some measure of all radical thought. For the belief that man is moulded by his environment, and can himself engineer his environment to the moral and material advantage of his descendants, strengthens the belief in the possibility of progress; it also denies the inevitability of man's subjection to economic or political laws written in nature or by God.

Owen trod part of this way: he made frequent though largely rhetorical gestures towards egalitarianism. But in the event the long-term influence of the work was wholly conservative. All the working man would have got from the *New View*[13] would have been a simple, if an impressive, faith in the power of reason. 'Expose [error] but for an instant to the clear light of intellectual day,' Owen wrote; 'and, as

13. In its later editions and as its theme was amplified in later Owenite literature: when first published, the work would have had no working-class readership.

though conscious of its own deformity, it will instantaneously vanish, never to reappear.' (See p. 166). Perhaps it was the later reiterations of this belief which helps to explain that peculiar non-militancy of Owenism in the 1830s which constituted the despair of all those who sought change in a direct confrontation with the social order. It could lead only, as we shall see later, to a doctrine of political passivity. The book's immediate and positive importance, then, lay first in its specific recommendation of educational reform, and secondly, more intimately, in the impetus and direction it gave Owen's subsequent concern with the possibility and advisability of social reconstruction.

He sets out with the thesis that man is born with a three-fold inheritance: a self-interested desire to obtain happiness ('the primary cause of all his actions'); natural inclinations born of the appetites and instincts; and 'faculties, which, in their growth, receive, convey, compare, and become conscious of receiving and comparing ideas'. These inclinations and faculties vary from person to person: here, if he is at all conscious of them, Owen bypasses the full egalitarian implications of his theory. But it is with what *happens* to the faculties in the course of life that he is most concerned.

Through them, man acquires ideas which constitute knowledge, or mind. These ideas are 'derived from the objects around him, and chiefly from the example and instruction of his immediate predecessors'. They differ in extent and truth, therefore, according not only to the quality of the individual's innate faculties, but also to the kind and degree of knowledge possessed by the community. If that knowledge is 'true', man has a greater chance of being happy; if wrong, 'his misery will be in proportion to the extent of those erroneous opinions'. Therefore it is necessary to teach men to distinguish truth from error by developing the faculty of reason, and by protecting it from the injury it receives from notions not derived from 'reality'.[14]

How to do this? If human character is moulded by the external environment, and particularly by the ideas shared by society, and if (as Owen took for granted) the end of government is to secure the greatest happiness of the greatest number, it follows that government must ensure that the principles by which society conducts its business are free from error. This conclusion is summarized in general terms as follows:

Any character, from the best to the worst, from the most ignorant to the most enlightened, may be given to any community, even to the world at large, by applying certain means; which are to a great extent at the command and under the control, or easily made so, of those who possess the government of nations.[15]

One specific conclusion follows. What government must immediately assail, he argues, is the restriction on truth exerted by religion. In asserting that men form their own individual characters and are responsible for them to God and their fellow-men, religion is responsible for all the inconsistencies and miseries in the world. This is particularly so since it is not in the interests of the churches to educate people into full rationality, lest the power of reason 'effectually and rapidly undermine the errors not only of their own, but of every other ecclesiastical establishment'. Therefore it follows that government must undermine the churches by reforming the educational system.[16] Education should not, as at present, be denominational, nor, like the monitorial systems of Bell and Lancaster,[17] should it reflect a

14. Text, pp. 152–5.

15. Title-page of first edition. The wording was slightly altered in the text (pp. 99, 101).

16. Text, pp. 183–4.

17. Andrew Bell (1753–1832) and Joseph Lancaster (1778–1838) independently developed systems of mutual education by scholars

preoccupation with the manner of teaching rather than its substance: 'Memory, in this mockery of learning, is all that is required.' Rather, it should be imparted through 'a national plan for the formation of character', which 'should *include* all the modern improvements of education, without regard to the system of any one individual; and should not *exclude* the child of any one subject in the empire.'[18]

In his development of this theme, Owen was at his most convincing. Perhaps he was also at his most original. It is true that the educational principles he outlined were virtually identical to those expounded in Rousseau's *Émile* (1762) and put into practice by Rousseau's Swiss disciple Pestalozzi. It is true too that Rousseau's educational theories were well known in polite English society: it was not unfashionable for cultivated gentlemen of advanced views to bring up their children in accordance with them.[19] Since, however, there is no evidence that Owen had read Rousseau, and since certainly he had not heard of Pestalozzi until he met him on his continental tour of 1818, it is at least conceivable that he came to similar conclusions simply because his premises were the same. If so it was a considerable achievement, because what Owen said was in very marked contrast to the standard practice of English education.

Particularly unorthodox was his conception of the nature and the potential of childhood. It was directly opposed to that belief in the child's original sin by which even long into

---

which were both cheap and within limits effective in the teaching of large numbers. Under the aegis of the established and nonconformist churches respectively their methods came to dominate popular education in the first decades of the nineteenth century. For Owen's strictures on their methods, see text, pp. 177–9.

18. Text, pp. 179, 129.

19. Ironically the father of Thomas Malthus, whose rationality should thereby have been assured, was one of them. But see below for the incompatibility of Owenism and Malthusianism.

the century the grosser maltreatments of the pupil were commonly justified.

Not one of [the] causes of character is at the command, or in any manner under the control, of infants, who (whatever absurdity we may have been taught to the contrary) cannot possibly be accountable for the sentiments and manners which may be given to them. ... Children are, without exception, passive and wonderfully contrived compounds; which, by an accurate previous and subsequent attention, *founded on a correct knowledge of the subject*, may be formed collectively to have any human character ... [and] be ultimately moulded into the very image of rational wishes and desires.

Unlike the adult's, the child's mind is an open book upon which new ideas could be inscribed at will. Its character would only be distorted if learning were encouraged by punishment or by the incentives of competition: he must merely be taught with the utmost kindness and patience. To remove him from the 'erroneous treatment of the yet untrained and untaught parents', he should be admitted to school as soon as he could walk. He was to learn through the exercise of his senses rather than of his intellect, by dancing, play, and practical experiment. Book-learning should be postponed until the age of ten. Nonetheless, constant appeals must be made to his reason, the end of education being not the accumulation of fact, but an appreciation of the 'clear and inseparable connexion which exists between the interest and happiness of each individual and the interest and happiness of every other individual'.[20] From this understanding will stem all that is moral and generous in human nature, for the child

will have acquired reasons sufficient to exhibit to him forcibly the irrationality of being angry with an individual for possessing qualities which, as a passive being during the formation of

20. Text, pp. 109–10, 125–6, 133–7, 143–5.

those qualities, he had not the means of preventing. . . . Thus
shortly, *directly* and *certainly* may mankind be taught the
essence, and to attain the *ultimate object*, of all former *moral*
and *religious* instruction.[21]

As an educational tract the *New View* had a modest
influence in its day.[22] But was it anything more? In no
apparent sense was it the work of a political radical, let alone
a future socialist. In intention and in content, it was one of
the most conservative documents of its time. The essays
were dedicated, *inter alia*, to William Wilberforce and the
Prince Regent. Their message was more generally addressed
to 'those who have influence in society' and to 'those who
possess the government of nations'. Its urgency was justified by the fear that if certain reforms were longer delayed,
'general disorder must ensue'.[23] And in purporting to attack
the 'false notions' which caused not only 'superstition,
biogotry, hypocrisy, hatred, revenge, wars, and all their evil
consequences', but also 'all the evil and misery, except those
of accidents, disease, and death, with which man has been
and is afflicted',[24] the work raised, but left unanswered, two
very important questions.

First, Owen in 1814 was blind to the realities of economic

21. Text, pp. 110–11. Compare Rousseau: 'The first impulses of
nature are always right: there is no original sin in the human heart:
the how and why of the entrance of every vice can be traced.' Education therefore should be directed to 'preserving the heart from vice
and the spirit of error' by beginning very early in life. Corporal
punishment should be eschewed since it was falsely justified by the
belief in original sin. And because 'man's first reason is a reason of
sense-experience' (Pestalozzi), learning should initially be encouraged
by the exercise of the senses, in experimentation, handicrafts, dancing,
and play. Book-learning should begin only at the age of twelve.
22. Schools on Owenite principles were established in Westminster
by Owen's friend Brougham, in Spitalfields by the Society of Friends;
an Infant School Society was founded in 1822.
23. Text, pp. 102, 31, 100.
24. Text, pp. 149, 154.

and social injustice. He found his scapegoat for the world's ills, accordingly, in religion.

> The church and its doctrines . . . involve considerations of the highest interest and importance; inasmuch as a knowledge of truth on the subject of religion would permanently establish the happiness of man; for it is the inconsistencies alone, proceeding from the want of this knowledge, which have created, and still create, a great proportion of the miseries which exist in the world.[25]

The condemnation was unconvincing. It was left as a mere assertion unsubstantiated by either sustained argument or historical illustration. It is a comment on its effect that the work met with the approval of the Archbishop of Canterbury. This, in 1813–14, was the limit of Owen's critique of his age.

The weakness was compounded, secondly, in Owen's failure to examine his assumptions about government. Quite uncritically, he had thus repeated Bentham's best known premise:

> The end of government is to make the governed and the governors happy. That government then is the best, which in practice produces the greatest happiness to the greatest number; including those who govern and those who obey.[26]

Having done so, he omitted to consider whether government was at all capable of attaining that end, and this despite the fact that he was writing in a period of recent and widespread political and social discontent – despite the fact, also, that he had a precedent for such an analysis in William Godwin's *Enquiry Concerning Political Justice*.

Of Godwin's work he could scarcely have been ignorant because it was published in 1793 and it must frequently have been discussed at the meetings of the Manchester Literary

25. Text, pp. 148–9. See also pp. 168, 182–4.
26. Text, p. 163.

and Philosophical Society. The contrast between the *Political Justice* and the *New View* is instructive. Both started from the premise that man's character could be regenerated only through the reform of the external environment. But Godwin was quite clear that that reform should begin with an attack on government, an institution born of past violence and injustice, and therefore always defensive of those institutions opposed to justice, including inequality of wealth and property. Together with all agencies of law and authority, therefore, government should be abolished entirely and be replaced by a collectivity of free and independent persons fulfilling their lives in the pursuit of reasons. Owen avoided the issue altogether:

The British constitution, in its present outline, is admirably adapted to effect these changes, without the evils which always accompany a coerced or ill-prepared change.[27]

The *New View*, then, might seem to have been something of a false start in the career of a man who was so intimately to affect the thought of the poor and the discontented: to their position it had no direct relevance at all. But two points are clear. First, it did express that compassion for their plight which informed his best writing in later years:

Shall the well-being of millions of the poor, half-naked, half-famished, untaught and untrained, hourly increasing to a most alarming extent in these islands, not call forth *one* petition, *one* delegate, or *one* rational effective legislative measure?[28]

More important, we can detect in the *New View* a portent of what was soon to emerge as the dominant theme of his thought: a still only half-defined sense that society was disintegrating into a situation of conflict, and an antithetical conviction that it should be integrated and 'organic': that the individual's interest, in short, should be related to that

27. Text, p. 168. See also below, p. 46.
28. Text, p. 108.

of the public: that 'the happiness of self ... can only be attained by conduct that must promote the happiness of the community.'[29]

Over the half-dozen years after the publication of the *New View*, Owen's perception of the proper source of the community's happiness broadened. He turned increasingly to the language of 'harmony', 'cooperation', 'community', 'union'. In doing so he came to give a new definition to the effect of environment upon character. Less and less did he argue that all the world's miseries stemmed from the domination of religion over men's understanding of the formation of their own character. More and more he argued that they stemmed from 'false notions' about the economic relationship of man to man, class to class. The firm conjunction of his environmentalist premises and his organic ideal was achieved around 1817. Reform, he argued then, could not be effected

by individualizing man in his proceedings, either in a cottage or in a palace; for while his character shall be so formed, and while the circumstances around him shall be, as they then must be, in unison with that character, he cannot but be an enemy to all men, and all men must be in enmity and opposed to him. . . . Individualized man, and all that is truly valuable in Christianity, are so separated as to be utterly incapable of union through all eternity.[30]

By the time he wrote the *Report to the County of Lanark* the definition was complete. 'The principle of individual interest' was 'opposed ... perpetually to the public good'.

It can never be that the universal division of men's pursuits can create any cordial union of interests among mankind. It can never be that a notion which necessarily separates, in a greater

29. Text, p. 103. See also pp. 161, 145, etc.

30. *Address Delivered at the City of London Tavern* (21 August 1817), reprinted in *The Life of Robert Owen, Supplementary Appendix* Vol. 1A (London, 1858), p. 112. Henceforth referred to as Owen: *Appendix*.

or less degree, every human being from his fellows, can ever be productive of practical benefit to society.[31]

To explain this radical change of emphasis we have to turn back to biography, and define the character of his very particular form of conservatism, in particular as it was exemplified at New Lanark.

NEW LANARK AND THE IDEA OF HARMONY

TODAY it is a seeming paradox that Owen, the first to declare himself opposed to the 'principle of individual interest', was a manufacturer. Similarly ambiguous was his achievement at New Lanark. In one sense it was a magnificent exercise in labour management, and under certain circumstances he felt no delicacy in confessing as much. In a preface to the third essay of the *New View* he assured the master manufacturers of Britain that:

> From the commencement of my management I viewed the population, with the mechanism and every other part of the establishment, as a system composed of many parts, and which it was my duty and interest so to combine, as that every hand, as well as every spring, lever, and wheel, should effectually co-operate to produce the greatest pecuniary gain to the proprietors.

He went on to recommend his principles to them as follows:

31. Text, pp. 231, 264. A note on Owen's terminology. *Individualized man* and *the principle of individual interest* are clear precursors of de Tocqueville's *individualism*, first used by him in English in 1835. More directly, the English language and English social thought owe to Owen the following: *cooperation* and *cooperative* (viz., as used in his sense); *socialist* and *communionist* (=*communist*) (as above, p. 14); *social system* (*Report to the County of Lanark*, p. 231 below); possibly also the novel juxtaposition of *science of society* (as above, p. 13).

I have thought it legitimate to use *environment* for Owen's *surrounding circumstances*, though the word is strictly an anachronism: to denote what Owen meant it was first used by Carlyle in 1827.

If, then, due care as to the state of your inanimate machines can produce ... beneficial results, what may not be expected if you devote equal attention to your vital machines, which are far more wonderfully constructed? ... From experience which cannot deceive me, I venture to assure you, that your time and money so applied, if directed by a true knowledge of the subject, would return you not five, ten, or fifteen per cent for your capital so expended, but often fifty and in many cases a hundred per cent.[32]

We need have no doubt that this was a deliberate, perhaps ironic, argument *ad homines*: Owen knew well how to touch the interest of his fellow-manufacturers. These quotations represent everything to which within a very few years he was most bitterly hostile. It remains true, however, that they come uncomfortably close to expressing the apparent substance of his achievement. At New Lanark he managed the largest spinning establishment in Britain. It was inevitable that in confronting there the same problems as those which faced the great manufacturers who were his southern counterparts – the Gregs, for example, at Quarry Bank, the Strutts at Belper – he should in many instances project the same solutions as they did, and be as necessarily preoccupied with production and profit. His workforce at the beginning of his management was about 1,800 strong, collected by Dale 'from anywhere and anyhow'. They were given to drunkenness, improvidence, and prolific conception out of wedlock. They were hostile to a new and non-Scottish employer with new-fangled methods brought from Manchester. Accordingly, like the Gregs and like the Strutts under similar circumstances, Owen had to enforce a humane discipline in the mills, regulate the sale of alcohol, curb the profits of the village store, insist on cleanliness in the houses and mills and good order in the streets, teach thrift and domestic economy to the wives. The disciplinary motif

32. Text, pp. 94, 95–6.

of this work was candid, and the end attained was in all cases comparable, a mechanical routine of life geared to production. It was also profitable. The value of the mills increased between 1799 and 1813 from £60,000 to £114,000; profits of £160,000 were produced in the period 1809 to 1813, of £15,000 in 1820–21 alone.[33]

But even after he had left New Lanark, Owen saw no inconsistency between this régime and his attack on individualism. For he was sure he was not seeking his own self-interest: it was only in a community over which he had absolute control that he could initiate what he firmly believed to be 'the most important experiment for the happiness of the human race that had yet been instituted at any time in any part of the world'. Whatever we may think of his naïvety, it remains true that there was a resonance to his management which was quite alien to that of his fellow manufacturers, and if it was not always apparent in practice, it certainly was in the statement of his intentions. His colleagues might justify their rule (benevolent or otherwise) in terms of the dictates of the productive system, in the terms indeed in which Owen had addressed them in the *New View*. They believed either that labour had to be looked after because it was a valuable asset, or else that it had to be exploited because that way lay profit and the nation's prosperity. In both cases labour was conceived as a commodity, defined as such by its role in the creation of wealth. For Owen, by contrast, labour was never merely a commodity. And he looked beyond the productive system to justify his rule by a wider purpose: he was trying, at New Lanark, to create not only a profitable community, but also one which was integrated and rigidly hierarchical, one, moreover,

33. Harrison, op. cit., p. 155, footnote. For a general account of the problems Owen faced at New Lanark, and his solutions, see the Second Essay of the *New View*, especially pp. 114–27. Also *Life*, pp. 78–85, 117–27, 186–204.

which would be the model of the good society at large. Where all had been 'distrust, disorder, and disunion . . . he wished to introduce confidence, regularity, and harmony'.[34]

Certainly he rarely expressed his aims quite as directly as this. When he said that he intended not to be 'a mere manager of cotton mills . . . [but] to change the conditions of the people', he meant to do so, predictably, by ascertaining 'whether by replacing evil conditions by good, man might not be relieved from evil, and transformed into an intelligent, rational, and good being'. But it is equally clear in other contexts that his interest in his workpeople was deeply personal, and it implied the acceptance of an obligation towards them. Thus when he reminded them of his predecessor, David Dale, that 'his wishes and intentions towards you all were those of a father towards his children. . . . His memory must be deeply engraven upon your hearts,'[35] this was more than manufacturer's cant. Dale's mantle Owen deliberately assumed himself, with a seriousness, and on certain assumptions about the proper moral bond between father and children, and by extension between master and men, which the Strutts and the Greggs would not have shared. Accordingly, too, he expected from his hands a return in kind: sober living, obedience, deference, a reciprocal acknowledgement on their part of their rightful place within the community. Even his educational experiments were designed not only to enlighten them, but to enlighten them in ways which would conduce to this reciprocity of feeling. From the earliest years children were to be made 'rational'. One of the things this meant was that they were to be shown the absurdity of passion and self-indulgence and conflict: conflict, implicitly, not only between man and man, but also between rich and poor, master and employees. As they

34. Text, p. 120.

35. *Life*, pp. 78, 82, 83; *Address to the Inhabitants of New Lanark* (1816), Cole (ed.), op. cit., p. 96.

came to recognize their true interests – as, in the words of the *New View*, their insight into the formation of human character removed any 'conceivable foundation for private displeasure or public enmity' – social resentment and antagonism would wither away completely. They were to be taught a doctrine not only of rationality but also of social acquiescence. At New Lanark, the integrated society was to be instituted in microcosm, and education was called to its service. More than this, the part, eventually, would become the model for the whole: rational education, 'properly understood', would be the cement of a harmonious society throughout the nation as well.

It was because many people recognized this wider purpose in what Owen was doing that New Lanark, rather than Belper or Quarry Bank, became one of the great showplaces of the decade. Here, particularly through the agency of Owen's Institution for the Formation of Character, a 'system of happiness' was being established which very clearly took the privileged into account.

It will . . . be the essence of wisdom in the privileged classes to cooperate sincerely and cordially with those who desire not to touch one iota of the supposed advantages which they *now* possess; and whose first and last wish is to increase the particular happiness of those classes as well as the general happiness of society. A very little reflection on the part of the privileged will insure this line of conduct; whence, without domestic revolution – without war or bloodshed – nay, without prematurely disturbing any thing which exists, the world will be prepared to receive principles which are alone calculated to build up a system of happiness.[36]

The message was driven home not only in the *New View*. One day he showed the Dukes of York and Sussex an ascending series of cubes representing the relative numerical

36. Text, p. 106.

strengths of the social orders. The smallest cube, representing the Royal Family and the Peerage,

appeared so strikingly insignificant, compared with all below, and especially when compared with the cubes representing the working and pauper classes, that the Duke of Sussex impulsively pushed the elbow of his royal brother, saying – 'Edward, do you see that?' And the whole party for the moment seemed confused.[37]

The results of this kind of unsubtle propaganda were always gratifying.

For a dozen years, accordingly, some 2,000 visitors went to New Lanark annually, all very eminent people, the Tsar of Russia among them. They were all duly impressed by the way in which the educational principles of the *New View* had been there implemented. Most of them, and always those who had met the force of one of Owen's parables, also took his wider point. Not only were the population becoming rational, they were also becoming productive, diligent, and peaceful. Illegitimacy had dropped, drunkenness and theft were all but banished, 'sprees' were a thing of the past. Most impressive was their relationship with Owen. He had become something of a father, perhaps, too, something of an industrialist squire, even though he wore manufacturer's clothing. In this achievement, of which there are numerous testimonies other than Owen's, New Lanark defined his close relationship with conservative feeling. What the village portended was clear: that the relationships, close, deferential, and interdependent, which were thought peculiar to pastoral Britain, were capable of reconstitution within industrial society. They could, in short, be reconciled with the machine and not least with the growing numbers of the poor. In this, every conservative instinct of the age could find hope for the survival of its values.

Owen's deep-seated assumptions about the proper cement

37. *Life*, p. 209.

of society, to which New Lanark attested, help to explain much that is otherwise puzzling in a man who has been posthumously assigned a role in history for which he was ill-fitted. It was as a result of no inconsistency on his part that after the publication of the *New View* he received the flattery and hospitality of the highest tories in the land. That book alone had understandably proved a passport to their drawing-rooms. Liverpool, the Prime Minister, had introduced him to his wife, whom Owen found both 'amiable and intelligent', and who duly expressed the hope that on the basis of his views 'much would be now done to ameliorate the condition of the working classes, and to raise their characters'. Sidmouth, the Home Secretary, endeared himself to Owen by sending 200 copies of the *New View* to the governments and universities of Europe and America. (One reached Napoleon on Elba.) Owen was befriended by the bishops of England and Ireland, and the 'most liberal' Sutton of Canterbury solicited a private reading at Lambeth of the third and fourth essays while they were still in manuscript. This mutual flirtation continued until 1817. In every action until then he could legitimately have claimed that he received the patronage of the most eminent and the most conservative statesmen and philanthropists in England.

This, moreover, is a relationship which does not wholly have to be explained in terms either of the *New View* or New Lanark. Owen acquired a quite genuine sympathy with the rural squirearchy and aristocracy in whom he found the exemplars of those values to which he himself instinctively subscribed. Even towards the end of his life he could still declare his allegiance to 'the old Conservative system of governing with more ignorance, but with greatly more humanity to the poor, their dependants, and the working classes'. 'The old aristocracy of birth,' he went on, 'as I recollect them in my early days, were in many respects superior to the money-making and money-seeking aristocracy of modern times.' He never quite lost his faith in them, nor in the political structure they upheld. More than this, the obverse of this attitude was fundamental to his assault on economic liberalism. It followed that the whigs and the political economists were creatures to whom his own philanthropic and paternalist instincts were alien. The whigs, he announced in 1817, were 'mere theorists', 'involved in a maze of false intelligence', misguided by the 'pushing, busy, and ever-active political economists' and their 'system of universal repulsion'. Implied in these judgements, further, was a characteristic position shared with his tory patrons towards contemporary social problems. In the dominant preoccupations of his public life in the next years, educational, factory, and poor law reform, not only did he advocate the implementation of the principles whose efficacy he had established at New Lanark, but he did so always in terms which were closely attuned to those of tory philanthropy. Thus it had been quite proper for him to address the original dedication of the *New View* to William Wilberforce, convinced as he was even then, after 'contemplating the public characters of the day [that] no one among them appears to have more nearly adopted in practice the principles which this Essay develops than yourself.'[38]

Finally, we may see now why Owen did not believe in democracy. Like his tory patrons he desired to restore harmony to society, and this could never be achieved by unleashing the untaught mob. That democracy would initiate conflict, the clamour for democracy was already proving. Demands for parliamentary reform, moreover, challenged the right and capacity of the old hierarchy to govern, but only the old hierarchy would govern on the principles to which he subscribed. Hence his hostility to and incomprehension of every radical movement which exploited class division to attain a political end. He could contemplate the

38. *Life*, pp. 179–80; Owen: *Appendix*, p. 107; text, p. 87.

London radicals who at his public meetings in 1817 raised their objections to his plans 'with precisely the same feelings with which I should have noticed so many individuals in a very ill-managed lunatic asylum'. In 1834 as its nominal leader he urged the Grand National Consolidated Trades Union 'to take up its true and constitutional position at once in society, and announce itself openly as the conservator of peace'. In the 1840s he condemned Chartism as leading to 'universal disunion . . . a pandemonium state of society'. He announced his justification for these views in 1817, and he adhered to it until his death:

> Should greater liberty be now given than the British Constitu-
> tion can with safety afford to all its subjects, the lives and
> properties of the well-disposed, and the safety of the State, would
> be put to imminent hazard; and until better training, more use-
> ful knowledge, and productive constant employment shall be
> given to the poor and working classes, no really intelligent per-
> son could venture to give more freedom to such a population as
> ours has gradually become, than the British Constitution in its
> ordinary state now admits.[39]

This might have been the pronouncement of the prime minister.

It is difficult in the light of these attitudes and associations to see Owen quite simply as a socialist – least of all as 'the first British socialist who did not turn to the past for inspira-tion'. It is also pointless to deplore, though it is necessary to point out, his 'fatal evasion' of the realities of political power in his age, or his assertion of 'a political doctrine which ran counter to the experience of those for whom his social message had real meaning'.[40] His social message, as it was

39. *Address Delivered at the City of London Tavern* (21 August 1817), Owen: *Appendix*, p. 109. For another of many similar justifi-cations see text, p. 128, and above, p. 36.

40. M. Beer, *A History of British Socialism* (London, 1919), Vol. 1, p. 162; E. P. Thompson, *The Making of the English Working Class*

first conceived, was indissolubly linked with his political doctrine. Conservative and retrospective values were the basis of the judgements he passed on contemporary society, and even of the communitarian ideal. They underlay, also, Owen's growing perception that contemporary ills were caused not so much by religious error as by the false notions of *laissez-faire*. He had refuted them at New Lanark. He set out now to refute them in the nation at large. It was this change of emphasis which – almost incidentally – made him the spokesman of working people.

THE REPORT TO THE COUNTY OF LANARK

THE conclusion of the Napoleonic Wars in 1815, and the subsequent rise in poverty and unemployment and mass discontent, brought most of the thinking nation to face what Carlyle later called that Condition-of-England Question which was to perplex its councils for three decades to come. It brought Owen in particular to the conviction that the greatest problems of his own time were the effects of the machine – the huge wealth it brought to some, the accompanying impoverishment of the rest – and the new spirit engendered in a competitive society, which divided men into classes bound not by reciprocal obligation but solely by the impersonal ties of the market. This awareness, and less and less the premises of the *New View*, came to dominate his thought. So much was the definition of principle which took place in 1815 a prerequisite of the position he adopted in the *Report to the County of Lanark* and beyond, that it must be seen as the real climacteric of his career. What had hitherto been merely a diffuse and somewhat doctrinaire preoccupation with the effects of environment on the formation of character now acquired both substance and a particular focus.

(London, 1964), p. 805; R. Miliband, 'The Politics of Robert Owen', *Journal of the History of Ideas,* Vol. XV, p. 245.

This new definition was the result of the first real setback in Owen's career, the reception accorded the factory bill he entrusted to the first Sir Robert Peel to present to parliament in 1815. Certain that it 'would be comparatively an easy task' to reform the nation, he had drafted his bill with high hopes. It was designed to restrict the working day in factories for those under eighteen to ten and a half hours, to limit the age of admission to ten, to forbid night work, and to set up a system of enforcement by inspection. He need not have been surprised, but he was, to find that it encountered immediate and highly effective opposition from the manufacturers' lobby. Outside parliament, he was not in a position long to persist in his agitation. After being subjected to personal abuse for his religious unorthodoxies, in the knowledge too that spies had been sent to cull what scandal they could at New Lanark, within a very few months he gave up the agitation in disgust, convinced, as he had not been before, that 'the rapid accumulation of wealth ... [had] created capitalists who were among most ignorant and injurious of the population ... totally unequal to their position'.[41] His presentiments were not unjustified. In the course of the next four years his recommendations were so diluted that when the bill was passed in 1819 it was virtually nugatory in its effects.

It was this experience which gave point to the judgements he passed in his *Observations upon the Effect of the Manufacturing System*, which he published in 1815. They are familiar enough to us now. They were to become the stock-in-trade of nineteenth-century conservative and socialist thought alike. Here we have a not too remote foretaste of Carlyle and Ruskin, and indeed of Marx. They are among the most eloquent passages Owen wrote.

The general diffusion of manufactures throughout a country generates a new character in its inhabitants. ... The acquisition

41. *Life*, p. 177.

of wealth, and the desire which it naturally creates for a continued increase, have introduced a fondness for essentially injurious luxuries among a numerous class of individuals who formerly never thought of them, and they have also generated a disposition which strongly impels its possessors to sacrifice the best feelings of human nature to this love of accumulation. To succeed in this career, the industry of the lower orders, from whose labour this wealth is now drawn, has been carried by new competitors striving against those of longer standing, to a point of real oppression, reducing them by successive changes, as the spirit of competition increased and the ease of acquiring wealth diminished, to a state . . . infinitely more degraded and miserable than they were before the introduction of these manufactories, upon the success of which their bare subsistence now depends.

This process entails not only the increasing misery of the poor, but also the corruption of the rich.

The governing principle of trade, manufactures, and commerce is immediate pecuniary gain, to which on the great scale every other is made to give way. All are sedulously trained to buy cheap and to sell dear; and to succeed in this art, the parties must be taught to acquire strong powers of deception; and thus a spirit is generated through every class of traders, destructive of that open, honest sincerity, without which man cannot make others happy, nor enjoy happiness himself.

Above all, the consequences of the competitive ethic are iniquitous in proportion as they debase human relationships into those of the market.

All ties between employers and employed are frittered down to the consideration of what immediate gain each can derive from the other. The employer regards the employed as mere instruments of gain, while these acquire a gross ferocity of character, which, if legislative measures shall not be judiciously devised to prevent its increase, and ameliorate the condition of this class, will sooner or later plunge the country into a formidable and perhaps inextricable state of danger.

These, then, the judgements: that the huge productivity consequent on technological change entailed the exploitation and increasing misery and moral degradation of labour; that it had unleashed in the rich an unprecedented acquisitiveness of spirit and an instinct for competition which divided men; that, in sum, the wage bond had destroyed the 'best feelings in human nature'. As important as the judgements was the retrospective ideal which informed them. In a highly significant passage Owen went on to contrast the contemporary malaise with the social harmony of the world which was even then almost lost. In the past, he wrote, the poor

were generally trained by the example of some landed proprietor, and in such habits as created a mutual interest between the parties, by which means even the lowest peasant was generally considered as belonging to, and forming somewhat of a member of, a respectable family. Under these circumstances the lower orders experienced not only a considerable degree of comfort, but they had also frequent opportunities of enjoying healthy rational sports and amusements; and in consequence they became strongly attached to those on whom they depended; their services were willingly performed; and mutual good offices bound the parties by the strongest ties of human nature to consider each other as friends in somewhat different situations; the servant indeed often enjoying more solid comfort and ease than his master.[42]

The pamphlet won no particular renown, yet in it Owen declared more explicitly than elsewhere a verdict and an interpretation of the social good which were long to inform the English imagination. In no ambiguous sense, he meant his reference to the pre-industrial past to be an objective description of those values which he might have felt he had known in boyhood, whose corrosion he had witnessed in

42. *Observations upon the Effect of the Manufacturing System* (1818), Owen: *Appendix*, pp. 38–41.

dramatic form in Manchester, and to which at New Lanark he was even then attempting to give new expression. Mutual interest and mutual good offices, attachment and dependence, the strongest ties of human nature – these were the indispensable values with which newly armed he resumed his role on the philanthropic stage in 1816.

He did so under conditions which threatened to destroy them all. With the conclusion of war, Britain's twenty-five-year-long monopoly of the world's markets and carrying trade drew to a close. Government orders for supplies were cut. The overproduction of the last war years glutted markets which were already contracting. Agriculture, in distress since 1813, entered a period of chronic and severe depression which lasted until 1823. From 1815 to 1817 textile wages were halved. In 1816, heavy unemployment, coupled in the later months of the year with rising food prices, precipitated a succession of disturbances and strikes which revived again in 1818. Spinners and weavers demanded a minimum wage. The agitation for parliamentary reform in London and the provincial cities culminated in 1819 in the fiasco of Peterloo and the imposition of the Six Acts by Owen's friend, the Home Secretary Sidmouth. The countryside was afflicted with outbreaks of rick-burning and machine-breaking comparable with those of the worst months of the Luddite protests in 1813. Finally, bringing the crisis home to the householder, the poor rates rose from over five million pounds in 1815 to nearly seven in 1817 and nearly eight in 1818. It was under these circumstances that Owen, by now in high repute, was put upon the Committee of the Association for the Relief of the Manufacturing Poor, presided over by the Archbishop of Canterbury and the Duke of York. Thus, under tory auspices, he joined in the debate about the proper measures by which to relieve the nation's unprecedented poverty. Under these auspices, too, he conceived the idea of the cooperative community.

His attitude to the problem of pauperism was quite distinctive. The existing poor law was an outdated inheritance from Elizabeth's reign which by the late eighteenth-century had been variously interpreted and haphazardly applied throughout the country. The catalyst of the contemporary debate on the subject had been the decision of the magistrates of Speenhamland in Berkshire (1795) to pay outdoor allowances to agricultural workers whose wages were inadequate to support their families, without obliging them to enter a workhouse. As the system spread throughout the south and east of England, Owen came to share the conviction of the commercial classes that it was destructive of the recipients' moral fibre and self-sufficiency. Even in Manchester, where it did not apply in the same form, he had found that poor relief afforded 'direct encouragement to idleness and profligacy of every description'.

In my own experience I have known workmen who in the years 1791 and 1792 could and often did earn from three to four pounds per week, and in 1793 were upon the parish, and themselves and families supported regularly from the funds raised under the name of the poor rate, in the town of Manchester. If those individuals had not been led to depend upon the support from this adventitious fund when they were in the practice of earning from three to four pounds per week, they would have made a different domestic arrangement, and expended 20 or 25 shillings a week, and put by the remainder, against a time of difficulty.[43]

So far Owen's opinion was utterly orthodox. It was in the conclusions he drew from it that he set himself apart from the usual attitude of his class. His fellow manufacturers might argue that the poor law should be abolished, or (as

43. Select Committee on the State of the Police in the Metropolis, *Parliamentary Papers* (1816), Vol. V, pp. 234–5. See also text, pp. 171–2.

was in fact effected in 1834) that the workhouse system
should be more rigorously applied. These measures, it was
calculated, would either create a free labour market by
obliging the agricultural poor to move into the towns, or at
the very least diminish the burden of the nation's poor rates.
Such were extreme views: Owen never countenanced them.
His alternative solution is important.

He presented it in a paper submitted to his Committee in
1816. Here he began by arguing that the immediate cause of
the current distress lay in 'the depreciation of human labour
... by the general introduction of mechanism'. There followed a reasoned analysis, one of the first indeed, of the
phenomenon we know as technological unemployment.
Mechanical invention, he argued, reduced commodity prices,
increased consumer demand, and for a while, therefore, increased also the demand for labour. Further invention, however, stimulated by the increase in the entrepreneur's
profits, led to overproduction, a consequent contraction of the
source of supply, and ultimately to unemployment. 'Under
these circumstances it soon proved that mechanical power
was much cheaper than human labour; the former, in consequence, was continued at work, while the latter was
superseded.' If they were not to starve therefore, 'advantageous occupation must be found for the poor and unemployed working classes, to whose labour mechanism must
be rendered subservient'. The existing poor laws could not
achieve this: in any case they encouraged idleness and
improvidence at the expense of the wealthy and industrious.
His proposal was very much more comprehensive:

Any plan for the amelioration of the poor should combine
means to prevent their children from acquiring bad habits, and
to give them good ones – to provide useful training and instruction for them – to provide proper labour for the adults – to direct
their labour and expenditure so as to produce the greatest benefit
to themselves and to society; and to place them under such

circumstances as shall remove them from unnecessary temptations, and closely unite their interest and duty.

These advantages cannot be given either to individuals or to families separately, or to large congregated numbers.

They can be effectually introduced into practice only under arrangements that would unite in one establishment a population of from 500 to 1,500 persons, averaging about 1,000.[44]

Thus was conceived the idea of the 'Village of Cooperation'. Acknowledging the obligation of the rich to the poor, concerned to bring the poor to self-sufficiency and 'rationality', Owen was seeking in the cooperative community a compromise between past ideal and present necessity, a substitute for that community relationship which had existed in the past. This was the strange but indubitable paternity of one of the main currents of socialist thought: the ideal of communal endeavour, collectivity, and cooperation.

Within a couple of years it was to become Owen's obsession. And this process was assisted by a second check to his optimism even more profound than that he had experienced over the factory bill. In its initial form, the Village of Cooperation was well attuned to the assumptions of the Committee which had indirectly brought it forth. To be sure, it was not greeted in tory and government circles with quite the enthusiasm which Owen had probably expected. Discontent in the country, the riot at Spa Fields in late 1816, and in 1817 the march of the Blanketeers and an 'insurrection' in Derbyshire, all induced a certain wariness in government circles which could only have been increased when presented with proposals which even remotely smacked of the communism of the Spencean Philanthropists. But these last, small in number if highly notorious, wanted the complete abolition of private property: Owen, more acceptably, wanted to assist, but also to control, the poor. His plan's

44. *Report to the Committee for the Relief of the Manufacturing and Labouring Poor* (March 1817), Owen: *Appendix*, pp. 53ff., 57.

credentials were confirmed, if anything, by the reception it received from working men themselves. Given its lineage, and Owen's reputation by 1816, the hostility of the London radicals was quite predictable. They tried to break up his public meetings. The editors of the radical press, William Cobbett included, poured scorn on what they conceived to be its underlying purpose: the preservation of order by the regimentation of the poor into 'parallelograms of paupers', into 'nurseries for men'. Under these circumstances, the plan met with the tentative approval of the Archbishop, the Prime Minister, and *The Times*. The Archbishop advised Owen to submit it to the parliamentary committee just convened to consider the poor laws. With some confidence he did so. What happened next marked the turning point in Owen's public career. He was kept waiting for two days in the committee's antechamber. Then he was told that his evidence would not after all be required.

For a man by now much accustomed to flattery this shock must have been profound. His rejection was both un-expected and unexplained. Owen later accounted for it by parliament's subjection to the false notions of whigs and political economists: and indeed it is very likely that the committee had already made up its mind that the Villages of Cooperation would only serve to increase the pauper population by making it too comfortable. More to the point is the effect the refusal had on Owen himself. He had already absorbed the first check to his early hopes in parlia-ment's handling of his factory bill. To this second setback he reacted in a quite unprecedented way. Very sure of his reputation, he proceeded, modestly, to turn demagogue.

First, he published his report in the London papers, and sent 30,000 copies to the minister of every parish, to every Member of Parliament and peer, and to every chief magis-trate and important banker in the kingdom. Then, as fully in the public eye as he was ever to be throughout his life, having in two months spent £4,000 in this form of publicity, he went on to perpetrate what was, given his earlier purposes, the most decisive tactical mistake of his career. In August 1817 he delivered a public attack in the City of London Tavern on 'the errors – gross errors – of every religion that has hitherto been taught to man'. He believed the occasion to be that on which 'bigotry, superstition, and all false religions received their death blow'.

Instead it provided the excuse which a growing number of sceptics were looking for. He had said little at the meeting which he had not said more sedately in the *New View*, but now he had noised it abroad to a mass audience, and this in a time of high political excitement. Almost overnight *The Times* turned against him, episcopal friendships froze. Respectable society was never to forgive him. He was soon officially classified as a subversive. In 1819 the Commons overwhelmingly rejected a motion to take his plans for poor relief into consideration. In the course of the debate, the Chancellor of the Exchequer declared that they were 'not only visionary and impracticable, but in the highest degree dangerous to the country'. They were, in short, 'subversive of . . . religion and government'. In an unpleasant and pious speech, William Wilberforce concurred.

In retrospect we can see that this was Owen's political epitaph, the end of half-a-dozen years' dalliance with the favours of the great. But more than this, it marked the beginning also of the process by which his idea sloughed off in the popular mind the taint of its origins, and by which Owen himself turned from the polite classes to a very much wider public. He did not deliberately plan this reorientation: it was imposed upon him. Nor as yet did he fully realize its implications. Despite mounting public scepticism about his plans they were still seriously considered as late as 1823 by a select committee on the Irish poor; New Lanark still received its quota of visitors, among them a deputation of

Leeds manufacturers; he still believed himself even after the speech to be among all classes the 'most generally popular character living'; and the *Report to the County of Lanark* itself was written in 1820 at the behest of Lanarkshire magistrates concerned at rising poor rates. Thus it was not by deliberate intent that the *Report* expressed some of the seminal ideas of what were to be exclusively working-class movements. Nonetheless with the luxury of hindsight we can sense in this last consummation a certain inevitability. Owen now had only one attentive audience to write for. Whether he knew it or not, already regarded by his intellectual betters with little more than sympathetic and amused tolerance, by most manufacturers with positive hostility, he was from 1817, with the loss of the confidence of his tory patrons, irrevocably committed to a political and social wilderness. Equally, although he still directed his appeals to government (and this on his continental tour as well), he began to identify himself with the interests of the poor with an explicitness which he had not yet ventured:

The value of mere manual labour has been so much reduced, that the working man ... is now [1818] placed under circumstances far more unfavourable to his happiness than the serf or villein was under the feudal system, or than the slave was in any of the nations of antiquity. . . . Yet it is from this class the wealthy derive all which they hold. The rich wallow in an excess of luxuries injurious to themselves, solely by the labour of men who are debarred from acquiring for their own use a sufficiency even of the indispensable articles of life, – much less any of those numberless comforts which they see around them. ... Past history exhibits no combination of circumstances which bears any analogy to the present crisis; the time never existed when knowledge and misery were closely and extensively united.[45]

But the change in the orientation of Owen's appeals was

45. *Letter to the Earl of Liverpool on the Employment of Children in Manufactories* (1818), Owen: *Appendix*, pp. 187–8.

more certain, perhaps, because he had discovered in the idea of the cooperative village a mechanism by which to implement his greatest plans, and one which had hitherto been lacking. A system which was originally conceived as a means to relieve and incidentally to discipline the poor became imbued in his mind with the wider purpose which had been latent ever since the publication of the *New View*: no less than the regeneration of mankind. Parliament had failed him. The good society would have to be instituted piecemeal, and, as at New Lanark, *in parvo*. For this purpose, the small scale community was ideally suited.

Thus upon the idea of the cooperative village Owen came to rest a very heavy responsibility indeed. It was to be the means whereby men would be educated into rationality; it was to exemplify the proper relations which were attainable only in a close community, where man would not compete with man; and by showing up the absurdity of the hostile prognostications of political economy it was to destroy 'false notions' whose effects upon human character were demonstrably more pernicious than any which, in his innocence, he had once assailed in the *New View*. In encompassing these three themes within the *Report to the County of Lanark*, Owen clarified the reorientation of thought and the channelling of feeling which had taken place over the past half-dozen years.

Just as Owen's condemnation of the capitalist ethic and his belief in the harmonious society heralded characteristic themes of nineteenth-century conservativism, so, in advocating the communitarian idea and attempting to refute political economy, the *Report* constitutes the unintentioned precursor of socialist thought as well. It assumes this status because it challenged at once what had to be challenged before any viable critique of early capitalist society could be developed: the seemingly incontrovertible and logical structure of economic theory upon whose side, with varying degrees of commitment, were ranged the intellectual giants of the age: Adam Smith and Bentham, James Mill and Ricardo. Ricardo's work especially constituted the gospel interpretation of economic mechanisms to which in the 1820s a good half of the educated public might have confessed some allegiance. The *Report* also challenged the grounds of what was perhaps the deepest social fear of the early decades of the century. This was embodied in Thomas Malthus's theory of population growth.

Malthus's argument had about it a devastating simplicity. Since population increased by a geometric progression, while food supply increased only arithmetically, population must so far expand beyond the means of subsistence that unless checked by disease or war, or by 'moral restraint' on the part of the working classes, the poor would ever be condemned to starvation. In the face of this harsh reality, every utopian scheme which rested on assumptions about the perfectability of man or the feasibility of large-scale social reorganization must be doomed to failure.[46] In the sixth edition of his *Essay on the Principle of Population* (published in 1817), Malthus applied his strictures very directly to the Villages of Cooperation. They would, he made it clear, reward the industrious and the profligate equally; and by encouraging the reproduction of the latter in particular, they would increase poverty, not lessen it. Such was Malthus's reputation, that it was deemed more than obscurantist to disbelieve him.

Owen was the first in any would-be systematic way to challenge these revelations. The debate thus initiated between the pessimism of political economy and the forces, as Owen conceived them, of reason and progress, was in some

46. Malthus first wrote his *Essay on the Principle of Population* in 1798 deliberately to deflate the utopian optimism of Condorcet and William Godwin.

form to last for thirty years. In very different forms it may be said to have lasted into our own century. It began, properly speaking, with a full-scale attack on the Villages of Cooperation published by Robert Torrens in the *Edinburgh Review* of October 1819. The *Report to the County of Lanark* may be seen as Owen's fullest reply.

The burden of Torrens's article lay in the demonstration that Owen's plans 'do not touch, nay, they do not have the most distant bearing on, the causes of our present distress'. He rested his case largely on an amplification of Malthus, showing that mass starvation would be inevitable, if proper measures were not applied, as the returns from land diminished with the quantity and quality of soil available for cultivation. Employment and prosperity, he argued, were controlled by the size of the capitalists' profit; this in turn was controlled by the returns upon the cultivation of land and the skill and economy with which labour was employed by the entrepreneur. At first, these two factors balanced each other: the return from land decreased as poorer soils were taken under cultivation, but at the same time a larger population could be supported by more specialized division of labour and thus higher productivity and cheaper goods. Nonetheless the time must come when the land would approach exhaustion and capital be deprived of an outlet on the soil. Then the economy would become stationary and the population would be checked by famine. This state of affairs Britain was now fast approaching. Herein lay the explanation of the present distress.

It was clear, Torrens went on, that to the inevitable and progressive impoverishment of the soil and its consequences for the profitability of capital, Owen's pauper communities offered no solution. To the contrary, since 'every increase of food and material which he obtains will be raised at an additional expense', capital accumulation in his Villages would be restricted. Shortage of capital would spell the end of his projects, since 'the net produce, or surplus of return above expenditure, *is the only fund to which he can look*' for the means with which to pay taxes, rent and interest, and to employ a growing population. In any case, a communitarian society could never, as Owen hoped, be a viable basis for the growth of manufacturing industry, even on a small scale. If the communities intended to trade their products with the rest of society, their prosperity would still be subject to the fluctuations in supply and demand in the nation at large; if they intended to trade overseas, they would still be subject to the legislative restrictions on free imports; and finally if they intended to be self-sufficient, their internal consumption would be too low to facilitate the division of labour upon which economy in manufacturing depended. It was not, in short, 'in the nature of things that Mr Owen's establishments should increase the effective powers of industry so as to afford beneficial occupation to capital, and adequate reward to labour'. A more realistic solution to distress than that proposed by Owen lay in the reduction of taxation and in the repeal of import duties, measures which would encourage British investment at home rather than abroad and discourage foreign competition. Such would be the effect of those measures if applied, that Britain would then be 'yet a long way removed from the degree of wealth to which it is in our power to attain before arriving at the stationary state'.

For a quarter of a century the Malthusian argument was used in this way to prove the inevitability of the labourer's situation in society; for a quarter of a century, too, the free trade solution was held out to woo working men from their more drastic panaceas. As it was, this was a substantial enough case for Owen to refute; but Torrens had not directly deployed all the arsenal at his disposal even yet. He made only oblique reference to the bleaker deductions from the Malthusian prediction, which, in Ricardo's *Principles of*

Political Economy (1817), had contributed to the theory of the subsistence wage. This was not directly relevant to the Villages of Cooperation. It was relevant, however, to Owen's growing concern that the labourer should receive a proper reward for what he produced. In the *Report*, therefore, Owen would have to try to counter political economy on these grounds as well.

Ricardo's wage theory was supported by two distinct arguments, and its implications confirmed by another. He drew first on Malthus. In times when the demand for labour exceeded its supply, he argued, it was usually the case that labour was in a strong enough bargaining position to effect a rise in wages. If this happened, however, the comforts of life thus attained would encourage a growth in the labouring population. The supply of labour would then exceed the demand, and wages would drop. But they could not drop very far. If they dropped below the level required to maintain subsistence, the population would decrease (by starvation, later marriage, or diminished fertility). This decrease of population would merely increase the value of labour once more, and the process would begin anew. In this way wages were balanced around subsistence level as by a natural law. The inevitability of this equilibrium was supported, secondly, by Ricardo's theory of value. This maintained that the value of a commodity depended on 'the relative quantity of labour necessary to its production'. Since labour was itself a commodity within the productive sphere, its value (customarily represented in wages) must be calculated on the same principle. Its value was therefore dependent on the quantity of labour (embodied in food, clothing, shelter, etc.) necessary to enable it to reproduce itself and subsist. If labour received more wages than was necessary for subsistence, it would be overvalued. This depressing edifice was completed, thirdly, when Ricardo added a chapter on machinery to the 1819 edition of his *Principles*, in which he accepted the likelihood of technological unemployment. Here he conceded that while mechanical invention might increase both the net revenue of the country and the fund from which land-lord and capitalist drew their revenue, it would remain im-possible for the labourer's wage to benefit likewise, since money invested in machinery must be deducted from the circulating capital from which wages were paid. There was, as a result, no prospect of an increase in the workman's wage beyond the subsistence level even as a result of greater mechanical productivity.

The whole structure of orthodox economic thought was against Owen. Even if it were true that international free trade might mitigate its harshest implications (as, inci-dentally, Owen himself believed), the prospects it held out for the poor and the unemployed remained grim. Labour was a commodity doomed to a struggle for subsistence; population expansion bore with it the threat of famine and economic stagnation. Within such a society there was no hope of progress as Owen conceived progress, and an experi-ment in community building was a luxury the nation could not afford. His plan must in any case fail: it expected too much of human nature. 'Can any reasonable person believe, with Owen,' Ricardo wrote to a friend,

that a society, such as he projects, will flourish and produce more than has ever yet been produced by an equal number of men, if they are to be stimulated to exertion by a regard to the com-munity, instead of by a regard to their private interest? Is not the experience of ages against him?[47]

To convert the world, Owen had not only to assail a theory, he had also to subvert the scepticism of men who could conceive of no economic order which was not built upon the principles of competition and self-interest.

At heart Owen's antagonism to these propositions was a

47. D. Ricardo, *Letters to Trower,* ed. Bonar and Hollander (Oxford, 1899), p. 80.

simple and a moralistic one, and it turned on the characteristic structure of values which we have seen define itself in
his mind over the previous half-dozen years. 'The political
economists,' he wrote in later years,

by reasoning from a false principle, knowing little of human
nature, and less of the powers of society when rightly directed,
had hardened their hearts against the natural feelings of
humanity, and were determined, aided by their disciples the
Whigs, to starve out the poor from the land.[48]

Gross simplification of the truth though this was, it was a
verdict which moved not only Owen but countless others
to protest against a system of thought which in its harshest
form appeared to condemn labour in perpetuity to the subsistence wage and the merciless struggle of the market. It
was a verdict born of feeling, but as time went on it acquired
its own logical authority.

This last, however, was not Owen's achievement. The
Report to the County of Lanark had little authority which
would have been recognized as such by educated readers.
He understood neither the complexities of political
economy nor the depth of the assumptions about human
nature on which it was partly based. In the *Report*, he took
the only alternative open to him. He ignored, or else
simply denied, the truth of what he did not believe, adapted
the terminology of the orthodox economists to his own
convenience, and blandly asserted premises which stood in
direct contradiction to those of economic liberalism. It was
an achievement of intuition rather than of logic that he was
often right to do so. Formally, the *Report* was a totally inadequate answer to the Ricardian structure. But it did mark
the beginning of an alternative and a viable system of
economic thought which could attempt to meet political
economy on its own ground. It also projected an alternative

48. *Life*, p. 177.

vision of society to which humble men, at least, could subscribe, often with passion.

It was the communitarian and cooperative ideal (most
fully set out in Part III of the *Report*), which evoked the
strongest popular response in subsequent years. Owen made
little attempt to prove the practicality of the Villages of
Cooperation in terms which would have satisfied either
Torrens or Ricardo. He conceded that taxes would still have
to be paid to the state, but failed to show from what source;
he did not consider Torrens's most telling argument that the
communities would still be subject to the laws of supply and
demand and competition operating outside them. Instead, in
the course of a full discussion of their size, location, and
domestic arrangement, he summed up the whole assault
against the individualist and competitive ethic which had
been germinating in his mind for five years.

It has been, and still is, a received opinion among theorists
in political economy, that man can provide better for himself,
and more advantageously for the public, when left to his own
individual exertions, opposed to and in competition with his
fellows, than when aided by any social arrangement which shall
unite his interests individually and generally with society.

The principle of individual interest, opposed as it is perpetually
to the public good, is considered, by the most celebrated political
economists, to be the corner-stone to the social system, and without which, society could not subsist.

Yet when they shall know themselves, and discover the wonderful effects which combination and union can produce, they will
acknowledge that the present arrangement of society is the most
anti-social, impolitic, and irrational, that can be devised. ... It
is one of those magnificent errors ... that when enforced in
practice brings ten thousand evils in its train. The principle on
which these economists proceed, instead of adding to the wealth
of nations or of individuals, is itself the sole cause of poverty.[49]

The reason for this was clear.

49. Text, pp. 231–2.

Under the present system there is the most minute division of mental power and manual labour in the individuals of the working classes; private interests are placed perpetually at variance with the public good.

What was necessary was a system which would lead to the combination of extensive mental and manual powers in the individuals of the working classes; to a complete identity of private and public interest; and to the training of nations to comprehend that their power and happiness cannot attain their full and natural development but through an equal increase of the power and happiness of all other states. These, therefore, are the real points at variance between that which *is* and that which *ought to be*.[50]

That which ought to be would be attained only in a communal society, one, moreover, in which each individual before he is twelve years old ... may with ease be trained to acquire a correct view of the outline of all the knowledge which men have yet attained.

By this means he will early learn what he is in relation to past ages, to the period in which he lives, to the circumstances in which he is placed, to the individuals around him, and to future events. *He will then only have any pretensions to the name of a rational being.*[51]

Once, in short, men learnt that 'impressions, combined with their natural qualities ... do truly determine the character of the individual through every period of life'. then:

Instead of the unhealthy pointer of a pin, – header of a nail, – piecer of a thread – or clodhopper, senselessly gazing at the soil or around him, without understanding or rational reflection, there would spring up a working class full of activity and useful knowledge, with habits, information, manners, and dispositions, that would place the lowest in the scale many degrees above the

50. Text, pp. 238–9.
51. Text, p. 251

best of any class which has yet been formed by the circumstances of past or present society.[52]

The consequences of this revolution in the human mind would be immeasurable. Government would become 'a mere recreation'. 'Courts of law, prisons, and punishments would not be required.' 'Evils, of course, will permanently cease, soon to be known only by description.' 'The smallest desire for what are now called honours and peculiar privileges' will vanish; the inhabitants of the communities 'will therefore have every motive not to interfere with the honours and privileges of the existing higher orders, but to remain well satisfied with their own station in life.' Conflict, competition, and war would vanish from the face of the earth.[52a]

In passages such as these, we may recognize the imaginative content of Owen's thought, that apocalyptic note which in his later writings became more and more overt, and which sought acquiescence by virtue of its cumulative emotive appeal alone. The vision was a grand one, but its theoretical justification had still to be presented. Here his path became more treacherous.

It was clearly necessary to deal first with the Malthusian prediction, because if it were true Owen's vision would be meaningless. What he did was simply deny its validity. Malthus, he had already written in the New View....

has not told us how much more food an intelligent and industrious people will create from the same soil, than will be produced by one ignorant and ill-governed. . . . Human labour, properly directed, may be made far more than sufficient to enable

52. Text, pp. 245, 252. Thirty-two years later Ruskin was to echo Owen's words very closely indeed: 'It is not, truly speaking, the labour that is divided; but the men: – Divided into mere segments of men – broken into small fragments and crumbs of life; so that all the little piece of intelligence that is left in a man is not enough to make a pin, or a nail, but exhausts itself in making the point of a pin or the head of a nail.' *(The Stones of Venice, Vol. II (1853), ch. VI. ¶ 16.)*
52a. Text, pp. 255, 261, 235, 256, 262.

the population of the world to live in the highest state of human enjoyment.[53]

He went on in the *Report* to argue that more intensive agriculture would enable food supply to keep pace with population increase; and in elaborating this assertion he devoted a good deal of Part II to the advocacy of cultivation by the spade rather than by the plough. This particular theme was not as idiosyncratic as it sounds: even Ricardo had given it serious consideration in the Parliamentary debate of 1819. But although we happen to know now that Owen was right to be optimistic about food supply, the fact remains that the simple contradiction of Malthus remained the weakest link in his argument: denial constituted no refutation.[54] Its only effect was to liberate Owen himself from the most pervasive social fear of the age. This was a prerequisite for the further development of his argument as follows. First, he turned the subsistence wage theory against Ricardo by arguing that it was precisely the paucity of wages which accounted for the current distress, and this simply because low wages led to 'underconsumption' on the domestic market. Secondly, he explained that paucity, not in terms of the natural balance between the supply of and demand for labour, but as a consequence of a deficient medium of exchange: of legislative error, in other words, rather than of natural law.

The underconsumptionist argument Owen had first sketched in a pamphlet of 1818:[55] the *Report* itself ampli-

53. Text, pp. 192–3.

54. Owen did attempt a more ambitious refutation of Malthus in his *Catechism of the New View of Society* (July, 1817), in which he suggested that population increased by an arithmetic, not a geometric, progression. Even there, however, his argument was not very convincing. See Owen: *Appendix*, pp. 74–5.

55. *To the British Master Manufacturers on the Employment of Children in Manufactories* (1818), Owen: *Appendix*, pp. 200–201. Like *environment*, *underconsumption* was not a word used by Owen himself, but it had gained currency in French through Sismondi's presen-

fied the theme. Britain's present difficulties, he had then
argued, derived from the lack of an adequate domestic
market for manufactured goods: domestic consumer
demand was low because wages were low. The result was
overproduction of goods, the glutting of markets, the closure
of factories, unemployment, and finally the further diminu-
tion of what demand there was. It was necessary, therefore,
deliberately to raise the wages of labour to increase its pur-
chasing power in the market. By thus enabling consumer
demand to keep pace with supply, overproduction and its
attendant miseries would be averted. To this theme he
returned in the *Report*.

It is the want of a profitable market that alone checks the
successful and otherwise beneficial industry of the working
classes. The markets of the world are created solely by the
remuneration allowed for the industry of the working classes,
and those markets are more or less extended and profitable in
proportion as these classes are well or ill remunerated for their
labour. But the existing arrangements of society will not permit
the labourer to be remunerated for his industry, and in consequence all markets fail.[56]

The Ricardian subsistence wage, therefore, was the source
of distress not only for the labourer, but ultimately for the
capitalist as well.

From this Owen went on to argue that the inadequacy of
the labourer's wage, and the shortage of employment,

cannot proceed from a want of wealth or capital, or of the means
of greatly adding to that which now exists, but from some defect
in the mode of distributing this extraordinary addition of new
capital throughout society, or, to speak commercially, from the

tation of an underconsumptionist argument in 1819, and very shortly
it was to denote the whole argument which Owen and Sismondi had
presented in rudimentary form.

56. Text, p. 210. Also pp. 203–4.

want of a ... means of exchange, coexistensive with the means of production.[57]

On this all-important subject he was probably influenced by the proposal of the 1819 Select Committee that Britain should return to the gold standard. To this there was a good deal of hostility. Introduced initially as a war-time measure, paper currency had for over twenty years proved itself a medium of exchange elastic enough to expand with the growth of population and wealth. It was defended by the manufacturing community because it was feared that a return to gold would limit the supply of money and the credit facilities necessary to an expanding economy. There was an underconsumptionist argument implicit in their case, and Owen agreed with it. But in the *Report* he took it to a more extreme conclusion. The objections to gold, he pointed out, applied also to paper currency. Both were artificial standards of value, and both were sometimes in short supply: gold because of its rarity, paper because its issue was subject to the policy of the directors of the Bank of England. The only 'natural' standard of value, therefore, which could expand without limit as wealth and population increased, was the very constituent of that wealth, the amount of human labour embodied within it.[58]

Owen may have discovered this idea in John Bellers, the seventeenth-century pamphleteer whose advocacy of a labour standard of value he had reprinted in 1817, or of course in Ricardo himself: the concept of labour value had both an ancient and a respectable ancestry. Where he was original was in his appropriation of the idea not to justify the subsistence wage as Ricardo had done, but to show how labour might receive a higher remuneration than it did at present. Characteristically, however, he argued his case with

57. Text, p. 204.
58. Text, pp. 205–7, 221–4.

question-begging rhetoric. Metallic and paper currency (by virtue presumably of its short supply)

has made man ignorantly, individually selfish; placed him in opposition to his fellows; engendered fraud and deceit; blindly urged him forward to create, but deprived him of the wisdom to enjoy.

By contrast, the substitution of the labour standard would 'let prosperity loose on the country', exalt the dignity of labour, remove it from its subjection to the demands of the market, open the whole world to peaceful trade, and 'materially improve human nature'.[59] The mechanism of this transformation he failed to discuss in detail. But concealed behind the rhetorical fervour of his exposition lay the following thought. The fair remuneration of the labourer according to the amount of work he put into his product would increase his power as a consumer. Since the domestic market would so far be stimulated, overproduction and thus unemployment would be averted. As population increased and more labour became productive,

there will be in the same proportion a perpetually extending market or demand for all the industry of society, whatever may be its extent. Under such arrangements what are technically called 'bad times' can never occur.[60]

The shortcomings of the *Report* as an exercise in economic theory are clear. Owen's formulation of the underconsumptionist and labour value theories fell far short of the complete. Eloquence hid its ragged ends, and repeatedly in the work he shied away from the logical deductions which were to be drawn from it by subsequent socialists.[61] He

59. Text, pp. 223, 204–8.
60. Text, p. 259.
61. One example: Marx used the underconsumptionist argument to demonstrate an inherent contradiction of purpose in capitalism. The entrepreneur was obliged to produce in excess and exploit labour

countered the Malthusian argument with mere denial. He left Torrens's assault of 1819 largely unanswered. He failed also to demonstrate how his communities were to be integrated within the revolution which would result from the new value system: to all intents and purposes in the communitarian idea and in the recommendation of a better medium of exchange he advocated two distinct solutions to contemporary ills, and left the connexion between them undefined.

The most conspicuous weakness of the *Report* lay in its ambiguity about the role of the capitalist. Owen neither visualized his extinction from the economic order, nor questioned the legitimacy of his profits. Under the new value system, we are told, the labourer would receive a '*fair* proportion' of the wealth he created. What this implied is conveyed in the suggestion that the capitalist and the landlord would benefit from this fair remuneration by the 'high profits [which] can [then] be paid for agricultural and manufactured produce'.[62] In thus tacitly accepting capitalist profit, Owen betrayed a belief that the final product of industry embodied not only the work of the labourer but also the skills and enterprise of management. He would in other words have been in tacit if muddled agreement with Ricardo's own distinction between labour as a true measure of value and labour as its sole creator. On the second alternative Owen never insisted. By this omission he failed both to formulate a theory of exploitation and to legitimize the prospect of total economic revolution. By so much, then, he was separated from his successors, men like Hodgskin,

---

in order to create the profits necessary to capital formation. But he also had to avert overproduction by encouraging consumer demand: this in turn, as Owen had suggested, was possible only by paying labour more than a subsistence wage.

62. Text, pp. 222, 224.

Bray, and Thompson,[63] who were much more directly to anticipate Marx in their insistence that even the capital used by the entrepreneur was the product of past labour, that accordingly he had no right to it nor to the interest accruing from it.

It is possible of course that Owen did not intend to challenge the capitalist order at all. The communities were to contain 'a whole population engaged in agriculture, with manufacturers as an appendage':[64] they were, after all, born of a rural ideal. And as he had insisted in the *New View*, so he still insisted in the *Report* that a failure to adopt his recommendations would be 'calculated to derange the whole of the existing social system'. He even envisaged that the 'higher classes' would be supported by the communities' surplus produce.[65] But in view of his denunciations of the competitive ethic we can accept this only as a characteristic inconsistency. The overall failure is one of intellect. He failed to see that the social order was intimately bound to the economic. He failed also to set himself an adequate framework of reference. To inquire into the laws which determined the distribution of wealth, Ricardo had attempted a comprehensive theory of the 'natural course of rent, profit, and wages'. Purporting to inquire into the same laws, Owen excluded a consideration of rent and profit, landlord and capitalist, from his theory entirely. To the Ricardians, then, Owen's theory was no theory at all. To subsequent socialists, for the same reason, it left many of the important things unsaid.

63. On the later socialists who learnt from Owen, see G. D. H. Cole, *A History of Socialist Thought*, Vol. I: *The Forerunners, 1789–1850*, (London, 1953), Ch. X and XII.
64. Text, p. 228.
65. Text, pp. 209, 228.

Introduction

IT is by now needless to point out that Owen takes his place in the roll-call of political and social thinkers under dubious colours. His mind was very confused indeed. But his historical importance is unquestionable. He was the first in the industrial age to provide ordinary men with a secular doctrine which attempted both to explain their present situation in the economic order and to offer a persuasive alternative to it. Unlike any previous thinker, for example, he was in a position to come to terms with the machine. He accepted the machine as an irrevocable fact, welcoming the wealth it brought if properly distributed. But he saw the dangers it represented in subverting the morality upon which society ought to rest; and in proposing certain practical solutions he attempted to surmount them. By comparison, therefore, those radical thinkers who immediately preceded him seem to belong to another era: William Godwin, for example, confident that man's rationality must inevitably prompt him towards the good once he understood wherein the good consisted, and that this would result in the abolition of government and authority; or Thomas Paine, with his assertion in *The Rights of Man* (1791–2) that only a government fully representative of the people could permit the expression of natural rights. It is true that this last thesis exercised a profound influence upon the sophisticated artisan culture of the larger cities, and more than any other single work it helps to account for the channelling of popular expectations over the next half-century upon parliamentary solutions. But though Godwin wanted to abolish private property, and Paine (in his *Agrarian Justice*, 1795–6) to tax it, both were pre-eminently concerned with man as a political animal, with his relationship in particular to the formal mechanisms of political power. Neither gave much attention to the proper regulation of his life as a producer of wealth. In this context Owen had something quite new to say, and something which was, in an unprecedented way, relevant to the lives of more and more people. More than this, as they had never done so overtly, he intruded value judgements into his diagnosis of contemporary ills, value judgements which in more sophisticated form we have ourselves inherited.

What he said was nonetheless patently ambiguous. This, paradoxically, for many years only widened its appeal. Unlike Marx's fifty years later, Owen's case did not rest on an intentionally coherent and logical system of reasoning. It was far from being a 'closed' ideology. Even modest minds might have felt unconvinced by his attack against Ricardo, not to mention his bland contradiction of Malthus. Nor, despite his claim to have established 'a science of society', did he do any such thing in a sense meaningful to people who increasingly looked at society in terms of an irreconcileable antagonism, which Owen would not have acknowledged, between capital and labour, propertied and propertyless. Nor was his faith in the old social and political hierarchy one which the masses could share. Not least, Owen himself lapsed into the Godwinian fallacy: it was to beg a mighty question to make the nation's regeneration depend not upon a political struggle against property and privilege, but upon a moral and spiritual revolution, bloodless and rational, which by some means he never explained should actually strengthen the existing social system while it purged it of erroneous principles.

For a while all this did not matter. Though Owenite thought was inconsistent, it was in a particular sense resilient as well. Since it did not pose as a coherent dogma, the questions and qualifications it invited did not destroy it. Resting not so much on logic as on values, the allegiance it evoked turned not so much on intellectual as emotional and intuitive acquiescence. Thus for some it came to acquire almost the force of a religion. For the more judicious it permitted a quite healthy eclecticism of belief. The trade unionists of the 1830s, for example, rejected Owen's quite absurd requirement that the unions should constitute the nuclei of communities encompassing eventually both masters and men. Chartists likewise resolved, in the words of one of their leaders, William Lovett,

to take up such parts of his system as they believed would be appreciated by the working classes, and be the means of uniting them for specific purposes, taking care that these purposes should not interfere more than was possible with ... matters on which great differences of opinion prevailed.

But few of these men, while disagreeing profoundly with Owen on particular issues, and those usually political, would have denied that they owed to him a great deal of their enlightenment. It would never have occurred to them to reject him outright.

In this way Owenism became an umbrella ideology, exerting its appeal at many different levels and upon many different types of men. So far from fragmenting working-class culture thereby, it immensely enriched its traditions of collectivity and self-reliance. Perhaps, too, it provided its only possible cement in an age when the distance between the skilled artisan and the handloom weaver was at times as manifest as that between the classes. Whatever the case, it remains true that where Paine had appealed chiefly to the sophisticated urban artisan, Owen appealed also to the domestic outworker, the skilled factory hand, the shopkeeper. The apocalyptic note which came to dominate his later writings won over the illiterate. His rationalism reassured the religious sceptic, and thus played its part in the history of nineteenth-century popular secularism. And the breadth of this appeal was assisted by the fact that Owen could exploit new channels of communication. Where Paine's ideas were confined to the discussions of the Corresponding Societies of the 1790s, Owen's, from the late 1820s onwards, were spread abroad in a multitude of tracts and journals, and were debated in Mechanics' Institutes and Halls of Science and at Socialist Congresses across the country. Most important, they were expressed, as Paine's could never be, in institutional form. This was an inestimable source of strength: it meant that Owenite ideas could be put into practice within the context of everyday life, and that men could register their principled protest against prevalent economic and social *mores* in terms eminently practical but also dramatic. Hence the communities established at Motherwell, Orbiston, and Queenwood; the Labour Exchanges set up in London, Birmingham, and Liverpool between 1830 and 1832; the Grand National Consolidated Trades Union; and above all the cooperative societies, some 500 of which had been founded in England by 1832 with perhaps 20,000 members. 'Owenism,' a hostile observer wrote in 1839, 'as those are aware who habitually watch the progress of opinion, is at present in one form or another, the actual creed of a great proportion of the working classes.'

But the open ideology always meets its due nemesis under changed social conditions. Owenism was strong only as long as men did want to register their protest against society. Permitting dissent, demanding no rigorous and doctrinaire loyalty of its supporters, it could not survive mid-century. Owenite idealism was at its most vulnerable when capitalism brought its eventual rewards, when individualism – self-help – became the creed of many of the poor themselves. Then the cooperative idea in its original form became redundant.

In one context this process was particularly clear. The cooperative retailing movement, Owenism's most important single monument, was initiated in 1828. Its original purpose was to bypass the middleman, and eventually, as the *Cooperator* put it in 1830, to raise a capital sufficient to purchase and cultivate land and establish manufactories of such goods as the members can produce for themselves, and to exchange for the production of others; likewise to form a community, thereby giving equal rights and privileges to all.

The last phrase was the important one. For over a decade, even after the original impetus of the movement was weakened during Owen's involvement in trade unionism, the sense that cooperative trading was merely a means to a wider end was not entirely lost. But in 1844, to the greater and more immediate prosperity of members, the Rochdale Pioneers' Society decided to pay prompt dividends on purchases. Thus began a gradual erosion of purpose. More and more conspicuously the attraction of the movement came to lie in the immediate personal benefits it held out, and these were understood increasingly in terms of the criteria of capitalist society itself. By 1860 the vision of eventual social transformation was gone. In that year the President of the Pioneers' Society was able candidly to confess that the movement joined together 'the means, the energies, and the talent of all for the benefit of each' by 'a common bond, that of self-interest'.[66]

That the Owenite ideal should thus disintegrate under changed economic conditions was doubtless unavoidable, but it is not unreasonable to account for its fate as well by looking back to its source in Owen himself. In 1844 Friedrich Engels castigated the Owenites for being 'too intellectual and too metaphysical' in preaching a doctrine of 'philanthropy and universal love'. Thirty years later in his *Anti-Dühring* he softened his criticisms, and even the *Communist Manifesto*, in repeating them, conceded that Owen's teachings, along with those of his French counterparts Fourier

66. See S. Pollard, 'Nineteenth Century Cooperation ...' in *Essays in Labour History*, ed. A. Briggs and J. Saville (London, 1960), pp. 85, 98.

and St Simon, were 'full of the most valuable materials for the enlightenment of the working class'. But the point of the earlier attack is clear, and we do not have to subscribe to Engels' own premises to see it.

A New View of Society was the last influential statement of a rationalist doctrine to be published in England. Reprinted many times, its theme repeated frequently in Owenite journalism and Owen's later writings, it was also the first such doctrine indirectly to affect the actions and beliefs of large numbers of hitherto inarticulate people. This was a strange conjunction and it had complex results. Owen's advocacy of change failed because he abhorred 'pandemonium' and conflict, the *sine qua non* of change, and because his communities failed to face up to the realities of the economic structure in which they would have to exist. But these failures were themselves manifestations of a deeper conviction, and one which Ricardo was not alone in suggesting expected too much of men: the conviction that each individual was susceptible to rational persuasion, and that once persuaded of the truth he would readily change his life for the sake of himself, his fellows, and posterity. At the heart of Owen's system was a confidence in the perfectibility of the individual which precluded the necessity of any systematic, or truly sociological interpretation of social processes. To an indefinable but possibly important extent this confidence could only have weakened working-class political militancy. For if change could take place by the force of example – and Owen had no doubt that once people saw how good the life was in the communities, they would hasten to join them – then there was no need for democracy, or class conflict, or for a movement with a defined and single-minded political end. The solutions he offered were to be implemented outside the existing social system, which by that fact alone would be gradually purified. Thus in essence, Owen's communities, the original cooperative societies, his Labour Exchange, rested all of them on a faith that men would take one splendid imaginative leap into the new moral world. In bad times this was a fine vision for the poor and discontented. But once they found they were able to buy more bread, the vision paled, faith in it wilted. Owen had built a castle of sand. Upon his incomprehension of men's need for defined political ends, whether constitutional or revolutionary, his magnificent system collapsed.

So that although it survives in vestigial form in the modern cooperative movement, Owenism today remains chiefly a phenomenon of past history. Owen himself, however, is something very much more than a historical curiosity. It is true that he cannot be said to live on in his more explicitly formulated ideas. He left the socialist tradition the labour theory of value and the underconsumptionist argument, and showed his successors, very roughly, how to turn them against political economy. But he bequeathed them in their most primitive forms. They evolved into a degree of sophistication which he probably would not have understood, just as he would not have agreed with their implications, at the hands of later socialists, for the established social and political hierarchy. His utopian expectations were destroyed in the failure, one by one, of New Harmony, Orbiston, Queenwood. Though his educational principles are 'modern' in a sense which needs little elaboration, they were not in his own day to be embodied, as he wanted them to be, in a national educational system. By mid-century, too, the great hopes which had been pinned to the cooperative system had lost the battle against prosperity and individualism.

But what does in some form live on is the criterion of the social good which Owen attempted to express in the communitarian and the cooperative ideal, and it does so more or less in the terms in which he first articulated it. We have been examining the way in which a man with an almost childlike innocence, the least introspective of beings, tried to analyse the meaning of one of the most profound changes in history. He did not have the conceptual tools we have for doing so; he did not possess the mastery of language of Carlyle or Ruskin, nor yet of Marx or Engels. But in suggesting that men should strive for harmony, and oppose an economic system which entailed the division of their interests and the depersonalization of their relationships, he was the first to imply a judgement which from a diversity of sources, not merely socialist, many of us inherit.

Further Reading

THE fullest bibliography of works by and about Owen and his followers is contained in J. F. C. Harrison, *Robert Owen and the Owenites in Britain and America*, (London, 1968). It is over a hundred pages long. Harrison's book is itself a refreshing attempt to correct the exclusive emphasis of most historians on Owen's 'socialism' and to relate his achievement to contemporary British and American society.

There are two collections of Owen's writings: for the period 1813–20, *A New View of Society and Other Writings*, edited by G. D. H. Cole (Everyman, 1927); and, less accessible, the supplementary appendix (Volume IA) to Owen's autobiography. This, the *Life of Robert Owen Written by Himself* (London, 1857; another edition London, 1920) is inaccurate but invaluable. Nowhere else does Owen's character define itself so clearly. The reminiscences of those who knew him are also useful: G. J. Holyoake, *Life and Last Days of Robert Owen of New Lanark ...* (London, 1859), and Lloyd Jones, *The Life, Times, and Labours of Robert Owen* (two volumes, London, 1889–90).

Basic biographies, all of them more or less preoccupied with Owen's relationship to the 'working class movement': G. D. H. Cole, *Robert Owen* (London, 1925; further editions 1930, 1965); Margaret Cole, *Robert Owen of New Lanark 1771–1858* (London, 1953); Frank Podmore, *Robert Owen: A Biography* (two volumes, London, 1906; two volumes in one, 1923) – still indispensible.

For the standard interpretations of Owen's contribution to socialist thought, see M. Beer, *A History of British Socialism* (two volumes, London, 1919) and G. D. H. Cole, *A History of Socialist Thought*. Volume I: *The Forerunners, 1789–1850* (London, 1953). The most persuasive presentation, but a brief one, of his relationship to a wider, not exclusively socialist, tradition of English social thought is contained in Raymond Williams's *Culture and Society 1780–1950* (Pelican, 1963). E. P. Thompson discusses to great effect Owenism's contribution to working-class culture in the early nineteenth century in *The*

Making of the English Working Class (London, 1964, Pelican, 1968). Amid a welter of literature on the cooperative movement, the shortest analysis is the best: S. Pollard, 'Nineteenth Century Cooperation: From Community Building to Shopkeeping', in *Essays in Labour History*, edited by A. Briggs and J. Saville (London, 1960).

Note on the Texts

A New View of Society: Owen attached the following note to the third edition:

The First Essay was written in 1812, and published early in 1813. The Second Essay was written and published at the end of 1813. The Third and Fourth Essays were written about the same time, and printed and circulated among the principal political, literary and religious characters in this country and on the continent, as well as among the governments of Europe, America, and British India. They were first printed for sale [as the Second Edition] in July 1816.

The third edition was published in 1817, the fourth in 1818. The text published here is that of these editions, all of which were identical apart from rearrangements of the dedications (indicated below) and minor alterations on the title page. There have been six further editions in Britain and three in America.

The *Report to the County of Lanark* was presented to the Lanarkshire magistrates on 1 May 1820, and published in Glasgow the following year. Another edition was published in London in 1832. The text here is taken from Owen's reprint of the original edition which he included in the supplementary appendix to his autobiography, 1858.

Facsimile title page to the First Edition.

A New View of Society:

OR,

ESSAYS

ON THE PRINCIPLE OF THE

FORMATION OF THE HUMAN CHARACTER,

AND

THE APPLICATION OF THE PRINCIPLE

TO

PRACTICE.

" Any character, from the best to the worst, from the most ignorant to the most enlightened, may be given to any community, even to the world at large, by applying certain means; which are to a great extent at the command and under the controul, or easily made so, of those who possess the government of nations."

BY ONE OF HIS MAJESTY'S JUSTICES OF PEACE FOR
THE COUNTY OF LANARK.

London:
PRINTED FOR CADELL AND DAVIES, STRAND;
BY RICHARD TAYLOR AND CO., PRINTERS' COURT, SHOE LANE.

1813.

WILLIAM WILBERFORCE, Esq., M.P.[1]

My Dear Sir, –

In contemplating the public characters of the day, no one among them appears to have more nearly adopted in practice the principles which this Essay develops than yourself.

In all the most important questions which have come before the senate since you became a legislator, you have not allowed the mistaken considerations of sect or party to influence your decisions; so far as an unbiased judgement can be formed of them, they appear generally to have been dictated by comprehensive views of human nature, and impartiality to your fellow-creatures. The dedication, therefore, of this Essay to you, I consider not as a mere compliment of the day, but rather as a *duty* which your benevolent exertions and disinterested conduct *demand*.

Yet permit me to say that I have a peculiar personal satisfaction in fulfilling this *duty*. My experience of human nature, *as it is now trained*, does not, however, lead me to expect that even *your* mind, without personal inspection, can instantaneously give credit to the *full* extent of the *practical advantages* which are to be derived from an undeviating adherence to the principles displayed in the following pages. And far less is such an effect to be anticipated from the first ebullition of public opinion.

The proposer of a *practice* so *new* and *strange must be content* for a time to be ranked among the *good kind of people*, the speculatists and visionaries of the day, for such it is probable will be the ready exclamations of those who merely skim the surface of all subjects; exclamations, however, in direct contradiction to the fact, that he has not brought the practice into public notice until he patiently for twenty years proved it upon an extensive scale, even to the conviction of inspecting incredulity itself.

And he *is so content*, knowing that the result of the most ample

1. In the first edition this was the dedication of the First Essay; in subsequent editions it was omitted altogether.

investigation and free discussion will prove to a still greater extent than he will yet state, the beneficial consequences of the introduction of the principles for which he now contends.

With confidence, therefore, that you will experience this conviction, and, when experienced, will lend your aid to introduce its influence into *legislative practice*, I subscribe myself, with much esteem and regard,

My dear Sir,

Your obliged and obedient Servant,

ROBERT OWEN

New Lanark Mills

Sir,

The following pages are dedicated to Your Royal Highness, not to add to the flattery which has generally been addressed to those of our fellow men who have filled elevated stations; but they claim your protection because they proceed from a Subject of the empire over which you preside, and from one who disregards every inferior consideration in order that he may accomplish the greatest practical good to that empire.

Your Royal Highness, and all who govern the nations of the world, must be conscious that those of high rank, as well as those of inferior situations in life, now experience much misery.

These Essays have been written to show that the origin of that misery may be traced to the ignorance of those who have ruled, and of those who have been governed; to make that ignorance known and evident to all; and to sketch the outlines of a practical Plan, founded altogether on a preventive system, and derived from principles directly opposed to the errors of our forefathers. Should the outlines which have been sketched be formed into a legislative system, and adhered to without deviation, the most important benefits may be anticipated, not only to the subjects of these realms but to the whole human race.

Your Royal Highness and those who direct the polity of other nations have been taught that you have duties to execute; duties, which, with the highest ability and best intentions, cannot, under the prevailing systems of error, be performed.

Hence the dissatisfaction of those for whose benefit Govern-

1. In the first edition this was the dedication of the Fourth Essay; in subsequent editions it was the first dedication of the complete work.

ments were, or ought to have been, established, and the perplexity and danger of those who govern.

It is concluded with confidence equal to certainty itself, that the principles unfolded in these Essays are competent to develop a practice which, without much apparent change, and without any public disorder, will progressively remove the difficulties of those who in future may rule, and the discontent of those who may be governed.

The language now addressed to Your Royal Highness is the result of a patient observation and extensive experience of human nature; of human nature, not indeed as it is explained in legendary tales of old, but as it now may be read in the living subject – in the words and actions of those among whom we exist.

It is true that many myriads of human beings have been conscientiously deceived; and it may be said, it is most probable that another is now added to the number: it is equally true, however, that similar language has been applied to many, and might have been applied to all who have been the instruments of beneficial improvements.

It may also be said that the principles herein advocated, may nevertheless, like all former theories which have misled mankind, originate in error; in the wild and perverted fancy of a well meaning enthusiast. They have, however, not only been submitted to several of the most intelligent and acute minds of the present day, and who, although urged to the task, have candidly declared they could find no fallacy in the inductions, but they are such, as few, if any, will venture to deny, or scruple to declare that they already admit.

If these principles shall demonstrate themselves to be in unison with every fact which is accessible to us in the present stage of human experience, they will soon prove themselves of a value permanent and substantial, beyond any of the discoveries which have hitherto been made.

Great however as the advantages may prove, the introduction of principles and practices so new, unless they are well understood, may create a temporary ferment.

To prevent the possibility of any such alarm, the leaders of all the sects and parties in the state are invited to canvass these principles, and to endeavour to find error in them, or evil in the consequences which might follow from their admission into practice.

The encouragement of such fair discussion and examination is all that is now solicited from Your Royal Highness.

Should that discussion and examination prove them to be erroneous, they will then be, as they ought to be for the public good, universally condemned. On the contrary, should they bear the test of that investigation to which they are submitted, and be found, without a single exception, uniformly consistent with all the known facts of the creation, and consequently true; then, under the auspices of Your Royal Highness's Administration, mankind will naturally look for the establishment of such a system in the conduct of public affairs as may introduce and perpetuate advantages so eminently important.

That these principles, if true, may give birth to the measures which they immediately recommend; and that Your Royal Highness and the Subjects of these Realms, and the Rulers and Subjects of all other Realms, may in the present age enjoy the advantages of them in practice, is the sincere wish of

Your Royal Highness's faithful Servant,

THE AUTHOR

Friends and Countrymen,

I address myself to you, because your primary and most essential interests are deeply involved in the subjects treated of in the following Essays.

You will find existing evils described, and remedies proposed; but as those evils proceed from the errors of our forefathers, they seem to call for something like veneration from their successors. You will therefore not attribute them to any of the individuals of the present day; neither will you for your own sakes wish or require them to be prematurely removed. Beneficial changes can only take place by well-digested and well-arranged plans temperately introduced and perseveringly pursued.

It is however an important step gained when the cause of evil is ascertained. The next is to devise a remedy, which shall create the least possible inconvenience. To discover this, and try its efficacy in practice, have been the employments of my life; and having found a remedy which experience proves to be safe in its application, and certain in its effects, I am now anxious that you should all partake of its benefits.

But be satisfied, fully and completely satisfied, that the principles on which the New View of Society is founded are true; that no specious error lurks within them, and that no sinister motive gives rise to their publicity. Let them therefore be investigated to their foundation. Let them be scrutinized with the eye of penetration itself; and let them be compared with every fact which the history of the past or the experience of the present may offer to our view. Let this be done, to give you full confidence, beyond the shadow of doubt or suspicion, in the proceedings which are or may

1. In the first edition this was the dedication of the Second Essay; in subsequent editions it was the second dedication of the complete work.

be recommended to your attention. For they will bear this test; and such investigation and comparison will fix them so deeply in your hearts and affections, that never but with life will they be removed from your minds, and from those of your children to the end of time.

Enter therefore fearlessly on the investigation and comparison; startle not at apparent difficulties, but persevere in the spirit and on the principles recommended; you will then speedily overcome those difficulties, your success will be certain, and you will eventually establish the happiness of your fellow-creatures.

That your immediate and united exertions in this cause may be the means of commencing a new system of action, which shall gradually remove the unnecessary evils which afflict the present race of men, is the ardent wish of

THE AUTHOR

An Address[1]

To the Superintendents of Manufactories, and to those Individuals generally, who, by giving Employment to an aggregated Population, may easily adopt the Means to form the Sentiments and Manners of such a Population.

LIKE you, I am a manufacturer for pecuniary profit. But having for many years acted on principles the reverse in many respects of those in which you have been instructed, and having found my procedure beneficial to others and to myself, even in a pecuniary point of view, I am anxious to explain such valuable principles, that you and those under your influence may equally partake of their advantages.

In two Essays, already published, I have developed some of these principles, and in the following pages you will find still more of them explained, with some detail of their application to practice, under the particular local circumstances in which I undertook the direction of the New Lanark Mills and Establishment.

By those details you will find, that from the commencement of my management I viewed the population, with the mechanism and every other part of the establishment, as a system composed of many parts, and which it was my duty and interest so to combine, as that every hand, as well as every spring, lever, and wheel, should effectually cooperate to produce the greatest pecuniary gain to the proprietors.

Many of you have long experienced in your manufacturing operations the advantages of substantial, well-contrived, and well-executed machinery.

Experience has also shown you the difference of the results between mechanism which is neat, clean, well

1. In all editions this Address was included within the text as a preface to the Third Essay.

arranged, and always in a high state of repair; and that which is allowed to be dirty, in disorder, without the means of preventing unnecessary friction, and which therefore becomes, and works, much out of repair.

In the first case, the whole economy and management are good; every operation proceeds with ease, order, and success. In the last, the reverse must follow, and a scene be presented of counteraction, confusion, and dissatisfaction among all the agents and instruments interested or occupied in the general process, which cannot fail to create great loss.

If then due care as to the state of your inanimate machines can produce such beneficial results, what may not be expected if you devote equal attention to your vital machines, which are far more wonderfully constructed?

When you shall acquire a right knowledge of these, of their curious mechanism, of their self-adjusting powers; when the proper main spring shall be applied to their varied movements, you will become conscious of their real value, and you will be readily induced to turn your thoughts more frequently from your inanimate to your living machines; you will discover that the latter may be easily trained and directed to procure a large increase of pecuniary gain, while you may also derive from them high and substantial gratification.

Will you then continue to expend large sums of money to procure the best devised mechanism of wood, brass, or iron; to retain it in perfect repair; to provide the best substance for the prevention of unnecessary friction, and to save it from falling into premature decay? Will you also devote years of intense application to understand the connexion of the various parts of these lifeless machines, to improve their effective powers, and to calculate with mathematical precision all their minute and combined movements? And when in these transactions you estimate time by minutes, and the money expended for the chance of increased gain

95

by fractions, will you not afford some of your attention to consider whether a portion of your time and capital would not be more advantageously applied to improve your living machines?

From experience which cannot deceive me, I venture to assure you, that your time and money so applied, if directed by a true knowledge of the subject, would return you not five, ten, or fifteen per cent for your capital so expended, but often fifty and in many cases a hundred per cent.

I have expended much time and capital upon improvements of the living machinery; and it will soon appear that the time and money so expended in the manufactory at New Lanark, even while such improvements are in progress only, and but half their beneficial effects attained, are now producing a return exceeding fifty per cent, and will shortly create profits equal to cent per cent on the original capital expended in them.

Indeed, after experience of the beneficial effects, from due care and attention to the mechanical implements, it became easy to a reflecting mind to conclude at once, that at least equal advantages would arise from the application of similar care and attention to the living instruments. And when it was perceived that inanimate mechanism was greatly improved by being made firm and substantial; that it was the essence of economy to keep it neat, clean, regularly supplied with the best substance to prevent unnecessary friction, and, by proper provision for the purpose, to preserve it in good repair; it was natural to conclude that the more delicate, complex, living mechanism would be equally improved by being trained to strength and activity; and that it would also prove true economy to keep it neat and clean; to treat it with kindness, that its mental movements might not experience too much irritating friction; to endeavour by every means to make it more perfect; to supply it regularly with a sufficient quantity of wholesome food and other necessaries of life, that the body might be preserved in good working condition, and prevented from being out of repair, or falling prematurely to decay.

These anticipations are proved by experience to be just.

Since the general introduction of inanimate mechanism into British manufactories, man, with few exceptions, has been treated as a secondary and inferior machine; and far more attention has been given to perfect the raw materials of wood and metals than those of body and mind. Give but due reflection to the subject, and you will find that man, even as an instrument for the creation of wealth, may be still greatly improved.

But, my friends, a far more interesting and gratifying consideration remains. Adopt the means which ere long shall be rendered obvious to every understanding, and you may not only partially improve those living instruments, but learn how to impart to them such excellence as shall make them infinitely surpass those of the present and all former times.

Here then is an object which truly deserves your attention; and instead of devoting all your faculties to invent improved inanimate mechanism, let your thoughts be, at least in part, directed to discover how to combine the more excellent materials of body and mind, which, by a well-devised experiment, will be found capable of progressive improvement.

Thus seeing with the clearness of noon-day light, thus convinced with the certainty of conviction itself, let us not perpetuate the really unnecessary evils, which our present practices inflict on this large proportion of our fellow subjects. Should your pecuniary interests somewhat suffer by adopting the line of conduct now urged, many of you are so wealthy, that the expense of founding and continuing at your respective establishments the institutions necessary to improve your animate machines, would not be felt. But when you may have ocular demonstration that, instead of any pecuniary loss, a well-directed attention to form the character and increase the comforts of those who are so entirely at your mercy will essentially add to your gains, prosperity, and happiness; no reasons except those founded on ignorance of your self-interest, can in future prevent you from bestowing your chief care on the living machines which you employ; and by so doing you will prevent an accumulation of human misery, of which it is now difficult to form an adequate conception.

That you may be convinced of this most valuable truth, which due reflection will show you is founded on the evidence of unerring facts, is the sincere wish of

THE AUTHOR

ESSAY FIRST

on The Formation of Character

Any general character, from the best to the worst, from the most ignorant to the most enlightened, may be given to any community, even to the world at large, by the application of proper means; which means are to a great extent at the command and under the control of those who have influence in the affairs of men.

ACCORDING to the last returns under the Population Act, the poor and working classes of Great Britain and Ireland have been found to exceed twelve millions of persons, or nearly three fourths of the population of the British Islands.

The characters of these persons are now permitted to be very generally formed without proper guidance or direction, and, in many cases, under circumstances which directly impel them to a course of extreme vice and misery; thus rendering them the worst and most dangerous subjects in the empire; while the far greater part of the remainder of the community are educated upon the most mistaken principles of human nature, such indeed as cannot fail to produce a general conduct throughout society totally unworthy of the character of rational beings.

The first thus unhappily situated are the poor and the uneducated profligate among the working classes, who are now *trained* to *commit* crimes, for the commission of which they are afterwards *punished*.

The second is the remaining mass of the population, who are not *instructed* to *believe*, or at least to acknowledge, that certain principles are *unerringly true*, and to *act* as though they were *grossly false*; thus filling the world with *folly* and *inconsistency*, and making society, throughout all its ramifications, a scene of insincerity and counteraction.

In this state the world has continued to the present time; its evils have been and are continually increasing; they cry aloud for efficient corrective measures, which if we longer delay, general disorder must ensue.

'But,' say those who have not deeply investigated the subject, 'attempts to apply remedies have been often made, yet all of them have failed. The evil is now of a magnitude not to be controlled; the torrent is already too strong to be stemmed; and we can only wait with fear or calm resignation, to see it carry destruction in its course by confounding all distinctions of right and wrong.'

Such is the language now held, and such are the general feelings on this most important subject.

These, however, if longer suffered to continue, must lead to the most lamentable consequences. Rather than pursue such a course, the character of legislators would be infinitely raised, if, forgetting the petty and humiliating contentions of sects and parties, they would thoroughly investigate the subject, and endeavour to arrest and overcome these mighty evils.

The chief object of these Essays is to assist and forward investigations of such vital importance to the well-being of this country, and of society in general.

The view of the subject which is about to be given has arisen from extensive experience for upwards of twenty years, during which period its truth and importance have been proved by multiplied experiments. That the writer may not be charged with precipitation or presumption, he has had the principle and its consequences, examined, scrutinized, and fully canvassed by some of the most learned, intelligent, and competent characters of the present day; who on every principle of duty as well as of interest, if they had discovered error in either, would have exposed it; – but who, on the contrary, have fairly acknowledged their incontrovertible truth and practical importance.

Assured, therefore, that his principles are true, he proceeds with confidence, and courts the most ample and free discussion of the subject; courts it for the sake of humanity – for the sake of his fellow creatures – millions of whom experience sufferings, which, were they to be unfolded, would compel those who govern the world to exclaim, 'Can these things exist and we have no knowledge of them?' But they do exist – and even the heart-rending statements which were made known to the public during the discussions upon Negro-slavery, do not exhibit more afflicting scenes than those which, in various parts of the world, daily arise from the injustice of society towards itself; from the inattention of mankind to the circumstances which incessantly surround them, and from the want of a correct knowledge of human nature in those who govern and control the affairs of men.

If these circumstances did not exist to an extent almost incredible, it would be unnecessary *now* to contend for a principle regarding Man, which scarcely requires more than to be fairly stated to make it self-evident.

This principle is, that 'ANY GENERAL CHARACTER, FROM THE BEST TO THE WORST, FROM THE MOST IGNORANT TO THE MOST ENLIGHTENED, MAY BE GIVEN TO ANY COMMUNITY, EVEN TO THE WORLD AT LARGE, BY THE APPLICATION OF PROPER MEANS; WHICH MEANS ARE TO A GREAT EXTENT AT THE COMMAND AND UNDER THE CONTROL OF THOSE WHO HAVE INFLUENCE IN THE AFFAIRS OF MEN.'

The principle as now stated is a broad one, and, if it should be found to be true, cannot fail to give a new character to legislative proceedings, and *such* a character as will be most favourable to the well-being of society.

That this principle is true to the utmost limit of the terms is evident from the experience of all past ages and from every existing fact.

Shall misery, then, most complicated and extensive, be experienced, from the prince to the peasant, throughout all the nations of the world, and shall its cause, and the means of its prevention, be known, and yet these means withheld? The undertaking is replete with difficulties, which can only be overcome by those who have influence in society; who, by foreseeing its important *practical* benefits, may be induced to contend against those difficulties; and who, when its advantages are clearly seen and strongly felt, will not suffer individual considerations to be put in competition with their attainment. It is true their ease and comfort may be for a time sacrificed to those prejudices; but, if they persevere, the principles on which this knowledge is founded must ultimately universally prevail.

In preparing the way for the introduction of these principles, it cannot now be necessary to enter into the detail of facts to prove that children can be trained to acquire '*any language, sentiments, belief, or any bodily habits and manners, not contrary to human nature.*'

For that this *has* been done, the history of every nation of which we have records abundantly confirms; and that this is, and may be again done, the facts which exist around us and throughout all the countries in the world prove to demonstration.

Possessing then the knowledge of a power so important; which, when understood, is capable of being wielded with the certainty of a law of nature, and which would gradually remove the evils which now chiefly afflict mankind, shall we permit it to remain dormant and useless, and suffer the plagues perpetually to exist and increase?

No: the time is *now* arrived when the public mind of this country and the general state of the world call imperatively for the introduction of this all-pervading principle, not only in *theory*, but into *practice*.

Nor can any human power now impede its rapid progress.

Silence will not retard its course, and opposition will give increased celerity to its movements. The commencement of the work will, in fact, ensure its accomplishment; henceforth all the irritating, angry passions, arising from ignorance of the true cause of bodily and mental character, will gradually subside, and be replaced by the most frank and conciliating confidence and good-will.

Nor will it be possible hereafter for comparatively a few individuals, unintentionally to occasion the rest of mankind to be surrounded by circumstances which *inevitably* form such characters, as they afterwards deem it a *duty* and a *right to punish even to death; and that too, while they themselves have been the instruments of forming those characters.* Such proceedings not only create innumerable evils to the directing few, but essentially retard them and the great mass of society from attaining the enjoyment of a high degree of positive happiness. Instead of *punishing* crimes after they have *permitted* the human character to be formed so as to commit them, they will adopt the only means which can be adopted to *prevent* the existence of those crimes; means by which they may be most easily prevented.

Happily for poor traduced and degraded human nature, the principle for which we now contend will speedily divest it of all the ridiculous and absurd mystery with which it has been hitherto enveloped by the ignorance of preceding times: and all the *complicated* and *counteracting* motives for good conduct, which have been multiplied almost to infinity, will be reduced to *one single principle of action,* which, by its evident operation and sufficiency, shall render this intricate system *unnecessary,* and ultimately supersede it in all parts of the earth. That principle is THE HAPPINESS OF SELF CLEARLY UNDERSTOOD AND UNIFORMLY PRACTISED; WHICH CAN ONLY BE ATTAINED BY CONDUCT THAT MUST PROMOTE THE HAPPINESS OF THE COMMUNITY.

For that Power which governs and pervades the universe

has evidently so formed man, that he must progressively pass from a state of ignorance to intelligence, the limits of which it is not for man himself to define; and in that progress to discover, that his individual happiness can be increased and extended only in proportion as he actively endeavours to increase and extend the happiness of all around him. The principle admits neither of exclusion nor of limitation; and such appears evidently the state of the public mind, that it will now seize and cherish this principle as the most precious boon which it has yet been allowed to attain. The errors of all opposing motives will appear in their true light, and the ignorance whence they arose will become so glaring, that even the most unenlightened will speedily reject them.

For this state of matters, and for all the gradual changes contemplated, the extraordinary events of the present times have essentially contributed to prepare the way.

Even the late Ruler of France, although *immediately* influenced by the most mistaken principles of ambition, has contributed to this happy result, by shaking to its foundation that mass of superstition and bigotry, which on the continent of Europe had been accumulating for ages, until it had so overpowered and depressed the human intellect, that to attempt improvement without its removal would have been most unavailing. And, in the next place, by carrying the mistaken selfish principles in which mankind have been hitherto educated to the extreme in *practice*, he has rendered their error manifest, and left no doubt of the fallacy of the source whence they originated.

These transactions, in which millions have been immolated, or consigned to poverty and bereft of friends, will be preserved in the records of time, and impress future ages with a just estimation of the principles now about to be introduced into practice; and will thus prove perpetually useful to all succeeding generations.

For the direful effects of Napoleon's government have created the most deep-rooted disgust at notions which could produce a belief that such conduct was glorious, or calculated to increase the happiness of even the individual by whom it was pursued.

And the late discoveries, and proceedings of the Rev. Dr Bell and Mr Joseph Lancaster, have also been preparing the way in a manner the most opposite, but yet not less effectual, by directing the public attention to the beneficial effects, on the young and unresisting mind, of even the limited education which their systems embrace.

They have already effected enough to prove that all which is now in contemplation respecting the training of youth may be accomplished without fear of disappointment. And by so doing, as the consequences of their improvements cannot be confined within the British Isles, they will for ever be ranked among the most important benefactors of the human race. But henceforward to contend for any new *exclusive* system will be in vain: the public mind is already too well informed, and has too far passed the possibility of retrogression, much longer to permit the continuance of any such evil.

For it is now obvious that such a system must be destructive of the happiness of the excluded, by their seeing others enjoy what they are not permitted to possess; and also that it tends, by creating opposition from the justly injured feelings of the excluded, in proportion to the extent of the exclusion, to diminish the happiness even of the privileged: the former therefore can have no rational motive for its continuance. If however, owing to the irrational principles by which the world has been hitherto governed, individuals, or sects, or parties, shall yet by their plans of exclusion attempt to retard the amelioration of society, and prevent the introduction into PRACTICE of that truly just spirit which knows *no* exclusion, such facts shall yet be brought forward as cannot fail to render all their efforts vain. It will therefore be the essence of wisdom in the privileged classes to cooperate sincerely and cordially with those who desire not to touch one iota of the supposed advantages which they *now* possess; and whose first and last wish is to increase the particular happiness of those classes as well as the general happiness of society. A very little reflection on the part of the privileged will insure this line of conduct; whence, without domestic revolution – without war and bloodshed – nay, without prematurely disturbing any thing which exists, the world will be prepared to receive principles which are alone calculated to build up a system of happiness, and to destroy those irritable feelings which have so long afflicted society, – solely because society has hitherto been ignorant of the true means by which the most useful and valuable character may be formed.

This ignorance being removed, experience will soon teach us how to form character, individually and generally, so as to give the greatest sum of happiness to the individual, and to mankind.

These principles require only to be known in order to establish themselves: the outline of our future proceedings then becomes clear and defined, nor will they permit us henceforth to wander from the right path. They direct that the governing powers of all countries should establish rational plans for the education and general formation of the characters of their subjects. – *These plans must be devised to train children from their earliest infancy in good habits of every description (which will of course prevent them from acquiring those of falsehood and deception). They must afterwards be rationally educated, and their labour be usefully directed. Such habits and education will impress them with an active and ardent desire to promote the happiness of every individual, and that without the* shadow of exception *for sect, or party, or country, or climate. They will also insure, with the fewest possible exceptions, health, strength, and vigour of body; for the happiness of man can be erected only on the foundations of health of body and peace of mind.*

And that health of body and peace of mind may be preserved sound and entire, through youth and manhood, to old age, it becomes *equall*y necessary that the irresistible propensities which form part of his nature, and which now produce the endless and ever multiplying evils with which humanity is afflicted, should be so directed as to *increase* and not to *counteract* his happiness.

The knowledge however thus introduced will make it evident to the understanding, that by far the greater part of the misery with which man is encircled *may* be easily dissipated and removed; and that with mathematical precision he *may be* surrounded with those circumstances which must gradually increase his happiness.

Hereafter, when the public at large shall be satisfied that these principles *can* and *will* withstand the ordeal through which they must inevitably pass; when they shall prove themselves true to the clear comprehension and certain conviction of the unenlightened as well as the learned; and when by the irresistible power of truth, detached from falsehood, they shall establish themselves in the mind, no more to be removed but by the entire annihilation of the human intellects; then the consequent practice which they direct shall be explained, and rendered easy of adoption.

In the meantime, let no one anticipate evil, even in the slightest degree, from these principles; they are, not innoxious only, but pregnant with consequences to be wished and desired beyond all others by *every* individual in society.

Some of the best intentioned among the various classes in society may still say, 'All this is *very delightful and very beautiful* in *theory,* but *visionaries* alone can expect to see it *realized.*' To this remark only one reply *can* or *ought* to be made; that *these principles have been carried most successfully into practice*.[1] The present Essays therefore are not brought forward as mere matter of speculation, to amuse the idle visionary – who *thinks* in his closet and never *acts* in the world; but to create universal activity, pervade society with a knowledge of its true interests, and direct the public mind to the most important object to which it can be directed; to a national proceeding for rationally forming the characters of that immense mass of population which is now allowed to be so formed as to fill the world with crimes. Shall questions of merely local and temporary interest, whose ultimate results are calculated only to withdraw pecuniary profits from one set of individuals and give them to others, engage day after day the attention of politicians and ministers; call forth petitions and delegates from the widely spread agricultural and commercial interests of the empire; – and shall the well-being of millions of the poor, half-naked, half-famished, untaught and untrained, hourly increasing to a most alarming extent in these islands, not call forth *one* petition, *one* delegate, or *one* rational effective legislative measure? No! for such has been our education, that we hesitate not to devote years and expend millions in the *detection* and *punishment* of crimes, and in the attainment of objects whose ultimate results are in comparison with this insignificancy itself; and yet we have not moved one step in the true path to *prevent* crimes, and to diminish the innumerable evils with which mankind are now afflicted. Are these false principles of conduct in those who govern the world to influence mankind permanently, – and if not, *how* and *when* is the change to commence? These important considerations shall form the subject of the next essay.

1. The beneficial effects of this practice have been experienced for many years among a population of between two and three thousand at New Lanark in Scotland.

ESSAY SECOND

The Principles of the Former Essay Continued and Applied in Part to Practice

*It is not unreasonable to hope that hostility may cease,
even where perfect agreement cannot be established. If
we cannot reconcile all opinions, let us endeavour to
unite all hearts.*
Mr Vansittart's Letter to the Rev. Dr Herbert Marsh.

―――――

GENERAL principles only were developed in the First Essay. In this an attempt will be made to show the advantages which may be derived from the adoption of those principles into practice, and to explain the mode by which the practice may without inconvenience be generally introduced.

Some of the most important benefits to be derived from the introduction of those principles into practice are, that they will create the most cogent reasons to induce each man 'to have charity for *all* men'. No feeling short of this can indeed find place in any mind which has been taught clearly to understand, that children in all parts of the earth have been, are, and everlastingly will be, impressed with habits and sentiments similar to those of their parents and instructors; modified, however, by the circumstances in which they have been, are, or may be placed, and by the peculiar original organization of each individual. Yet not one of these causes of character is at the command, or in any manner under the control, of infants, who (whatever absurdity we may have been taught to the contrary) cannot possibly be accountable for the sentiments and manners which may be given to them. And here lies the fundamental error of society, and from hence have proceeded, and do proceed, most of the miseries of mankind.

Children are, without exception, passive and wonderfully contrived compounds; which, by an accurate previous and subsequent attention, *founded on a correct knowledge of the subject*, may be formed collectively to have any human character. And although these compounds, like all the other works of nature, possess endless varieties, yet they partake of that plastic quality, which, by perseverance under judicious management, may be ultimately moulded into the very image of rational wishes and desires.

In the next place, these principles cannot fail to create feelings, which without force, or the production of any counteracting motive, will irresistibly lead those who possess them to make due allowance for the difference of sentiments and manners, not only among their friends and country-men, but also among the inhabitants of every region of the earth, even including their enemies. With this insight into the formation of character, there is no conceivable founda-tion for private displeasure or public enmity. Say, if it be within the sphere of possibility that children can be trained to attain *that* knowledge, and at the same time to acquire feelings of enmity towards a single human creature? The child who from infancy has been rationally instructed in these principles, will readily discover and trace *whence* the opinions and habits of his associates have arisen, and *why* they possess them. At the same age he will have acquired reasons sufficient to exhibit to him forcibly the irrationality of being angry with an individual for possess-ing qualities which, as a passive being during the formation of those qualities, he had not the means of preventing. Such are the impressions these principles will make on the mind of every child so taught; and instead of generating anger or displeasure, they will produce commiseration and pity for those individuals who possess either habits or sentiments which appear to him to be destructive of their own comfort, pleasure, or happiness; and will produce on his part a desire to remove those causes of distress, that his own feelings of commiseration and pity may be also removed. The pleasure which he cannot avoid experiencing by this mode of conduct will likewise stimulate him to the most active endeavours to withdraw those circumstances which surround any part of mankind with causes of misery, and to replace them with others which have a tendency to increase happiness. He will then also strongly entertain the desire to 'do good to *all* men', and even to those who think themselves his enemies.

Thus *shortly, directly,* and *certainly* may mankind be taught the *essence,* and to attain the *ultimate object,* of all former *moral* and *religious* instruction.

These Essays, however, are intended to explain that which is *true,* and not to attack that which is *false.* For to explain that which is true may permanently improve, without creating even temporary evil; whereas to attack that which is false, is often productive of very fatal consequences. The former convinces the judgement, when the mind possesses full and deliberative powers of judging; the latter instantly arouses irritation, and renders the judgement unfit for its office, and useless. But why should we *ever* irritate? Do not these principles make it so obvious as to place it beyond any doubt, that even the present irrational ideas and practices prevalent throughout the world, are not to be charged as either a fault or culpable error of the existing generation? The immediate cause of them was the partial ignorance of our forefathers, who, although they acquired some vague disjointed knowledge of the principles on which character is formed, could not discover the connected chain of those principles, and consequently knew not how to apply them to practice. They taught their children that which they had acquired; and in so doing they acted like their forefathers; who retained the established customs of former generations until better and superior were discovered and made evident to them.

The present race of men have also instructed their children as they had been previously instructed, and are equally unblameable for any defects which their systems contain. And however erroneous or injurious that instruction and those systems may now be proved to be, the principles on which these Essays are founded will be misunderstood, and their spirit will be wholly misconceived, if either irritation, or the slightest degree of ill will, shall be generated against those who even tenaciously adhere to the worst parts of that instruction, and support the most pernicious of those systems. For such individuals, sects, or parties have been trained from infancy to consider it their duty and interest so to act, and in so acting they merely continue the customs of their predecessors. Let truth unaccompanied with error be placed before them; give them time to examine it, and see that it is in unison with all previously ascertained truths, and conviction and acknowledgement of it will follow of course. It is weakness itself to require assent *before* conviction, and *afterwards* it will not be withheld. To endeavour to force conclusions, without making the subject clear to the understanding, is most unjustifiable and irrational, and must prove useless or injurious to the mental faculties. In the spirit thus described we therefore proceed in the investigation of the subject.

The facts which by the invention of printing have gradually accumulated, now show the errors of the systems of our forefathers so distinctly, that they must be, when pointed out, evident to all classes of the community, and render it absolutely necessary that new legislative measures be immediately adopted, to prevent the confusion which must arise from even the most ignorant being competent to detect the absurdity and glaring injustice of many of those laws by which they are now governed.

Such are those laws which enact punishments for a very great variety of actions designated crimes; while those from whom such actions proceed, are regularly trained to acquire no other knowledge than that which compels them to conclude, that those actions are the best they could perform.

How much longer shall we continue to allow generation after generation to be taught crime from their infancy, and, when so taught, hunt them like beasts of the forests, until they are entangled beyond escape in the toils and nets of the law? when, if the circumstances of those poor unpitied sufferers had been reversed with those who are even surrounded with the pomp and dignity of justice, these latter would have been at the bar of the culprit, and the former would have been in the judgement seat.

Had the present Judges of these realms been born and educated among the poor and profligate of St Giles's, or some similar situation, is it not certain, inasmuch as they possess native energies and abilities, that ere this they would have been at the head of their *then* profession, and, in consequence of that superiority and proficiency, would have already suffered imprisonment, transportation, or death? Can we for a moment hesitate to decide, that if some of those men whom the laws, dispensed by the present Judges, have doomed to suffer capital punishments, had been born, trained, and circumstanced as these Judges were born, trained, and circumstanced; that some of those who had so suffered, would have been the identical individuals who would have passed the same awful sentences on the present highly esteemed dignitaries of the law?

If we open our eyes and attentively notice events, we shall observe these facts to multiply before us. Is the evil then of so small magnitude as to be totally disregarded and passed by as the ordinary occurrences of the day, and as not deserving of one reflection? And shall we be longer told, 'that the convenient time to attend to inquiries of this nature is not yet come; that other matters of far weightier import engage our attention, and it must remain over till a season of more leisure?'

To those who may be inclined to think and speak thus, I would say, 'Let feelings of humanity or strict justice induce you to devote a few hours to visit some of the public prisons of the metropolis, and patiently inquire, with kind commiserating solicitude, of their various inhabitants, the events of their lives, and the lives of their connexions. They will tales unfold that *must* arrest attention, that will disclose *sufferings, misery*, and *injustice*, upon which, for obvious reasons, I will not now dwell, but which, previously, I am persuaded, you could not suppose it possible to exist in any civilized state, far less that they should be permitted for centuries to increase around the very fountain of British jurisprudence.' The true cause however of this conduct, so contrary to the general humanity of the natives of these Islands, is, that a practicable remedy for the evil, on clearly defined and sound principles, had not yet been suggested. But the principles developed in this 'New View of Society' *will point out a remedy which is almost simplicity itself, possessing no more practical difficulties than many of the common employments of life: and such as are readily overcome by men of very ordinary practical talents*.

That such a remedy is easily practicable, may be collected from the account of the following very partial experiment.

In the year 1784 the late Mr Dale of Glasgow founded a manufactory for spinning of cotton near the falls of the Clyde, in the county of Lanark in Scotland; and about that period cotton mills were first introduced into the northern part of the kingdom.

It was the power which could be obtained from the falls of water which induced Mr Dale to erect his mills in this situation, for in other respects it was not well chosen; the country around was uncultivated; the inhabitants were poor, and few in number; and the roads in the neighbourhood were so bad, that the Falls now so celebrated were then unknown to strangers.

It was therefore necessary to collect a new population to supply the infant establishment with labourers. This however was no light task; for all the regularly trained Scotch peasantry disdained the idea of working early and late, day after day, within cotton mills. Two modes then only remained of obtaining these labourers: the one, to procure children from the various public charities of the country; and the other, to induce families to settle around the works.

To accommodate the first, a large house was erected, which ultimately contained about five hundred children, who were procured chiefly from workhouses and charities in Edinburgh. These children were to be fed, clothed, and educated; and these duties Mr Dale performed with the unwearied benevolence which it is well known he possessed.

To obtain the second, a village was built, and the houses were let at a low rent to such families as could be induced to accept employment in the mills: but such was the general dislike to that occupation at the time, that, with a few exceptions, only persons destitute of friends, employment, and character, were found willing to try the experiment; and of these a sufficient number to supply a constant increase of the manufactory could not be obtained. It was therefore deemed a favour on the part even of such individuals to reside at the village, and when taught the business they grew so valuable to the establishment, that they became agents not to be governed contrary to their own inclinations.

Mr Dale's principal advocations were at a distance from the works, which he seldom visited more than once for a few hours in three or four months: he was therefore under the necessity of committing the management of the establishment to various servants with more or less power.

Those who have a practical knowledge of mankind will readily anticipate the character which a population so collected and constituted would acquire; it is therefore scarcely necessary to state, that the community by degrees was formed under these circumstances into a very wretched society; every man did that which was right in his own eyes, and vice and immorality prevailed to a monstrous extent. The population lived in idleness, in poverty, in almost every kind of crime; consequently in debt, out of health, and in misery. Yet to make matters still worse, – although the cause proceeded from the best possible motive, a conscientious adherence to principle, – the whole was under a strong sectarian influence, which gave a marked and decided preference to one set of religious opinions over all others, and the professors of the favoured opinions were the privileged of the community.

The boarding-house containing the children presented a very different scene. The benevolent proprietor spared no expense to give comfort to the poor children. The rooms provided for them were spacious, always clean, and well ventilated; the food was abundant, and of the best quality; the clothes were neat and useful; a surgeon was kept in constant pay to direct how to prevent or to cure disease; and the best instructors which the country afforded were appointed to teach such branches of education as were deemed likely to be useful to children in their situation. Kind and well disposed persons were appointed to superintend all their proceedings. Nothing, in short, at first sight seemed wanting to render it a most complete charity.

But to defray the expense of these well devised arrangements, and support the establishment generally, it was absolutely necessary that the children should be employed within the mills from six o'clock in the morning till seven in the evening, summer and winter; and after these hours their education commenced. The directors of the public charities, from mistaken economy, would not consent to send the children under their care to cotton mills, unless the children were received by the proprietors at the ages of six, seven, and eight. And Mr Dale was under the necessity of accepting them at those ages, or of stopping the manufactory which he had commenced.

It is not to be supposed that children so young could remain, with the interval of meals only, from six in the morning until seven in the evening, in constant employment on their feet within cotton mills, and afterwards acquire much proficiency in education. And so it proved; for many of them became dwarfs in body and mind, and some of them were deformed. Their labour through the day, and their education at night, became so irksome, that numbers of them continually ran away, and almost all looked forward with impatience and anxiety to the expiration of their apprenticeship of seven, eight, and nine years; which generally expired when they were from thirteen to fifteen years old. At this period of life, unaccustomed to provide for themselves, and unacquainted with the world, they usually went to Edinburgh or Glasgow, where boys and girls were soon assailed by the innumerable temptations which all large towns present; and to which many of them fell sacrifices.

Thus Mr Dale's arrangements and kind solicitude for the comfort and happiness of these children were rendered in their ultimate effect almost nugatory. They were hired by him, and sent to be employed, and without their labour he could not support them; but, while under his care, he did all that any individual, circumstanced as he was, could do for his fellow-creatures. The error proceeded from the children being sent from the workhouses at an age much too young for employment; they ought to have been detained four years longer, and educated; and then some of the evils which followed would have been prevented.

If such be a true picture, not overcharged, of parish apprentices to our manufacturing system, under the best and most humane regulations, in what colours must it be exhibited under the worst?

Mr Dale was advancing in years; he had no son to succeed him; and finding the consequences just described to be the result of all his strenuous exertions for the improvement and happiness of his fellow-creatures, it is not surprising that he became disposed to retire from the cares of the establishment. He accordingly sold it to some English merchants and manufacturers; one of whom, under the circumstances just narrated, undertook the management of the concern, and fixed his residence in the midst of the population. This individual had been previously in the management of large establishments, employing a number of work-people in the neighbourhood of Manchester; and in every case, by the steady application of certain general principles, he succeeded in reforming the habits of those under his care, and who always among their associates in similar employment appeared conspicuous for their good conduct. With this previous success in remodelling English character, but ignorant of the local ideas, manners, and customs of those now committed to his management, the stranger commenced his task.

At that period the lower classes in Scotland, like those of other countries, had strong prejudices against strangers having any authority over them, and particularly against the English; few of whom had then settled in Scotland, and not one in the neighbourhood of the scenes under description. It is also well known that even the Scotch peasantry and working classes possess the habit of making observations and reasoning thereon with great acuteness; and in the present case, those employed naturally concluded that the new purchasers intended merely to make the utmost profit by the establishment, from the abuses of which many of themselves were then deriving support. The persons employed at these works were therefore strongly prejudiced against the new director of the establishment; prejudiced, because he was a stranger and from England; because he succeeded Mr Dale, under whose proprietorship they acted almost as they liked; because his religious creed was not theirs; and because they concluded that the works would be governed by new laws and regulations, calculated to squeeze, as they often termed it, the greatest sum of gain out of their labour.

In consequence, from the day he arrived among them, every means which ingenuity could devise was set to work to counteract the plan which he attempted to introduce; and for two years it was a regular attack and defence of prejudices and malpractices between the manager and population of the place; without the former being able to make such progress, or convince the latter of the sincerity of his good intentions for their welfare. He however did not lose his patience, his temper, or his confidence in the certain success of the principles on which he founded his conduct. These principles ultimately prevailed: the population could not continue to resist a firm well-directed kindness administering justice to all. They therefore slowly and cautiously began to give him some portion of their confidence; and, as this increased, he was enabled more and more to develop his plans for their amelioration. It may with truth be said, that at this period they possessed almost all the vices and very few of the virtues of a social community. Theft and the receipt of stolen goods was their trade, idleness and drunkenness their habit, falsehood and deception their garb, dissentions civil and religious their daily practice: they united only in a zealous systematic opposition to their employers.

Here, then, was a fair field on which to try the efficacy in practice of principles supposed capable of altering any characters. The manager formed his plans accordingly: he spent some time in finding out the full extent of the evil against which he had to contend, and in tracing the true causes which had produced, and were continuing, those effects. He found that all was distrust, disorder, and dis- union; and he wished to introduce confidence, regularity, and harmony: he therefore began to bring forward his various expedients to withdraw the unfavourable circum- stances by which they had been hitherto surrounded, and replace them by others calculated to produce a more happy result. He soon discovered that theft was extended through almost all the ramifications of the community, and the re- ceipt of stolen goods through all the country around. To remedy this evil, not one legal punishment was inflicted, not one individual imprisoned, even for an hour: but checks and other regulations of prevention were introduced: a short plain explanation of the immediate benefits they would derive from a different conduct was inculcated by those instructed for the purpose, who had the best powers of reasoning among themselves. They were at the same time instructed how to direct their industry in legal and useful occupations; by which, without danger or disgrace, they could really earn more than they had previously obtained by dishonest practices. – Thus, the difficulty of committing the crime was increased, the detection after- wards rendered more easy, the habit of honest industry formed, and the pleasure of good conduct experienced.

Drunkenness was attacked in the same manner: it was discountenanced on every occasion by those who had charge of any department: its destructive and pernicious effects were frequently stated by his own more prudent com- rades, at the proper moment, when the individual was soberly suffering from the effects of his previous excess: pot- and public-houses were gradually removed from the immedi- ate vicinity of their dwellings: the health and comfort of temperance were made familiar to them: by degrees drunkenness disappeared, and many who were habitual bacchanalians are now conspicuous for undeviating sobriety.

Falsehood and deception met with a similar fate; they were held in disgrace, their practical evils were shortly explained; and every countenance was given to truth and open conduct. The pleasure and substantial advantages derived from the latter, soon overcame the impolicy, error, and consequent misery which the former mode of acting had created.

Dissentions and quarrels were undermined by analogous expedients. When they could not be readily adjusted between the parties themselves, they were stated to the manager; and as in such cases both disputants were usually more or less in the wrong, that wrong was in as few words as possible explained, forgiveness and friendship recommended, and one simple and easily remembered precept inculcated, as the most valuable rule for their whole conduct, and the advantages of which they would experience every moment of their lives: – viz. 'That in future they should endeavour to use the same active exertions to make each other happy and comfortable, as they had hitherto done to make each other miserable; and, by carrying this short memorandum in their mind, and applying it on all occasions, they would soon render that place a paradise, which, from the most mistaken principles of action, they now made the abode of misery.' – The experiment was tried, the parties enjoyed the gratification of this new mode of conduct; references rapidly subsided, and now serious differences are scarcely known.

Considerable jealousies also existed on account of one religious sect possessing a decided preference over the others. This was corrected by discontinuing that preference, and giving an uniform encouragement to those who conducted themselves well, among all the various religious persuasions;

by recommending the same consideration to be shown to the conscientious opinions of each sect, on the ground that all must believe the particular doctrines which they had been taught, and consequently all were in that respect upon an equal footing, nor was it possible yet to say which was right, or which wrong. It was likewise inculcated, that all should attend to the essence of religion, and not act as the world was now taught and trained to do: that is, to overlook the substance and essence of religion, and devote their talents, time, and money, to that which is far worse than its shadow, sectarianism, another term for something very injurious to society, and very absurd, which one or other well meaning enthusiast has added to *true religion*; which, without these defects, would soon form those characters which every wise and good man is anxious to see.

Such statements and conduct arrested sectarian animosity and ignorant intolerance; each retains full liberty of conscience, and in consequence each partakes of the sincere friendship of many sects instead of one. They act with cordiality together in the same departments and pursuits, and associate as though the whole community were not of different sectarian persuasions: and not one evil ensues.

The same principles were applied to correct the irregular intercourse of the sexes; – such conduct was discountenanced and held in disgrace; fines were levied upon both parties for the use of the support fund[1] of the community. But because they had once unfortunately offended against the established laws and customs of society, they were not forced to become vicious, abandoned, and miserable. The door was left open for them to return to the comforts of kind friends and respected acquaintance; and, beyond any previous expectation, the evil became greatly diminished.

1. This fund arose from each individual contributing one sixtieth part of their wages, which, under their own management, was applied to support the sick, the injured by accident, and the aged.

The system of receiving apprentices from public charities was abolished; permanent settlers with large families were encouraged, and comfortable houses were built for their accommodation.

The practice of employing children in the mills, of six, seven, and eight years of age, was discontinued, and their parents advised to allow them to acquire health and education until they were ten years old.[2]

The children were taught reading, writing, and arithmetic, during five years, that is, from five to ten, in the village school, without expense to their parents. All the modern improvements in education have been adopted, or are in process of adoption.[3] They may therefore be taught and well trained before they engage in any regular employment. Another important consideration is, that all their instruction is rendered a pleasure and delight to them; they are much more anxious for the hour of school time to arrive than to end: they therefore make a rapid progress; and it may be safely asserted, that if they shall not be trained to form such characters as may be the most desired, the fault will not proceed from the children; the cause will be in the want of a true knowledge of human nature in those who have the management of them and their parents.

During the period that these changes were going forward,

2. It may be remarked, that even this age is too early to keep them at constant employment in manufactories from six in the morning to seven in the evening. Far better would it be for the children, their parents, and for society, that the first should not commence employment until they attain the age of twelve, when their education might be finished, and their bodies would be more competent to undergo the fatigue and exertions required of them. When parents can be trained to afford this additional time to their children without inconvenience, they will, of course, adopt the practice now recommended.

3. To avoid the inconveniences which must ever arise from the introduction of a particular creed into a school, the children are taught to read in such books as inculcate those precepts of the Christian religion which are common to all denominations.

attention was given to the domestic arrangements of the community. Their houses were rendered more comfortable, their streets were improved, the best provisions were purchased, and sold to them at low rates, yet covering the original expense; and under such regulations as taught them how to proportion their expenditure to their income. Fuel and clothes were obtained for them in the same manner; and no advantage was ever attempted to be taken of them, or means used to deceive them.

In consequence, their animosity and opposition to the stranger subsided, their full confidence was obtained, and they became satisfied that no evil was intended them: they were convinced that a real desire existed to increase their happiness, upon those grounds alone on which it could be permanently increased. All difficulties in the way of future improvement vanished. They were taught to be rational, and they acted rationally; thus both parties experienced the incalculable advantages of the system which had been adopted. Those employed became industrious, temperate, healthy; faithful to their employers, and kind to each other; while the proprietors were deriving services from their attachment, almost without inspection, far beyond those which could be obtained by any other means than those of mutual confidence and kindness. Such was the effect of these principles on the adults; on those whose previous habits had been as ill formed as habits could be; and certainly the application of the principles to practice was made under the most unfavourable circumstances.[4]

I have thus given a detailed account of this experiment,

4. It may be supposed that this community was separated from other society; but the supposition would be erroneous, for it had daily and hourly communication with a population exceeding itself. The royal borough of Lanark is only one mile distant from the works; many individuals come daily from the former to be employed at the latter; and a general intercourse is constantly maintained between the old and new towns.

although a partial application of the principles is of far less importance than a clear and accurate account of the principles themselves, in order that they may be so well understood as to be easily rendered applicable to practice in any community, and under any circumstances. Without this, particular facts may indeed amuse or astonish, but they would not contain that substantial value which the principles will be found to possess. But if the relation of the narrative shall forward this object, the experiment cannot fail to prove the certain means of renovating the moral and religious principles of the world; by showing whence arise the various opinions, manners, vices and virtues of mankind; and how the best or the worst of them may, with mathematical precision, be taught to the rising generations.

Let it not, therefore, be longer said that evil or injurious actions cannot be prevented; or that the most rational habits in the rising generation cannot be universally formed. In those characters which now exhibit crime, the fault is obviously not in the individual, but the defect proceeds from the system in which the individual has been trained. Withdraw those circumstances which tend to create crime in the human character, and crime will not be created. Replace them with such as are calculated to form habits of order, regularity, temperance, industry, and these qualities will be formed. Adopt measures of fair equity and justice, and you will readily acquire the full and complete confidence of the lower orders: proceed systematically on principles of undeviating persevering kindness, yet retaining and using, with the least possible severity, the means of restraining crime from immediately injuring society; and by degrees even the crimes now existing in the adults will also gradually disappear; for the worst formed disposition, short of incurable insanity, will not long resist a firm, determined, well directed, persevering kindness. Such a proceeding, whenever practised, will be found the most powerful and effective corrector of crime, and of all injurious and improper habits.

The experiment narrated shows that this is not hypothesis and theory. The principles may be with confidence stated to be universal, and applicable to all times, persons, and circumstances. And the most obvious application of them would be, to adopt rational means to remove the temptation to commit crimes, and increase the difficulties of committing them; while, at the same time, a proper direction should be given to the active powers of the individual, and a due share provided of uninjurious amusements and recreation. Care must be also taken to remove the causes of jealousy, dissentions, and irritation; to introduce sentiments calculated to create union and confidence among all the members of the community; and the whole should be directed by a persevering kindness, sufficiently evident to prove that a sincere desire exists to increase, and not to diminish, happiness.

These principles, applied to the community at New Lanark at first under many of the most discouraging circumstances, but persevered in for sixteen years, effected a complete change in the general character of the village, containing upwards of two thousand inhabitants, and into which also, there was a constant influx of new comers. – But as the promulgation of new miracles is not for present times, it is not pretended that under such circumstances one and all are become wise and good; or, that they are free from error: but it may be truly stated, that they now constitute a very improved society, that their worst habits are gone, and that their minor ones will soon disappear under a continuance of the application of the same principles; that during the period mentioned, scarcely a legal punishment has been inflicted, or an application been made for parish funds by any individual among them. Drunkenness is not seen in their streets, and the children are taught and trained in the institution for forming their character without any punishment. The community exhibits the general appearance of industry, temperance, comfort, health, and happiness. – These are and ever will be the sure and certain effects of the adoption of the principles explained; and these principles, applied with judgement, will effectually reform the most vicious community existing, and train the younger part of it to any character which may be desired; and that, too, much more easily on an extended than on a limited scale. – To apply these principles, however, successfully to practice, both a comprehensive and a minute view must be taken of the existing state of the society on which they are intended to operate. The causes of the most prevalent evils must be accurately traced, and those means which appear the most easy and simple should be immediately applied to remove them.

In this progress the smallest alteration, adequate to produce any good effect, should be made at one time; indeed, if possible, the change should be so gradual as to be almost imperceptible, yet always making a permanent advance in the desired improvements. By this procedure the most rapid practical progress will be obtained, because the inclination to resistance will be removed, and time will be given for reason to weaken the force of long established injurious prejudices. The removal of the first evil will prepare the way for the removal of the second; and this facility will increase, not in an arithmetical, but in a geometrical proportion; until the directors of the system will themselves be gratified beyond expression with the beneficial magnitude of their own proceedings.

Nor while these principles shall be acted upon can there be any retrogression in this good work; for the permanence of the amelioration will be equal to its extent.

What then remains to prevent such a system from being immediately adopted into national practice? Nothing surely, but a general distribution of the knowledge of the practice.

For, with the certain means of preventing crimes, can it be supposed that British legislators, as soon as these means shall be made evident, will longer withhold them from their fellow subjects? No: I am persuaded that neither prince, ministers, parliament, nor any party in church or state, will avow inclination to act on principles of such flagrant injustice. Have they not on many occasions evinced a sincere and ardent desire to ameliorate the condition of the subjects of the empire, when practicable means of amelioration were explained to them, which could be adopted without risking the safety of the state? They have, it is true, refused one measure called a reform, and most wise have they been in persevering in that refusal. But the advocates for that measure, well-intentioned and patriotic as many of them are, cannot show any good practical effects to be derived from it in the present state of ignorance in which the mass of the British population has been hitherto allowed to be trained. On the contrary, no rational being can attentively observe the scenes exhibited during every general election, and wish for those scenes to be extended. That, indeed, would be to wish anything but a reform of the manners, habits and principles of our abused and deluded fellow subjects. Nor is it easy to say which most deserve our pity and commiseration; those who, with some pretensions to knowledge, adopt every low art to deceive, – to engender the most pernicious habits, – nay, to foster crime, which they afterwards enact laws to punish, – or those whose welfare and substantial comforts are sacrificed to such proceedings.

Away then with this abuse of terms! It would not, and while the present circumstances continue, it could not be reform; but, if now adopted, it would soon terminate in anarchy and confusion.

For some time to come there can be but one practicable, and therefore one rational reform, which without danger can be attempted in these realms; a reform in which all men and all parties may join – that is, a reform in the training and in the management of the poor, the ignorant, the untaught and untrained, or ill taught and ill trained among the whole mass of British population; and a plain, simple, practicable plan, which would not contain the least danger to any individual or to any part of society, may be devised for that purpose.

That plan is a national, well digested, unexclusive system for the formation of character, and general amelioration of the lower orders. On the experience of a life devoted to the subject I hesitate not to say, that the members of any community may by degrees be trained to live *without idleness, without poverty, without crime, and without punishment;* for each of these is the effect of error in the various systems prevalent throughout the world. *They are all the necessary consequences of ignorance.*

Train any population rationally, and they will be rational. Furnish honest and useful employments to those so trained, and such employments they will greatly prefer to dishonest or injurious occupations. It is beyond all calculation the interest of every government to provide that training and that employment: and to provide both is easily practicable.

The first, as before stated, is to be obtained by a national system for the formation of character; the second, by governments preparing a reserve of employment for the surplus working classes, when the general demand for labour throughout the country is not equal to the full occupation of the whole: that employment to be on useful national objects, from which the public may derive advantage equal to the expense which those works may require.

The national plan for the formation of character should *include* all the modern improvements of education, without regard to the system of any one individual; and should not *exclude* the child of any one subject in the empire. Anything short of this would be an act of intolerance and injustice to the excluded, and of injury to society, so glaring and manifest, that I shall be deceived in the character of my countrymen, if any of those who have influence in church or state should now be found willing to attempt it. Is it not indeed strikingly evident even to common observers, that any further effort to enforce religious exclusion would involve the certain and speedy destruction of the present church establishment, and would even endanger our civil institutions?

It may be said, however, that ministers and parliament have many other important subjects under discussion. This is evidently true; but will they not have high national concerns always to engage their attention? And can any question be brought forward of deeper interest to the community than that which affects the formation of character and the well-being of every individual within the empire? a question too which, when understood, will be found to offer the means of amelioration to the revenues of these kingdoms, far beyond any practical plan now likely to be devised. Yet, important as are considerations of revenue, they must appear secondary when put in competition with the lives, liberty, and comfort of our fellow subjects; which are now hourly sacrificed for want of an *effective legislative measure to prevent crime.* And is an act of such vital importance to the well-being of all to be longer delayed? *Shall yet another year pass in which crime shall be forced on the infant, who in ten, twenty, or thirty years hence shall suffer* DEATH *for being taught that crime?* Surely it is impossible. Should it be so delayed, *the individuals of the present parliament, the legislators of this day,* ought in strict and impartial justice to be amenable to the laws, for not adopting the means in their power to prevent the crime; rather than the poor, untrained, and unprotected culprit, whose previous years, if he had language to describe them, would exhibit a life of unceasing wretchedness, arising *solely* from the errors of society.

Much might be added on these momentous subjects, even to make them evident to the capacities of children: but for obvious reasons the outlines are merely sketched; and it is hoped these outlines will be sufficient to induce the well-disposed of all parties cordially to unite in this vital measure for the preservation of everything dear to society.

In the next Essay an account will be given of the plans which are in progress at New Lanark for the further comfort and improvement of its inhabitants; and a general *practical* system be described, by which the same advantages may be gradually introduced among the poor and working classes throughout the United Kingdom.

ESSAY THIRD

The Principles of the Former Essays Applied to a Particular Situation

Truth must ultimately prevail over Error

AT the conclusion of the Second Essay, a promise was made that an account should be given of the plans which were in progress at New Lanark for the further improvement of its inhabitants; and that a practical system should be sketched, by which equal advantages might be generally introduced among the poor and working classes throughout the United Kingdom.

This account became necessary, in order to exhibit even a limited view of the principles on which the plans of the author are founded, and to recommend them generally to practice.

That which has been hitherto done for the community of New Lanark, as described in the Second Essay, has chiefly consisted in WITHDRAWING SOME OF THOSE CIRCUMSTANCES WHICH TENDED TO GENERATE, CONTINUE, OR INCREASE EARLY BAD HABITS; THAT IS TO SAY, UNDOING THAT WHICH SOCIETY HAD FROM IGNORANCE PERMITTED TO BE DONE.

To effect this, however, was a far more difficult task than to train up a child from infancy in the way he should go, for that is the most easy process for the formation of character; while to unlearn and to change long acquired habits, is a proceeding directly opposed to the most tenacious feelings of human nature.

Nevertheless the proper application steadily pursued

132

did effect beneficial changes on the old habits, even beyond the most sanguine expectations of the party by whom the task was undertaken. The principles were derived from the study of human nature itself, and they could not fail of success.

Still, however, very little, comparatively speaking, had been done for them. They had not been taught the most valuable domestic and social habits: such as the most economical method of preparing food; how to arrange their dwellings with neatness, and to keep them always clean and in order; but what was of infinitely more importance, they had not been instructed how to train their children, to form them into valuable members of the community, or to know that principles existed, which, when properly applied to practice from infancy, would insure from man to man, without chance of failure, a just, open, sincere, and benevolent conduct.

It was in this stage of the progress of improvement, that it became necessary to form arrangements for surrounding them with circumstances, which should gradually prepare the individuals to receive and firmly retain those domestic and social acquirements and habits.

For this purpose a building, which may be termed the 'New Institution', was erected in the centre of the establishment, with an enclosed area before it. The area is intended for a play-ground for the children of the villagers, from the time they can walk alone until they enter the school.

It must be evident to those who have been in the practice of observing children with attention, that much of good or evil is taught to or acquired by a child at a very early period of its life; that much of temper or disposition is correctly or incorrectly formed before he attains his second year; and that many durable impressions are made at the termination of the first twelve or even six months of his existence.

The children therefore of the uninstructed and ill-instructed suffer material injury in the formation of their characters, during these and the subsequent years of childhood and of youth.

It was to prevent, or as much as possible to counteract, these primary evils, to which the poor and working classes are exposed when infants, that the area became part of the New Institution.

Into this play-ground the children are to be received as soon as they can freely walk alone; to be superintended by persons instructed to take charge of them.

As the happiness of man chiefly, if not altogether, depends on his own sentiments and habits, as well as those of the individuals around him; and as any sentiments and habits may be given to all infants, it becomes of primary importance that those alone should be given to them which can contribute to their happiness. Each child therefore, on his entrance into the play-ground, is to be told in language which he can understand, that 'he is never to injure his play-fellows, but on the contrary he is to contribute all in his power to make them happy'. This simple precept, when comprehended in all its bearings, and the habits which will arise from its early adoption into practice, *if no counter-acting principles shall be forced on the young mind*, will effectually supersede all the errors which have hitherto kept the world in ignorance and misery. So simple a precept, too, will be easily taught, and as easily acquired; for the chief employment of the superintendents will be to prevent any deviation from it in practice. The older children, when they shall have experienced the endless advantages from acting on this principle, will, by their example, soon enforce the practice of it on the young strangers; and the happiness which the little groups will enjoy from this rational conduct, will insure its speedy and general and willing adoption. The habit also which they will acquire at this early period of life, by continually acting on the principle, will fix it firmly; it will become easy and familiar to them, or as it is often termed, natural.

Thus, by merely attending to the evidence of our senses respecting human nature, and disregarding the wild, inconsistent, and absurd theories in which man has been hitherto trained in all parts of the earth, we shall accomplish with ease and certainty the supposed Herculean labour of forming a rational character in man, and that too, chiefly, before the child commences the ordinary course of education.

The character thus early formed will be as durable as it will be advantageous to the individual and to the community; for by the constitution of our nature, when once the mind fully understands that which is true, the impression of that truth cannot be erased except by mental disease or death; while error must be relinquished at every period of life, whenever it can be made manifest to the mind in which it has been received. This part of the arrangement therefore will effect the following purposes:

The child will be removed, so far as is at present practicable, from the erroneous treatment of the yet untrained and untaught parents.

The parents will be relieved from the loss of time, and from the care and anxiety which are now occasioned by attendance on their children from the period when they can go alone to that at which they enter the school.

The child will be placed in a situation of safety, where, with its future schoolfellows and companions, it will acquire the best habits and principles, while at meal times and at night it will return to the caresses of its parents; and the affections of each are likely to be increased by the separation.

The area is also to be a place of meeting for the children from five to ten years of age, previous to and after school-hours, and to serve for a drill ground, the object of which will be hereafter explained. And a shade will be formed, under which, in stormy weather, the children may retire for shelter.

These are the important purposes to which a play-ground attached to a school may be applied.

Those who have derived a knowledge of human nature from observation know that man in every situation requires relaxation from his constant and regular occupations, whatever they may be; and that, if he shall not be provided with or permitted to enjoy innocent and uninjurious amusements, he must and will partake of those which he can obtain, to give him temporary relief from his exertions, although the means of gaining that relief should be most pernicious. For man, irrationally instructed, is ever influenced far more by immediate feelings than by remote considerations.

Those, then, who desire to give mankind the character which it would be for the happiness of all that they should possess, will not fail to make careful provision for their amusement and recreation.

The Sabbath was originally so intended. It was instituted to be a day of universal enjoyment and happiness to the human race. It is frequently made, however, from the opposite extremes of error, either a day of superstitious gloom and tyranny over the mind, or of the most destructive intemperance and licentiousness. The one of these has been the cause of the other; the latter, the certain and natural consequences of the former. Relieve the human mind from useless and superstitious restraints, train it on those principles which facts, ascertained from the first knowledge of time to this day, demonstrate to be the only principles which are true, and intemperance and licentiousnesss will not exist; for such conduct in itself is neither the immediate nor the future interest of man; and he is ever governed by one or other of these considerations, according to the habits which have been given to him from infancy.

The Sabbath, in many parts of Scotland, is not now a day of innocent and cheerful recreation to the labouring man; nor can those who are confined all the week to sedentary occupations freely partake, without censure, of the air and exercise to which nature invites them, and which their health demands.

The errors of the times of superstition and bigotry still hold some sway, and compel those who wish to preserve a regard to their respectability in society to an overstrained demeanour; and this demeanour sometimes degenerates into hypocrisy, and is often the cause of great inconsistency. It is destructive of every open, honest, generous, and manly feeling. It disgusts many, and drives them to the opposite extreme. It is sometimes the cause of insanity. It is founded in ignorance, and defeats its own object.

While erroneous customs prevail in any country, it would evince an ignorance of human nature in any individual to offend against them, until he has convinced the community of their error.

To counteract, in some degree, the inconvenience which arose from this misapplication of the Sabbath, it became necessary to introduce on the other days of the week some innocent amusement and recreation for those whose labours were unceasing, and in winter almost uniform. In summer, the inhabitants of the village of New Lanark have their gardens and potato-grounds to cultivate; they have walks laid out to give them health, and the habit of being gratified with the ever-changing scenes of nature; for those scenes afford not only the most economical but also the most innocent pleasures which man can enjoy; and all men may be easily trained to enjoy them.

In winter, the community are deprived of these healthy occupations and amusements; they are employed ten hours and three quarters every day in the week, except Sunday, and generally every individual continues during that time at the same work; and experience has shown that the average health and spirits of the community are several degrees lower in winter than in summer, and this in part may be fairly attributed to that cause.

These considerations suggested the necessity of rooms for innocent amusements and rational recreation.

Many well-intentioned individuals, unaccustomed to witness the conduct of those among the lower orders who have been rationally treated and trained, may fancy such an assemblage will necessarily become a scene of confusion and disorder: instead of which, however, it proceeds with uniform propriety; it is highly favourable to the health, spirits, and dispositions of the individuals so engaged; and if any irregularity should arise, the cause will be solely owing to the parties who attempt to direct the proceedings, being deficient in a practical knowledge of human nature.

It has been and ever will be found far more easy to lead mankind to virtue, or to rational conduct, by providing them with well regulated innocent amusements and recreations, than by forcing them to submit to useless restraints, which tend only to create disgust, and often to connect such feelings even with that which is excellent in itself, merely because it has been injudiciously associated.

Hitherto indeed, in all ages, and in all countries, man seems to have blindly conspired against the happiness of man, and to have remained as ignorant of himself as he was of the solar system prior to the days of Copernicus and Galileo.

Many of the learned and wise among our ancestors were conscious of this ignorance, and deeply lamented its effects; and some of them recommended the partial adoption of those principles which can alone relieve the world from the miserable effects of ignorance.

The time, however, for the emancipation of the human mind was not then arrived, the world was not prepared to receive it. The history of humanity shows it to be an undeviating law of nature, that man shall not prematurely break the shell of ignorance; that he must patiently wait until the principle of knowledge has pervaded the whole mass of the interior, to give it life and strength sufficient to bear the light of day.

Those who have duly reflected on the nature and extent of the mental movements of the world for the last half century, must be conscious that great changes are in progress; that man is about to advance another important step towards that degree of intelligence which his natural powers seem capable of attaining. Observe the transactions of the passing hours; see the whole mass of mind in full motion; behold it momentarily increasing in vigour, and preparing ere long to burst its confinement. But what is to be the nature of this change? A due attention to the facts around us, and to those transmitted by the invention of printing from former ages, will afford a satisfactory reply.

From the earliest ages it has been the practice of the world, to act on the supposition that each individual man forms his own character, and that therefore he is accountable for all his sentiments and habits, and consequently merits reward for some, and punishment for others. Every system which has been established among men has been founded on these erroneous principles. When, however, they shall be brought to the test of fair examination, they will be found not only unsupported, but in direct opposition to all experience, and to the evidence of our senses. This is not a slight mistake which involves only trivial consequences; it is a fundamental error of the highest possible magnitude; it enters into all our proceedings regarding man from his infancy, and will be found to be the true and sole origin of evil. It generates and perpetuates ignorance, hatred, and revenge, where, without such error, only intelligence, confidence, and kindness would exist. It has hitherto been the Evil Genius of the world. It severs man from man throughout the various regions of the earth; and makes enemies of those who, but for this gross error, would have enjoyed each other's kind offices and sincere friendship. It is, in short, an error which carries misery in all its consequences.

This error cannot much longer exist; for every day will make it more and more evident THAT THE CHARACTER OF MAN IS, WITHOUT A SINGLE EXCEPTION, ALWAYS FORMED FOR HIM; THAT IT MAY BE, AND IS CHIEFLY, CREATED BY HIS PREDECESSORS; THAT THEY GIVE HIM, OR MAY GIVE HIM, HIS IDEAS AND HABITS, WHICH ARE THE POWERS THAT GOVERN AND DIRECT HIS CONDUCT. MAN, THEREFORE, NEVER DID, NOR IS IT POSSIBLE HE EVER CAN, FORM HIS OWN CHARACTER.

The knowledge of this important fact has not been derived from any of the wild and heated speculations of an ardent and ungoverned imagination; on the contrary, it proceeds from a long and patient study of the theory and practice of human nature, under many varied circumstances; it will be found to be a deduction drawn from such a multiplicity of facts as to afford the most complete demonstration.

Had not mankind been misinstructed from infancy on this subject, making it necessary that they should unlearn what they have been taught, the simple statement of this truth would render it instantaneously obvious to every rational mind. Men would know that their predecessors might have given them the habits of ferocious cannibalism, or of the highest known benevolence and intelligence: and by the acquirement of this knowledge they would soon learn that, as parents, preceptors, and legislators united, they possess the means of training the rising generations to either of those extremes; that they may with the greatest certainty make them the conscientious worshippers of Juggernaut, or of the most pure spirit possessing the essence of every excellence which the human imagination can conceive; that they may train the young to become effeminate, deceitful, ignorantly selfish, intemperate, revengeful, murderous, – of course ignorant, irrational, and miserable; or to be manly, just, generous, temperate, active, kind, and benevolent – that is, intelligent, rational, and happy. The knowledge of these principles having been derived from facts which perpetually exist, they defy ingenuity itself to confute them; nay, the most severe scrutiny will make it evident that they are utterly unassailable.

Is it then wisdom to think and to act in opposition to the facts which hourly exhibit themselves around us, and in direct contradiction to the evidence of our senses? Inquire of the most learned and wise of the present day, ask them to speak with sincerity, and they will tell you that they have long known the principles on which society has been founded to be false. Hitherto, however, the tide of public opinion in all countries has been directed by a combination of prejudice, bigotry, and fanaticism, derived from the wildest imaginations of ignorance; and the most enlightened men have not dared to expose those errors which to them were offensive, prominent, and glaring.

Happily for man, this reign of ignorance rapidly approaches to dissolution; its terrors are already on the wing, and soon they will be compelled to take their flight, never more to return. For now the knowledge of the existing errors is not only possessed by the learned and reflecting, but it is spreading far and wide throughout society; and ere long it will be fully comprehended even by the most ignorant.

Attempts may indeed be made by individuals, who through ignorance mistake their real interests, to retard the progress of this knowledge; but as it will prove itself to be in unison with the evidence of our senses, and therefore true beyond the possibility of disproof, it cannot be impeded, and in its course will overwhelm all opposition.

These principles, however, are not more true in theory than beneficial in practice whenever they are properly applied. Why, then, should all their substantial advantages be longer withheld from the mass of mankind? Can it, by possibility, be a crime to pursue the only practical means which a rational being can adopt to diminish the misery of man, and increase his happiness?

These questions, of the deepest interest to society, are now brought to the fair test of public experiment. It remains to be proved, whether the character of man shall continue to be formed under the guidance of the most inconsistent notions, the errors of which for centuries past have been manifest to every reflecting rational mind; or whether it shall be moulded under the direction of uniformly consistent principles, derived from the unvarying facts of the creation; principles, the truth of which no sane man will now attempt to deny.

It is then by the full and complete disclosure of these principles, that the destruction of ignorance and misery is to be effected, and the reign of reason, intelligence, and happiness, is to be firmly established.

It was necessary to give this development of the principles advocated, that the remaining parts of the New Institution, yet to be described, may be clearly understood. We now proceed to explain the several purposes intended to be accomplished by the School, Lecture-Room, and Church.

It must be evident to those who have any powers of reason yet undestroyed, that man is now taught and trained in a theory and practice directly opposed to each other. Hence the perpetual inconsistencies, follies and absurdities, which everyone can readily discover in his neighbour, without being conscious that he also possesses similar incongruities. The instruction to be given in the School, Lecture-Room, and Church, is intended to counteract and remedy the evil;

and to prove the incalculable advantages which society would derive from the introduction of a theory and practice consistent with each other. The uppermost story of the New Institution is arranged to serve for a School, Lecture-Room, and Church. And these are intended to have a direct influence in forming the character of the villagers.

It is comparatively of little avail to give to either young or old 'precept upon precept, and 'line upon line', EXCEPT THE MEANS SHALL BE ALSO PREPARED TO TRAIN THEM IN GOOD PRACTICAL HABITS. Hence an education for the untaught and ill-taught becomes of the first importance to the welfare of society; and it is this which has influenced all the arrangements connected with the New Institution.

The time the children will remain under the discipline of the play-ground and school will afford all the opportunity that can be desired, to create, cultivate, and establish those habits and sentiments which tend to the welfare of the individual and of the community. And in conformity to this plan of proceeding, the precept which was given to the child of two years old, on coming into the play-ground, 'that he must endeavour to make his companions happy', is to be renewed and enforced on his entrance into the school; and the first duty of the schoolmaster will be to train his pupils to acquire the practice of always acting on this principle. It is a simple rule, the plain and obvious reasons for which children at an early age may be readily taught to comprehend: as they advance in years, become familiarized with its practice, and experience the beneficial effects to themselves, they will better feel and understand all its important consequences to society.

Such then being the foundation on which the practical habits of the children are to be formed, we proceed to explain the superstructure.

In addition to the knowledge of the principle and practice of the abovementioned precept, the boys and girls are to be taught in the school to read well, and to understand what they read; to write expeditiously a good legible hand; and to learn correctly, so that they may comprehend, and use with facility, the fundamental rules of arithmetic. The girls are also to be taught to sew, cut out and make up useful family garments; and after acquiring a sufficient knowledge of these, they are to attend in rotation in the public kitchen and eating-rooms; to learn to prepare wholesome food in an economical manner, and to keep a house neat and well arranged.

It was said that the children are to be taught to read well, and to understand what they read.

In many schools, the children of the poor and labouring classes are never taught to understand what they read; the time therefore which is occupied in the mockery of instruction is lost; in other schools, the children, through the ignorance of their instructors, are taught to believe without reasoning, and thus never to think or to reason correctly. These truly lamentable practices cannot fail to indispose the young mind for plain, simple, and rational instruction.

The books by which it is now the common custom to teach children to read, inform them of anything except that which, at their age, they ought to be taught: hence the inconsistencies and follies of adults. It is full time that this system should be changed. *Can man, when possessing the full vigour of his faculties, form a rational judgement on any subject, until he has first collected all the facts respecting it, which are known? Has not this ever been, and will not this ever remain, the only path by which human knowledge can be obtained?* Then children ought to be instructed on the same principles. They should first be taught the knowledge of facts, commencing with those which are the most familiar to the young mind, and gradually proceeding to the most useful and necessary to be known by the respective individuals in the rank of life in which they are likely to be placed; and in all cases the children should have as clear an explanation of each fact as their minds can comprehend, rendering those explanations more detailed as the child acquires strength and capacity of intellect.

As soon as the young mind shall be duly prepared for such instruction, the master should not allow any opportunity to escape, that would enable him to enforce the clear and inseparable connexion which exists between the interest and happiness of each individual, and the interest and happiness of every other individual. This should be the beginning and end of all his instruction: and by degrees it will be so well understood by his pupils, that they will receive the same conviction of its truth, that those familiar with mathematics now entertain of the demonstrations of Euclid. And when thus comprehended, the all-prevailing principle of known life, the desire of happiness, will compel them without deviation to pursue it in practice.

It is much to be regretted that the strength and capacity of the minds of children are yet unknown: their faculties have been hitherto estimated by the folly of the instruction which has been given to them; while, if they were never taught to acquire error, they would speedily exhibit such powers of mind, as would convince the most incredulous how much human intellect has been injured by the ignorance of former and present treatment.

It is therefore indeed important that the mind from its birth should receive those ideas only, which are consistent with each other, which are in unison with all the known facts of the creation, and which are therefore true. Now, however, from the day they are born, the minds of children are impressed with false notions of themselves and of mankind; and in lieu of being conducted into the plain path leading to health and happiness, the utmost pains are taken to compel them to pursue an opposite direction, in which they can attain only inconsistency and error.

Let the plan which has now been recommended, be steadily put in practice from infancy, *without counteraction from the systems of education which now exist*; and characters even in youth may be formed, that in true knowledge and in every good and valuable quality, will not only greatly surpass the wise and learned of the present and preceding times, but appear, as they really will be, a race of rational, or superior beings. It is true, this change cannot be instantaneously established; it cannot be created by magic, or by a miracle; it must be effected gradually – and to accomplish it finally, will prove a work of labour and of years. For those who have been misinstructed from infancy, who have now influence, and are active in the world, and whose activity is directed by the false notions of their forefathers, will of course endeavour to obstruct the change. Those who have been systematically impressed with early errors, and conscientiously think them to be truths, will of necessity, while such errors remain, endeavour to perpetuate them in their children. Some simple but general method, therefore, becomes necessary to counteract as speedily as possible an evil of so formidable a magnitude.

It was this view of the subject which suggested the utility of preparing the means to admit of evening lectures in the New Institution; and it is intended they should be given, during winter, three nights in the week, alternately with dancing.

To the ill-trained and ill-taught these lectures may be made invaluable; and these are now numerous; for the far greater part of the population of the world has been permitted to pass the proper season of instruction without being trained to be rational; and they have acquired only the ideas and habits which proceed from ignorant association and erroneous instruction.

It is intended that the lectures should be familiar discourses, delivered in plain impressive language, to instruct the adult part of the community in the most useful practical parts of knowledge in which they are deficient, particularly in the proper method of training their children to become rational creatures; how to expend the earnings of their own labour to advantage; and how to appropriate the surplus gains which will be left to them, in order to create a fund which will relieve them from the anxious fear of future want, and thus give them, under the many errors of the present systems, that rational confidence in their own exertions and good conduct, without which, consistency of character or domestic comfort cannot be obtained, and ought not to be expected. The young people may be also questioned relative to their progress in useful knowledge, and allowed to ask for explanations. In short, these lectures may be made to convey, in an amusing and agreeable manner, highly valuable and substantial information to those who are now the most ignorant in the community; and by similar means, which at a trifling expense may be put into action over the whole kingdom, the most important benefits may be given to the labouring classes, and through them, to the whole mass of society.

For it should be considered, that *the far greater part of the population belong to or have risen from the labouring classes; and by them the happiness and comfort of all ranks, not excluding the highest, are very essentially influenced*; because even much more of the character of children in all families is formed by the servants, than is ever supposed by those unaccustomed to trace with attention the human mind from earliest infancy. It is indeed impossible that children in any situation can be correctly trained, until those from infancy shall be previously well instructed: and the value of good servants may be duly appreciated by those who have experienced the difference between the very good and very bad.

The last part of the intended arrangement of the New

Institution remains yet to be described. This is the church and its doctrines; and they involve considerations of the highest interest and importance; inasmuch as a knowledge of truth on the subject of religion would permanently establish the happiness of man; for it is the inconsistencies alone, proceeding from the want of this knowledge, which have created, and still create, a great proportion of the miseries which exist in the world.

The only certain criterion of truth is, that it is ever consistent with itself; it remains one and the same, under every view and comparison of it which can be made; while error will not stand the test of this investigation and comparison, because it ever leads to absurd conclusions.

Those whose minds are equal to the subject will, ere this, have discovered that the principles in which mankind have been hitherto instructed, and by which they have been governed, will not bear the test of this criterion. Investigate and compare them: they betray absurdity, folly, and weakness; hence the infinity of jarring opinions, dissensions, and miseries, which have hitherto prevailed.

Had any one of the various opposing systems which have governed the world, and disunited man from man, been true, without any mixture of error, – that system, very speedily after its public promulgation, would have pervaded society, and compelled all men to have acknowledged its truth.

The criterion however which has been stated shows that they are all, without an exception, in part inconsistent with the works of nature; that is, with the facts which exist around us. Those systems therefore must have contained some fundamental errors; and it is utterly impossible for man to become rational, or enjoy the happiness which he is capable of attaining, until those errors are exposed and annihilated.

Each of those systems contains some truth with more

error: hence it is that no one of them has gained, or is likely to gain, universality.

The truth which the several systems possess, serves to cover and perpetuate the errors which they contain; but those errors are most obvious to all those who have not, from infancy, been taught to receive them.

Is proof demanded? Ask, in succession, those who are esteemed the most intelligent and enlightened of every sect and party, what is their opinion of every other sect and party throughout the world. Is it not evident that without one exception, the answer of each will be, that they all contain errors so clearly in opposition to reason and to equity, that he can feel only pity and deep commiseration for the individuals whose minds have been thus perverted and rendered irrational? And this reply they will all make, unconscious that they themselves are of the number whom they commiserate.

The doctrines which have been taught to every known sect, combined with the external circumstances by which they have been surrounded, have been directly calculated, and could not fail, to produce the characters which have existed. And the doctrines in which the inhabitants of the world are now instructed, combined with the external circumstances by which they are surrounded, form the characters which at present pervade society.

The doctrines which have been and now are taught throughout the world must necessarily create and perpetuate, and they do create and perpetuate, a total want of mental charity among men. They also generate superstition, bigotry, hypocrisy, hatred, revenge, wars, and all their evil consequences. For it has been and is a fundamental principle in every system hitherto taught, with exceptions more nominal than real, 'That man will possess merit, and receive eternal reward, by believing the doctrines of that peculiar system; that he will be eternally punished if he disbelieves them; that all those innumerable individuals also, who, through time, have been taught to believe other than the tenets of this system, must be doomed to eternal misery.' Yet nature itself, in all its works, is perpetually operating to convince man of such gross absurdities.

Yes, my deluded fellow-men, believe me, for your future happiness, that the facts around us, when you shall observe them aright, will make it evident even to demonstration, that all such doctrines must be erroneous, because THE WILL OF MAN HAS NO POWER WHATEVER OVER HIS OPINIONS; HE MUST, AND EVER DID, AND EVER WILL, BELIEVE WHAT HAS BEEN, IS, OR MAY BE IMPRESSED ON HIS MIND BY HIS PREDECESSORS, AND THE CIRCUMSTANCES WHICH SURROUND HIM. It becomes therefore the essence of irrationality to suppose that any human being, from the creation to this day, could deserve praise or blame, reward or punishment, for the prepossession of early education.

It is from these fundamental errors in all systems which have been hitherto taught to the mass of mankind, that the misery of the human race has to so great an extent proceeded; for, in consequence of it, man has been always instructed from infancy to believe impossibilities; he is still taught to pursue the same insane course, and the result is still misery. Let this source of wretchedness, this most lamentable of all errors, this scourge of the human race, be publicly exposed; and let those just principles be introduced, which prove themselves true by their uniform consistency and the evidence of our senses: hence insincerity, hatred, revenge, and even a wish to injure a fellow-creature, will ere long be unknown; and mental charity, heartfelt benevolence, and acts of kindness to one another, will be the distinguishing characteristics of human nature.

Shall then misery most complicated and extensive be experienced, from the prince to the peasant, in all nations throughout the world, and shall its cause and prevention be known, and yet withheld? The knowledge of this cause, however, cannot be communicated to mankind without offending against the deep-rooted prejudices of all. The work is therefore replete with difficulties, which can alone be overcome by those who, foreseeing all its important practical advantages, may be induced to contend against them.

Yet, difficult as it may be to establish this grand truth generally throughout society, on account of the dark and gross errors in which the world to this period has been instructed, it will be found, whenever the subject shall undergo a full investigation, that the principles now brought forward cannot, by possibility, injure any class of men, or even a single individual. On the contrary, there is not one member of the great family of the world, from the highest to the lowest, that will not derive the most important benefits from its public promulgation. And when such incalculable, substantial, and permanent advantages are clearly seen and strongly felt, shall individual considerations be for a moment put in competition with its attainment? No! Ease, comfort, the good opinion of a part of society, and even life itself, may be sacrificed to those prejudices; and yet the principles on which this knowledge is founded must ultimately and universally prevail.

This high event, of unequalled magnitude in the history of humanity, is thus confidently predicted, because the knowledge whence that confidence proceeds is not derived from any of the uncertain legends of the days of dark and gross ignorance, but from the plain and obvious facts which now exist throughout the world. Due attention to these facts, to these truly revealed works of nature, will soon instruct, or rather compel, mankind to discover the universal errors in which they have been trained.

The principle then on which the doctrines taught in the New Institution are proposed to be founded, is, that they shall be in unison with universally revealed facts which cannot but be true.

The following are some of the facts which, with a view to this part of the undertaking, may be deemed fundamental.

That man is born with a desire to obtain happiness, which desire is the primary cause of all his actions, continues through life, and, in popular language, is called self-interest.

That he is also born with the germs of animal propensities, or the desire to sustain, enjoy, and propagate life; and which desires, as they grow and develop themselves, are termed his natural inclinations.

That he is born likewise with faculties, which in their growth receive, convey, compare, and become conscious of receiving and comparing, ideas.

That the ideas so received, conveyed, compared, and understood, constitute human knowledge, or mind, which acquires strength and maturity with the growth of the individual.

That the desire of happiness in man, the germs of his natural inclinations, and the faculties by which he acquires knowledge, are formed, unknown to himself, in the womb; and, whether perfect or imperfect, they are alone the immediate work of the Creator, and over which the infant and future man have no control.

That these inclinations and faculties are not formed exactly alike in any two individuals: hence the diversity of talents, and the varied impressions called liking, and disliking, which the same external objects make on different persons, and the lesser varieties which exist among men whose characters have been formed apparently under similar circumstances.

That the knowledge which man receives, is derived from the objects around him, and chiefly from the example and instruction of his immediate predecessors.

That this knowledge may be limited or extended, erroneous or true; limited when the individual receives few, and extended when he receives many, ideas; erroneous when those ideas are inconsistent with the facts which exist around him, and true when they are uniformly consistent with them.

That the misery which he experiences, and the happiness which he enjoys, depend on the kind and degree of knowledge which he receives, and on that which is possessed by those around him.

That when the knowledge which he receives is true, and unmixed with error, although it be limited, if the community in which he lives possesses the same kind and degree of knowledge, he will enjoy happiness in proportion to the extent of that knowledge. On the contrary, when the opinions which he receives are erroneous, and the opinions possessed by the community in which he resides are equally erroneous, his misery will be in proportion to the extent of those erroneous opinions.

That when the knowledge which man receives shall be extended to its utmost limit, and true without any mixture of error, then he may and will enjoy the happiness of which his nature will be capable.

That it consequently becomes of the first and highest importance that man should be taught to distinguish truth from error.

That man has no other means of discovering what is false, except by his faculty of reason, or power of acquiring and comparing the ideas which he receives.

That when this faculty is properly cultivated or trained from infancy, and the child is rationally instructed to retain no impressions or ideas which by his powers of comparing them appear to be inconsistent, then the individual will acquire real knowledge, or those ideas only which will leave an impression of their consistency, or truth, on all minds which have not been rendered irrational by an opposite procedure.

That the reasoning faculty may be injured and destroyed, during its growth, by reiterated impressions being made upon it of notions not derived from realities, and which it therefore cannot compare with the ideas previously received from the objects around it. And when the mind receives these notions which it cannot comprehend, along with those ideas which it is conscious are true and yet inconsistent with such notions, then the reasoning faculties become injured, the individual is taught or forced to believe, and not to think or reason, and partial insanity or defective powers of judging ensue.

That all men are thus erroneously trained at present, and hence the inconsistencies and misery of the world.

That the fundamental errors now impressed from infancy on the minds of all men, and from whence all their other errors proceed, are, that they form their own individual characters, and possess merit or demerit for the peculiar notions impressed on the mind during its early growth, before they have acquired strength and experience to judge of or resist the impressions of those notions or opinions, which on investigation appear contradictions to facts existing around them, and which are therefore false.

That these false notions have ever produced evil and misery in the world, and that they still disseminate them in every direction.

That the sole cause of their existence hitherto has been man's ignorance of human nature; while their consequences have been, all the evil and misery, except those of accidents, disease, and death, with which man has been and is afflicted; and that the evil and misery which arise from accidents, disease, and death, are also greatly increased and extended by man's ignorance of himself.

That in proportion as man's desire of self-happiness, or his self-love, is directed by true knowledge, those actions will abound which are virtuous and beneficial to man; that in proportion as it is influenced by false notions, or the absence of true knowledge, those actions will prevail which generate crimes, from whence arises an endless variety of misery; and consequently that every rational means should be now adopted to detect error and increase true knowledge among men.

That when these truths are made evident, every individual will necessarily endeavour to promote the happiness of every other individual within his sphere of action; because he must clearly, and without any doubt, comprehend such conduct to be the essence of self-interest, or the true cause of self-happiness.

Here then is a firm foundation on which to erect vital religion, pure and undefiled, and the only one which, without any counteracting evil, can give peace and happiness to man.

It is to bring into practical operation, in forming the characters of men, these most important of all truths, that the religious part of the Institution at New Lanark will be chiefly directed; and such are the fundamental principles upon which the Instructor will proceed.

They are thus publicly avowed before all men, that they may undergo discussion, and the most severe scrutiny and investigation.

Let those, therefore, who are esteemed the most learned and wise throughout the various states and empires of the world, examine them to their foundation, compare them with every fact which exists; and if the shadow of inconsistency or falsehood be discovered, let it be publicly exposed, that error may not more abound.

But should they withstand this extended ordeal, and prove themselves uniformly consistent with every known fact, and therefore true; then let it be declared, that man may be permitted by man to become rational, and that the misery of the world may be speedily removed.

Having alluded to the chief uses of the play-ground and

exercise-rooms, with the School, Lecture-room, and Church, it remains, to complete the account of the New Institution, that the object of the drill exercise, mentioned when stating the purposes of the play-ground, should be explained; and to this we proceed.

Were all men trained to be rational, the art of war would be rendered useless. While, however, any part of mankind shall be taught that they form their own characters, and continue to be trained from infancy to think and act irrationally; that is, to acquire feelings of enmity, and to deem it a duty to engage in war, against those who have been instructed to differ from them in sentiments and habits; even the most rational must, for their personal security, learn the means of defence; and every community of such characters, while surrounded by men who have been thus improperly taught, should acquire a knowledge of this destructive art, that they may be enabled to overrule the actions of irrational beings, and maintain peace.

To accomplish these objects to the utmost practical limit, and with the least inconvenience, every male should be instructed how best to defend, when attacked, the community to which he belongs. And these advantages are only to be obtained by providing proper means for the instruction of all boys in the use of arms and the arts of war.

As an example how easily and effectually this might be accomplished over the British Isles, it is intended that the boys trained and educated in the Institution at New Lanark shall be thus instructed; that the person appointed to attend the children in the play-ground shall be qualified to drill and teach the boys the manual exercise, and that he shall be frequently so employed. That afterwards fire-arms of proportionate weight and size to the age and strength of the boys, shall be provided for them; when also they might be taught to practise and understand the more complicated military movements.

This exercise, properly administered, will greatly contribute to the health and spirits of the boys, give them an erect and proper form, and habits of attention, celerity, and order. They will however be taught to consider this exercise an art rendered absolutely necessary by the partial insanity of some of their fellow-creatures, who, by the errors of their predecessors transmitted through preceding generations, have been taught to acquire feelings of enmity increasing to madness against those who could not avoid differing from them in sentiments and habits; that this art should never be brought into practice except to restrain the violence of such madmen; and in these cases that it should be administered with the least possible severity; and solely to prevent the evil consequences of those rash actions of the insane, and if possible cure them of their disease.

Thus, in a few years, by foresight and arrangement, may almost the whole expense and inconvenience attending the local military be superseded, and a permanent force created, which in numbers, discipline, and principles, would be superior beyond all comparison for the purposes of defence, always ready in case of need, yet without the loss which is now sustained by the community of efficient and valuable labour. The expenditure which would be saved by this simple expedient would be far more than competent to educate the whole of the poor and labouring classes of these kingdoms.

There is still another arrangement in contemplation for the community at New Lanark, and without which the establishment will remain incomplete.

It is an expedient to enable the individuals, by their own foresight, prudence, and industry, to secure themselves in old age a comfortable provision and asylum.

Those now employed at the establishment contribute to a fund which supports them when too ill to work, or when superannuated. This fund, however, is not calculated to give them more than a bare existence; and it is surely desirable that, after they have spent nearly half a century in unremitting industry, they should, if possible, in the decline of life, enjoy a comfortable independence.

To effect this object, it is intended that in the most pleasant situation near the present village, neat and convenient dwellings should be erected, with gardens attached; that they should be surrounded and sheltered by plantations, through which public walks should be formed, and the whole arranged to give the occupiers the most substantial comforts.

That these dwellings, with the privileges of the public walks, etc., shall become the property of those individuals who, without compulsion, shall subscribe such equitable sums monthly as, in a given number of years, will be equal to their purchase, and to create a fund from which, when these individuals become occupiers of their new residences, they may receive weekly, monthly, or quarterly payments sufficient for their support, the expenses of which may be reduced to a very low rate individually, by arrangements which may be easily formed to supply all their wants with little trouble to themselves; and by their previous instruction they will be enabled to afford the small additional subscription which will be required for these purposes.

This part of the arrangement would always present a prospect of rest, comfort, and happiness to those employed: in consequence their daily occupations would be performed with more spirit and cheerfulness, and their labour would appear comparatively light and easy. Those still engaged in active operations would of course frequently visit their former companions and friends, who after having spent their years of toil were in the actual enjoyment of this simple retreat; and from this intercourse each party would naturally derive pleasure. The reflections of each would be most gratifying. The old would rejoice that they had been trained in habits of industry, temperance, and foresight, to enable them to receive and enjoy in their declining years every reasonable comfort which the present state of society will admit; the young and middle-aged, that they were pursuing the same course; and that they had not been trained to waste their money, time, and health, in idleness and intemperance. These and many similar reflections could not fail often to arise in their minds; and those who could look forward with confident hopes to such certain comfort and independence would, in part, enjoy by anticipation these advantages. In short, when this part of the arrangement is well considered, it will be found to be most important to the community and to the proprietors: indeed, the extensively good effects of it will be experienced in such a variety of ways, that to describe them even below the truth would appear an extravagant exaggeration. They will not however prove the less true because mankind are yet ignorant of the practice, and of the principles on which it has been founded.

These, then, are the plans which are in progress or intended for the further improvement of the inhabitants of New Lanark: they have uniformly proceeded from the principles which have been developed through these Essays, restrained however, hitherto, in their operations by the local sentiments and unfounded notions of the community and neighbourhood, and by the peculiar circumstances of the establishment.

In every measure to be introduced at the place in question, for the comfort and happiness of man, the existing errors of the country were always to be considered; and as the establishment belonged to parties whose views were various, it became also necessary to devise means to create pecuniary gains from each improvement sufficient to satisfy the spirit of commerce.

All therefore which has been done for the happiness of this community, which consists of between two and three thousand individuals, is far short of what might have been easily effected in practice, had not mankind been previously trained in error. Hence, in devising these plans, the sole consideration was not what were the measures, dictated by these principles, which would produce the greatest happiness to man; but what could be effected in practice under the present irrational systems by which these proceedings were surrounded.

Imperfect however as these proceedings must yet be, in consequence of the formidable obstructions enumerated, they will yet appear, upon a full and minute investigation by minds equal to the comprehension of such a system, to combine a greater degree of substantial comfort to the individuals employed in the manufactory, and of pecuniary profit to the proprietors, than has hitherto been found attainable.

But to whom can such arrangements be submitted? Not to the mere commercial character, in whose estimation to forsake the path of immediate individual gain would be to show symptoms of a disordered imagination; for the children of commerce have been trained to direct all their faculties to buy cheap and sell dear; and consequently those who are the most expert and successful in this wise and noble art are in the commercial world deemed to possess foresight and superior acquirements, while such as attempt to improve the moral habits and increase the comforts of those whom they employ are termed wild enthusiasts.

Nor yet are they to be submitted to the mere men of the law; for they are necessarily trained to endeavour to make wrong appear right, or involve both in a maze of intricacies, and to legalize injustice. Nor to mere political leaders or their partisans; for they are embarrassed by the trammels of party, which mislead their judgement, and often constrain them to sacrifice the real well-being of the community and of themselves to an apparent but most mistaken self-interest.

Nor to those termed heroes and conquerors, or their followers; for their minds have been trained to consider the infliction of human misery, and the commission of military murders, a glorious duty, almost beyond reward.

Nor yet to the fashionable or splendid in their appearance; for these are from infancy trained to deceive and to be deceived; to accept shadows for substances; and to live a life of insincerity, and consequent discontent and misery.

Still less are they to be exclusively submitted to the official expounders and defenders of the various opposing religious systems throughout the world; for many of these are actively engaged in propagating imaginary notions, which cannot fail to vitiate the rational powers of man, and perpetuate his misery.

These principles, therefore, and the practical systems which they recommend, are not to be submitted to the judgement of those who have been trained under and continue in any of these unhappy combinations of circumstances; but they are to be submitted to the dispassionate and patient investigation and decision of those individuals of every rank and class and denomination in society, who have become in some degree conscious of the errors in which they exist; who have felt the thick mental darkness by which they are surrounded; who are ardently desirous of discovering and following truth wherever it may lead; and who can perceive the inseparable connexion which exists between individual and general, between private and public good!

It has been said, and it is now repeated, that these principles, thus combined, will prove themselves unerringly true against the most insidious or open attack; and ere long they will, by their irresistible truth, pervade society to the utmost bounds of the earth; for 'silence will not retard their progress, and opposition will give increased celerity to their movements'. When they shall have dissipated in some degree, as they speedily will dissipate, the thick darkness in which the human mind has been and is still enveloped, the endless beneficial consequences which must follow the general introduction of them into practice may then be explained in greater detail, and urged upon minds to which they will then appear less questionable. In the meantime we shall proceed to state, in a fourth Essay, of what immediate improvements the present state of the British population is susceptible in practice.

ESSAY FOURTH

The Principles of the Former Essays Applied to Government

It is beyond all comparison better to prevent than to punish crimes.

A System of Government therefore which shall prevent ignorance, and consequently crime, will be infinitely superior to one, which, by encouraging the first, creates a necessity for the last, and afterwards inflicts punishment on both.

THE end of government is to make the governed and the governors happy.

That government then is the best, which in practice produces the greatest happiness to the greatest number; including those who govern, and those who obey.

In a former Essay we said, and it admits of practical demonstration, that by adopting the proper means, man may, by degrees, be trained to live in any part of the world without poverty, without crime, and without punishment; for all these are the effects of error in the various systems of training and governing; error, proceeding from very gross ignorance of human nature.

It is of primary importance to make this ignorance manifest, and to show what are the means which are endowed with that transcendent efficacy.

We have also said that man may be trained to acquire any sentiments and habits, or any character; and no one now, possessing pretensions to the knowledge of human nature, will deny that the government of any independent community may form the individuals of that community into the best, or into the worst characters.

If there be one duty therefore more imperative than another, on the government of every country, it is, that it should adopt, without delay, the proper means to form those sentiments and habits in the people, which shall give the most permanent and substantial advantages to the individuals and to the community.

Survey the acquirements of the earliest ages; trace the progress of those acquirements, through all the subsequent periods, to the present hour; and say if there be anything of real value in them, except that which contributes in practice to increase the happiness of the world.

And yet, with all the parade of learning contained in the myriads of volumes which have been written, and which still daily pour from the press, the knowledge of the first step of the progress which leads to human happiness remains yet unknown, or disregarded by the mass of mankind.

The important knowledge to which we allude is, 'That the old collectively may train the young collectively, to be ignorant and miserable, or to be intelligent and happy'. And, on investigation, this will be found to be one of those simple yet grand laws of the universe which experience discovers and confirms, and which, as soon as men become familiar with it, will no longer admit of denial or dispute. Fortunate will be that government which shall first acquire this knowledge in theory, and adopt it in practice.

To obtain its introduction into our own country first, a mode of procedure is now submitted to the immediate governing powers of the British Empire; and it is so submitted with an ardent desire that it may undergo the most full and ample discussion; that if it shall, as on investigation it will, be found to be the only consistent, and therefore rational, system of conducting human beings, it may be temperately and progressively introduced, instead of those defective national practices by which the state is now governed.

We therefore proceed to explain how this principle may now be introduced into practice, without injury to any part of society. For it is the time and manner of introducing this principle, and its consequent practice, which alone constitute any difficulty.

This will appear evident, when it is considered that, although, from a plain statement of the most simple facts, the truth of the principle cannot fail to prove so obvious that no one will ever attempt openly to attack it; and although its adoption into practice will speedily accumulate benefits of which the world can now form no adequate conception: yet both theory and practice are to be introduced into a society, trained and matured under principles that have impressed upon the individuals who compose it the most opposite habits and sentiments; which have been so entwined from infancy in their bodily and mental growth, that the simplicity and irresistible power of truth alone can disentangle them, and expose their fallacy. It becomes then necessary, to prevent the evils of a too sudden change, that those who have been thus nursed in ignorance may be progressively removed from the abodes of mental darkness, to the intellectual light which this principle cannot fail to produce. The light of true knowledge therefore must be first made to dawn on those dwellings of darkness, and afterwards gradually to increase, as it can be borne by the opening faculties of their inhabitants.

To proceed on this plan, it becomes necessary to direct our attention to the actual state of the British population; to disclose the cause of those great and leading evils of which all now complain.

It will then be seen that the foundation on which these evils have been erected is ignorance, proceeding from the errors which have been impressed on the minds of the present generation by its predecessors; and chiefly by that *greatest of all errors, the notion, that individuals form their own characters.* For while this most inconsistent and therefore most absurd of all human conceptions shall continue to be forced upon the young mind, there will remain no foundation whatever on which to build a sincere love and extended charity from man to his fellow-creatures.

But destroy this hydra of human calamity, this immolator of every principle of rationality; this monster, which hitherto has effectually guarded every avenue that can lead to true benevolence and active kindness, and human happiness will be speedily established on a rock from whence it shall never more be removed.

This enemy of humanity may now be most easily destroyed. Let it be dragged forth from beneath the dark mysterious veil by which, till now, it has been hid from the eyes of the world; expose it but for an instant to the clear light of intellectual day; and, as though conscious of its own deformity, it will instantaneously vanish, never to reappear.

As a ground-work then of a rational system, let this absurd doctrine, and all the chain of consequences which follow from it, be withdrawn, and let that only be taught as sacred, which can be demonstrated by its never-failing consistency to be true.

This essential object being accomplished, and accomplished it must be before another step can be taken to form man into a rational being, the next is to withdraw those national laws which chiefly emanate from that erroneous doctrine, and now exist in full vigour; training the population to almost every kind of crime. For these laws are, without chance of failure, adapted to produce a long train of crimes, which crimes are accordingly produced.

Some of the most prominent to which allusion is made are such as encourage the consumption of ardent spirits, by fostering and extending those receptacles to seduce the ignorant and wretched, called gin-shops and pot-houses; – those which sanction and legalize gambling among the poor, under the name of a state lottery; – those which are insidiously destroying the real strength of the country under the name of providing for the poor; – and those of punishment, which, under the present irrational system of legislation, are supposed to be absolutely necessary to hold society together.

To prove the accuracy of this deduction, millions of facts exist around us, speaking in a language so clearly connected and audible, that it is scarcely credible any man can misunderstand it.

These facts proclaim aloud to the universe, that ignorance generates, fosters, and multiplies sentiments and actions which must produce private and public misery; and that when evils are experienced, instead of withdrawing the *cause* which created them, it invents and applies punishments, which, to a superficial observer, may appear to lessen the evils which afflict society, while, in reality, they greatly increase them.

Intelligence, on the contrary, traces to its source the cause of every evil which exists; adopts the proper measures to remove the *cause;* and then, with the most unerring confidence, rests satisfied that its object will be accomplished.

Thus then intelligence, or, in other words, plain unsophisticated reason, will consider the various sentiments and actions which now create misery in society, will patiently trace the cause whence those sentiments and actions proceed, and immediately apply the proper remedies to remove them.

And attention, thus directed, discovers that the cause of such sentiments and actions in the British population is the laws which have been enumerated, and others which shall be hereafter noticed.

To withdraw therefore the existing evils which afflict

society, these unwise laws must be progressively repealed or modified. The British constitution, in its present outline, is admirably adapted to effect these changes, without the evils which always accompany a coerced or ill-prepared change.

As a preliminary step, however, to the commencement of national improvement, it should be declared with a sincerity which shall not admit of any after deviation, that no individual of the present generation should be deprived of the emolument which he now receives, or of that which has been officially or legally promised.

The next step in national reform is to withdraw from the national church those tenets which constitute its weakness and create its danger. Yet still, to prevent the evils of any premature change, let the church in other respects remain as it is; because under the old established forms it may effect the most valuable purposes.

To render it truly a national church, all tests, as they are called, that is, declarations of belief in which all cannot conscientiously join, should be withdrawn: this alteration would tend more perhaps than any other which can be devised, to give stability both to the national church and to the state; and a conduct thus rational would at once terminate all the theological differences which now confound the intellects of men, and disseminate universal discord.

The next measure of national improvement should be to repeal or modify those laws which leave the lower orders in ignorance, train them to become intemperate, and produce idleness, gambling, poverty, disease, and murder. The production and consumption of ardent spirits are now legally encouraged; licences to keepers of gin-shops and unnecessary pot-houses are by thousands annually distributed; the laws of the state now direct those licences to be distributed; and yet perhaps not one of the authors or guardians of these laws has once reflected how much *each* of those houses daily contributes to public crime, disease, and weakness, or how much they add to the stock of private misery.

Shall we then continue to surround our fellow-creatures with a temptation which, as many of them are now trained, we know they are unable to resist? with a temptation too which predisposes its victims to proceed gradually from a state of temporary insanity, into which they had been led by the example and instruction of those around them, to one of madness and bodily disease, creating more than infantile weakness, which again produces mental torments and horrors, that silently, yet most effectually, undermine every faculty in man which can contribute to private or public happiness?

Can the British Government longer preserve such laws, or countenance a system which trains man to devise and enforce such laws?[1]

Enough surely has been said to exhibit the evil consequences of these laws in their true colours. Let the duties

---

1. In the year 1736, an act of parliament (stat. 9 Geo. II. c. 23) was passed. The preamble is as follows: 'Whereas the drinking of spirituous liquors or strong waters is become very common, especially amongst the people of lower and inferior rank, the constant and excessive use of which tends greatly to the destruction of their healths, rendering them unfit for useful labour and business, debauching their morals, and inciting them to perpetrate all manner of vices; and the ill consequences of the excessive use of such liquor are not confined to the present generation, but extend to future ages, and tend to the devastation and ruin of this kingdom.' It was therefore enacted, that no person should retail spirits without a licence, for which £50 was to be paid annually, with other provisions to restrain the sale of spirits. By a Report of His Majesty's Justices of the Peace for the county of Middlesex, made in January 1736, it appeared that there were then within Westminster, Holborn, the Tower, and Finsbury division, (exclusive of London and Southwark,) 7,044 houses and shops wherein spirituous liquors were publicly sold by retail, of which they had got an account, and that they believed it was far short of the true number.

therefore on the production of ardent spirits be gradually increased, until the price shall exceed the means of ordinary consumption; let the licences be progressively withdrawn from the present occupiers of gin-shops and unnecessary pot-houses; and let the duties on the production and consumption of malt liquor be diminished, that the poor and working classes may be the more readily induced to abandon their destructive habits of dram-drinking, and by degrees to withdraw altogether from this incentive to crime, and source of misery.

The next improvement should be to discontinue the state lottery.

The law which creates this measure is neither more nor less than a law to legalize gambling, entrap the unwary, and rob the ignorant.

How great must be the error of that system which can induce a state to deceive and injure its subjects, and yet expect that those subjects shall not be necessarily trained to injure and to deceive!

These measures may be thought detrimental to the national revenues.

Those who have reflected on the nature of public revenue, and who possess minds capable of comprehending the subject, know that revenue has but one legitimate source; that it is derived directly or indirectly from the labour of man, and that it may be more or less from any given number of men (other circumstances being similar) in proportion to their strength, industry and capacity.

The efficient strength of a state governed by laws founded on an accurate knowledge of human nature, in which the whole population are well trained, will greatly exceed one of equal extent and numbers, in which a large part of the population are improperly trained, and governed by laws founded in ignorance.

Thus were the small states of Greece, while governed by

laws comparatively wise, superior in national strength to the extended empire of Persia.

On this plain and obvious principle will the effective power and resources of the British empire be largely increased by withdrawing those laws which, under the plausible appearance of adding a few, and but a few, millions to the annual revenues of this kingdom, in reality feed on the very vitals of the state. For such laws destroy the energies and capacities of its population, which, so weakened and trained to crime, requires a far greater expenditure to protect and govern it.

Confidently may it be said, that a short experience in practice is alone necessary to make the truth of these positions self-evident even to the most common understandings.

The next measure for the general improvement of the British population should be to revise the laws relative to the poor. For, pure and benevolent as, no doubt, were the motives which actuated those with whom the poor laws originated, the direct and certain effects of these laws are to injure the poor, and, through them, the state, as much almost as they can be injured.

They exhibit the appearance of affording aid to the distressed, while, in reality, they prepare the poor to acquire the worst habits, and to practise every kind of crime; they thus increase the number of the poor, and add to their distress. It becomes therefore necessary that decisive and effectual measures should be adopted to remove those evils which the existing laws have created.

Benevolence says that the destitute must not starve, and to this declaration political wisdom readily assents. Yet can that system be right, which compels the industrious, temperate, and comparatively virtuous, to support the ignorant, the idle, and comparatively vicious? Such however is the effect of the present British poor laws; for they publicly proclaim greater encouragement to idleness, ignorance, extravagance, and intemperance, than to industry and good conduct: the evils which arise from a system so irrational, are hourly experienced, and hourly increasing.

It thus becomes necessary that some counteracting remedy be immediately devised and applied; for, injurious as these laws are, it is obviously impracticable, in the present state of the British population, to annul at once a system to which so large a portion of the people has been taught to look for support.

These laws should be progressively undermined by a system of an opposite nature, and ultimately rendered altogether nugatory.

The proper system to supersede these laws has been in part already explained, but we proceed to unfold it still more. It may be called 'A System for the Prevention of Crime, and the Formation of Human Character'; and under an established and well-intentioned government, it will be found more efficacious in producing public benefit than any of the laws now in existence.

The fundamental principle on which all these Essays proceed is, that 'Children collectively may be taught any sentiments and habits'; or, in other words, 'trained to acquire any character'.

It is of importance that *this principle should be ever present in the mind, and that its truth should be established beyond even the shadow of doubt.* To the superficial observer it may appear to be an abstract truth of little value; but to the reflecting and accurate reasoner it will speedily discover itself to be a power which ultimately must destroy the ignorance, and consequent prejudices, that have accumulated through all preceding ages.

For as it is a deduction from all the leading facts in the past history of the world, so it will be found, on the most extensive investigation, to be consistent with every fact which now exists. It is calculated therefore to become the foundation of a new system, which, because true and of unparalleled importance, must prove irresistible, will speedily supersede all those which exist, and itself become permanent.

It is necessary however, prior to the introduction of this system in all its bearings and consequences, that the public mind should be impressed with the deepest conviction of its truth.

For this purpose let us, in imagination, survey the various states and empires of the world, and attentively observe man, as in these arbitary divisions of the earth he is known to exist.

Compare the national character of each community with the laws and customs by which they are respectively governed, and, without an exception, the one will be found the archetype of the other.

Where, in former ages, the laws and customs established by Lycurgus formed man into a model for martial exploits, and a perfect instrument for war, he is now trained, by other laws and customs, to be the instrument of a despotism which renders him almost or altogether unfit for war. And where the laws and customs of Athens trained the young mind to acquire as high a degree of partial rationality as the history of preceding times records; man is now reduced, by a total change of laws and customs, to the lowest state of mental degradation. Also where, formerly, the superior native American tribes roamed fearlessly through their trackless forests, uniformly exhibiting the hardy, penetrating, elevated, and sincere character, which was at a loss to comprehend how a rational being could desire to possess more than his nature could enjoy; now, on the very same soil, in the same climate, characters are formed under laws and customs so opposite, that all their bodily and mental faculties are individually exerted to obtain, if possible, ten thousand times more than any man can enjoy.

But why proceed to enumerate such endless results as

these, of the never-failing influences of training over human nature, when it may be easily rendered self-evident even to the most illiterate, by daily examples around their own dwellings?

No one, it may be supposed, can now be so defective in knowledge as to imagine that it is a different human nature, which by its own power forms itself into a child of ignorance, of poverty, and of habits leading to crime and to punishment; or into a votary of fashion, claiming distinction from its folly and inconsistency; or to fancy that it is some undefined, blind, unconscious process of human nature itself, distinct from instruction, that forms the sentiments and habits of the men of commerce, of agriculture, the law, the church, the army, the navy, or of the private and illegal depredator on society; or that it is a different human nature which constitutes the societies of the Jews, of Friends, and of all the various religious denominations which have existed or which now exist. No! human nature, save the minute differences which are ever found in all the compounds of the creation, is one and the same in all; it is without exception universally plastic, and, by judicious training, THE INFANTS OF ANY ONE CLASS IN THE WORLD MAY BE READILY FORMED INTO MEN OF ANY OTHER CLASS; EVEN TO BELIEVE AND DECLARE THAT CONDUCT TO BE RIGHT AND VIRTUOUS, AND TO DIE IN ITS DEFENCE, WHICH THEIR PARENTS HAD BEEN TAUGHT TO BELIEVE AND SAY WAS WRONG AND VICIOUS, AND TO OPPOSE WHICH, THOSE PARENTS WOULD ALSO HAVE WILLINGLY SACRIFICED THEIR LIVES.

Whence then the foundation of your claim, ye advocates for the superiority of the early prepossessions of your sect or party, in opposition to those taught to other men? Ignorance itself, at this day, might almost make it evident that one particle of merit is not due to you for not possessing those notions and habits which you now the most contemn. Ought you not, and will you not then, have charity for those who have been taught different sentiments and habits from yourselves? Let all men fairly investigate this subject for themselves; it well merits their most attentive examination; they will then discover that it is from the errors of education, misinstructing the young mind relative to the true cause of early prepossessions, that almost all the evils of life proceed.

Whence then, ye advocates for the merit and demerit of early prepossessions of opinion, do you derive your principles?

Let this system of misery be seen in all its naked deformity! It ought to be so exposed; for the instruction which it inculcates at the outset of forming human character, is destructive of the genuine charity which can alone train man to be truly benevolent to all other men. The ideas of exclusive right and consequent superiority, which men have hitherto been taught to attach to the early sentiments and habits in which they have been instructed, are the chief cause of disunion throughout the society; such notions are, indeed, in direct opposition to pure and undefiled religion, nor can they ever exist together. The extent of the misery which they generate cannot however be much longer concealed; they are already hastening fast to meet the fate of all errors; for the gross ignorance on which this system of misery has been raised, is exposed to the world on its own proper foundation; and, so exposed, its supporters will shrink from the task of defence, and no rational mind will be found to give it support.

Having exhibited the error on which ignorance has erected the systems by which man has been governed, or compelled to become irrational and miserable; and having laid an immoveable foundation for a system devoid of that error, which, when fully comprehended and adopted into practice, must train mankind 'to think of and act to others as they would wish others to think of and act to them', – we proceed further to explain this *system without error*, and which may be termed a *system without mystery*.

As then children collectively may be formed into any characters, by whom ought their characters to be formed?

The kind and degree of misery or happiness experienced by the members of any community, depend on the characters which have been formed in the individuals which constitute the community. It becomes then the highest interest, and consequently the first and most important duty, of every state, to form the individual characters of which the state is composed. And if any characters, from the most ignorant and miserable to the most rational and happy, can be formed, it surely merits the deepest attention of every state to adopt those means by which the formation of the latter may be secured, and that of the former prevented.

It follows that every state, to be well governed, ought to direct its chief attention to the formation of character; and that the best governed state will be that which shall possess the best national system of education.

Under the guidance of minds competent to its direction, a national system of training and education may be formed, to become the most safe, easy, effectual, and economical instrument of government that can be devised. And it may be made to possess a power equal to the accomplishment of the most grand and beneficial purposes.

It is, however, by instruction only that the population of the world can be made conscious of the irrational state in which they now exist; and until that instruction is given, it is premature to introduce a national system of education.

But the time is now arrived when the British Government may with safety adopt a national system of training and education for the poor and uninstructed; and this measure alone, if the plan shall be well devised and executed, will effect the most importantly beneficial changes.

As a preliminary step, however, it is necessary to observe, that to create a well trained, united, and happy people, this national system should be uniform over the United Kingdom; it should be also founded in the spirit of peace and of rationality; and for the most obvious reasons, the thought of exclusion to one child in the empire should not for a moment be entertained.

Several plans have been lately proposed for the national education of the poor, but these have not been calculated to effect all that a national system for the education of the poor ought to accomplish.

For the authors and supporters of these systems we feel those sentiments which the principles developed throughout these Essays must create in any minds on which they have been early and effectually impressed; and we are desirous of rendering their labours for the community as extensively beneficial as they can be made. To fulfil, however, a great and important public duty, the plans which they have devised must be considered as though they had been produced and published in the days of antiquity.

The plans alluded to are those of the Reverend Dr Bell, Mr Joseph Lancaster, and Mr Whitbread.

The systems of Dr Bell and Mr Lancaster, for instructing the poor in reading, writing, and arithmetic, prove the extreme ignorance which previously existed in the *manner* of training the young; for it is in the manner alone of giving instruction that these new systems are an improvement on the modes of instruction which were formerly practised.

The arrangement of the room, and many of the details in Mr Lancaster's plan, are in some respects better calculated to give instruction in the elements enumerated, than those recommended by Dr Bell, although some of the details introduced by the latter are very superior, and highly deserving of adoption.

The essence, however, of national training and education is to impress on the young, ideas and habits which shall contribute to the future happiness of the individual and of the state; and this can be accomplished only by instructing them to become rational beings.

It must be evident to common observers, that children may be taught, by either Dr Bell's or Mr Lancaster's system, to read, write, account, and sew, and yet acquire the worst habits, and have their minds rendered irrational for life.

Reading and writing are merely instruments, by which knowledge, either true or false, may be imparted; and, when given to children, are of little comparative value, unless they are also taught how to make a proper use of them.

When a child receives a full and fair explanation of the objects and characters around him, and when he is also taught to reason correctly, so that he may learn to discover general truths from falsehood; he will be much better instructed, although without the knowledge of one letter or figure, than those are who have been compelled to *believe*, and whose reasoning faculties have been confounded, or destroyed, by what is most erroneously termed learning.

It is readily acknowledged, that the manner of instructing children is of importance, and deserves all the attention which it has lately received; that those who discover or introduce improvements which facilitate the acquirement of knowledge, are important benefactors to their fellow-creatures. Yet the *manner* of giving instruction is one thing, the *instruction* itself another, and no two objects can be more distinct. The *worst* manner may be applied to give the *best* instruction, and the *best* manner to give the *worst* instruction. Were the real importance of both to be estimated by numbers, the manner of instruction may be compared to one, and the matter of instruction to millions: the first is the means only; the last, the end to be accomplished by those means.

If therefore, in a national system of education for the poor, it be desirable to adopt the best *manner*, it is surely so much the more desirable to adopt also the best *matter*, of instruction.

Either give the poor a rational and useful training, or mock not their ignorance, their poverty, and their misery, by merely instructing them to become conscious of the extent of the degradation under which they exist. And therefore, in pity to suffering humanity, either keep the poor, *if you now can*, in the state of the most abject ignorance, as near as possible to animal life; or at once determine to form them into rational beings, into useful and effective members of the state.

Were it possible, without national prejudice, to examine into the matter of instruction which is now given in some of our boasted new systems for the instruction of the poor, it would be found almost as wretched as any which can be devised. In proof of this statement, enter any one of the schools denominated national, request the master to show the acquirements of the children; these are called out, and he asks them theological questions to which men of the most profound erudition cannot make a rational reply: the children, however, readily answer as they had been previously instructed, for memory in this mockery of learning is all that is required.

Thus the child whose natural faculty of comparing ideas, or whose rational powers, shall be the soonest destroyed, if, at the same time, he possess a memory to retain incongruities without connexion, will become what is termed the first scholar in the class; and three fourths of the time which ought to be devoted to the acquirement of useful instruction, will be really occupied in destroying the mental powers of the children.

To those accustomed attentively to notice the human countenance, from infancy to age, in the various classes and religious denominations of the British population, it is truly an instructive although melancholy employment, to observe in the countenances of the poor children in these schools, the evident expression of mental injury derived from the well intentioned, but most mistaken, plan of their instruction.

It is an important lesson, because it affords another recent and striking example to the millions which previously existed, of the ease with which children may be taught to receive any sectarian notions, and thence acquire any habits, however contrary to their real happiness.

To those trained to become truly conscientious in any of the present sectarian errors which distract the world, this free exposure of the weakness of the peculiar tenets in which such individuals have been instructed, will at first excite feelings of high displeasure and horror; and these feelings will be acute and poignant, in proportion to the obvious and irresistible evidence on which the disclosure of their errors is founded.

Let them, however, begin to think calmly on these subjects, to examine their own minds, and the minds of all around them, and they will become conscious of the absurdities and inconsistencies in which their forefathers have trained them; they will then abhor the errors by which they have been so long abused; and, with an earnestness not to be resisted, they will exert their utmost faculties to remove the cause of so much misery to man.

Enough surely has now been said of the manner and matter of instruction in these new systems, to exhibit them in a just and true light.

The improvements in the manner of teaching children

whatever may be deemed proper for them to learn; improvements which we may easily predict will soon receive great additions and amendments; have proceeded from the Reverend Dr Bell and Mr Lancaster; while the errors which their respective systems assist to engrave on the ductile mind of infancy and childhood, are derived from times when ignorance gave countenance to every kind of absurdity.

Mr Whitbread's scheme for the education of the poor, was evidently the production of an ardent mind possessing considerable abilities; his mind, however, had been irregularly formed by the errors of his early education; and was most conspicuous in the speech which introduced the plan he had devised to the House of Commons, and in the plan itself.

The first was a clear exposition of all the reasons for the education of the poor, which could be expected from a human being trained from infancy under the systems in which Mr Whitbread had been instructed.

The plan itself evinced the fallacy of the principles which he had imbibed, and showed that he had not acquired a practical knowledge of the feelings and habits of the poor, or of the only effectual means by which they could be trained to be useful to themselves and to the community.

Had Mr Whitbread not been trained, as almost all the Members of both Houses of Parliament have been, in delusive theories devoid of rational foundation, which prevent them from acquiring an extensive practical knowledge of human nature, he would not have committed a plan for the national education of the poor to the sole management and direction of the Ministers, Churchwardens, and Overseers of Parishes, whose present interests must have appeared to be opposed to the measure.

He would surely first have devised a plan to make it the evident interest of the Ministers, Churchwardens, and Overseers, to cooperate in giving efficacy to the system which he wished to introduce to their superintendence; and also to render them, by previous training, competent to that superintendence for which now they are in general unprepared. For, trained as these individuals have hitherto been, they must be deficient in the practical knowledge necessary to enable them successfully to direct the instruction of others. And had an attempt been made to carry Mr Whitbread's plan into execution, it would have created a scene of confusion over the whole kingdom.

Attention to the subject will make it evident that it never was, and that it never can be, the interest of any sect claiming exclusive privileges on account of professing high and mysterious doctrines, about which the best and most conscientious men may differ in opinion, that the mass of the people should be otherwise instructed than in those doctrines which were and are in unison with its peculiar tenets; and, that at this hour a national system of education for the lower orders on sound political principles is really dreaded, even by some of the most learned and intelligent members of the Church of England. Such feelings in the members of the national church are those only which ought to be expected; for most men so trained and circumstanced must of necessity acquire those feelings. Why therefore should any class of men endeavour to rouse the indignation of the public against them? Their conduct and their motives are equally correct, and therefore equally good with those who raise the cry against and oppose the errors of the Church. And let it ever be remembered, that an establishment which possesses the power of propagating principles, may be rendered truly valuable when directed to inculcate a system of self-evident truth, unobstructed by inconsistencies and counteractions.

The Dignitaries of the Church, and their adherents, foresaw that a national system for the education of the poor, unless it were placed under the immediate influence and management of individuals belonging to the Church, would effectually and rapidly undermine the errors not only of their own, but of every other ecclesiastical establishment. In this foresight, they evinced the superiority of their penetration over the sectaries by whom the unexclusive system of education is supported. The heads of the Church have wisely discovered that reason and inconsistency cannot long exist together; that the one must inevitably destroy the other, and reign paramount. They have witnessed the regular, and latterly the rapid progress which reason has made; they know that its accumulating strength cannot be much longer resisted; and as they now see the contest is hopeless, the unsuccessful attempt to destroy the Lancasterian system of education is the last effort they will ever make to counteract the dissemination of knowledge, which is now widely extending itself in every direction.

The establishment of the Reverend Dr Bell's system for initiating the children of the poor in all the tenets of the Church of England, is an attempt to ward off a little longer the yet dreaded period of a change from ignorance to reason; from misery to happiness.

Let us, however, not attempt impossibilities; the task is vain and hopeless; the Church, while it adheres to the defective and injurious parts of its system, cannot be induced to act cordially in opposition to its apparent interests.

The principles here advocated will not admit the application of any deception to any class of men; they countenance no proceedings in practice, but of unlimited sincerity and candour; they give rise to no one sentiment which is not in unison with the happiness of the human race; and they impart knowledge, which renders it evident that such happiness can never be acquired, until every particle of falsehood and deception shall be eradicated from the instructions which the old force upon the young.

Let us then, in this spirit, openly declare to the Church,

that a national unexclusive plan of education for the poor will, without the shadow of doubt, destroy all the errors which are attached to the various systems; and that, when this plan shall be fully established, not one of the tenets which is in opposition to facts can long be upheld.

This unexclusive system for the education of the poor has gone forth; and having found a resting place in the minds of its supporters, it will never more return even to the control of its projectors; but it will be speedily so improved, that by rapidly increasing strides it will firmly establish the reign of reason and happiness.

Seeing and knowing this, let us also make it equally evident to the Church, – warn it of its actual state, – cordially and sincerely assist its members quietly to withdraw those inconsistencies from the system, which now create its weakness and its danger; that it may retain those rational principles alone which can be successfully defended against attack, or which rather will prevent any attack from being attempted, or even meditated.

The wise and prudent then of all parties, instead of wishing to destroy national establishments, will use their utmost exertions to render them so consistent and reasonable in all their parts, that every well-disposed mind may be induced to give them their hearty and willing support.

For the first grand step towards effecting any substantial improvement in these realms, without injury to any part of the community, is to make it the clear and decided interest of the Church to cooperate cordially in all the projected ameliorations. Once found a national church on the true, unlimited, and genuine principles of mental charity, and all the members of the state will soon improve in every truly valuable quality. If the temperate and discerning of all parties will not now lend their aid to effect this change by peaceable means – which may with the greatest ease and with unerring certainty be done, – it is evident, to every calm observer, that the struggle by those who now exist in unnecessary misery to obtain that degree of happiness which they may attain in practice, cannot long be deferred. It will therefore prove true political wisdom to anticipate and guide these feelings.

To those who can reflect, and will attend to the passing scenes before them, the times are indeed awfully interesting; some change of high import, scarcely yet perhaps to be scanned by the present ill-taught race of men, is evidently in progress: in consequence, well founded, prompt, and decisive measures are now required in the British councils, to direct this change, and relieve the nation from the errors of its present systems.

It must surely then be the desire of every rational man, of every true friend to humanity, that a cordial cooperation and unity of action should be effected between the British Executive, the Parliament, the Church, and the People, to lay a broad and firm foundation for the future happiness of themselves and the world.

Say not, my countrymen, that such an event is impracticable; for, by adopting the evident means to form a rational character in man, there is a plain and direct road opened, which, if pursued, will render its accomplishment not only possible but certain. That road too will be found the most safe and pleasant that human beings have ever yet travelled. It leads direct to intelligence and true knowledge, and will show the boasted acquirements of Greece, of Rome, and of all antiquity, to be the mere weakness of mental infancy. Those who travel this road will find it so straight and well defined, that no one will be in danger of wandering from the right course. Nor is it yet a narrow or exclusive path; it admits of no exclusion, every colour of body and diversity of mind are freely and alike admitted. It is open to the human race, and it is broad and spacious enough to receive the whole, were they increased a thousand fold.

We well know that a declaration like the one now made must sound chimerical in the ears of those who have hitherto wandered in the dark mazes of ignorance, error, and exclusion; and who have been taught folly and inconsistencies only, from their cradle. But if every known fact connected with the subject proves that, from the day in which man first saw light to that in which the sun now shines, the old collectively have taught the young collectively the sentiments and habits which the young have acquired; and that the present generation, and every following generation, must in like manner instruct their successors; then do we say, with a confidence founded on certainty itself, that even much more shall come to pass than has yet been foretold, or promised. When these principles, derived from the unchangeable laws of nature, and equally revealed to all men, shall, as they soon will, be publicly established in the world, no conceivable obstacle can remain to prevent a sincere and cordial union and cooperation for every wise and good purpose, not only among all the members of the same state, but also among the rulers of those kingdoms and empires whose enmity and rancour against each other have been carried to the utmost stretch of melancholy folly, and even occasionally to a high degree of madness.

Such, my fellow men, are some, and yet but a few, of the mighty consequences which must result from the public acknowledgement of these plain, simple, and irresistible truths. They will not prove a delusive promise of mockery, but will in reality speedily and effectually establish peace, good-will, and an ever-active benevolence throughout the whole human race.

The public avowal of these principles, and their general introduction into practice, will constitute that invaluable secret, for which the human mind, from its birth, has been in perpetual search; its future beneficial consequences no man can yet foresee.

We will now show how these principles may be immediately and most advantageously introduced into general practice.

It has been said that 'the state which shall possess the best national system of education, will be the best governed'; and if the principle on which all the reasoning of these Essays is founded, be true, then is that sentiment also true. Yet (will future ages credit the fact?) to this day the British Government is without any national system of training and education, even for its millions of poor and uninstructed! ! The formation of the mind and habits of its subjects is permitted to go on at random, often in the hands of those who are the most incompetent in the empire; and the result is, the gross ignorance and disunion which now everywhere abound! ![2]

Instead of continuing such unwise proceedings, a national system for the training and education of the labouring classes ought to be immediately arranged, and, if judiciously devised, it may be rendered the most valuable improvement ever yet introduced into practice.

For this purpose, an act should be passed for the instruction of all the poor and labouring classes in the three kingdoms.

In this act provision should be made,

First, – For the appointment of proper persons to direct this new department of Government, which will be found ultimately to prove the most important of all its departments: consequently, those individuals who possess the highest integrity, abilities, and influence in the state, should be appointed to its direction.

2. Even the recent attempts which have been made are conducted on the narrow principle of debasing man to a mere irrational military machine, which is to be rapidly moved by animal force.

Second, – For the establishment of seminaries, in which those individuals, who shall be destined to form the minds and bodies of the future subjects of these realms, should be well initiated in the art and matter of instruction.

This is, and ought to be considered, an office of the greatest practical trust and confidence in the empire; for let this duty be well performed, and the government must proceed with ease to the people, and high gratification to those who govern.

At present, there are not any individuals in the kingdom who have been trained to instruct the rising generation, as it is for the interest and happiness of all that it should be instructed. The training of those who are to form the future man becomes a consideration of the utmost magnitude: for, on due reflection, it will appear that instruction to the young must be, of necessity, the only foundation upon which the superstructure of society can be raised. Let this instruction continue to be left, as heretofore, to chance, and often to the most inefficient members of the community, and society must still experience the endless miseries which arise from such weak and puerile conduct. On the contrary, let the instruction to the young be well devised and well executed, and no subsequent proceedings in the state can be materially injurious. For it may truly be said to be a wonder-working power; one that merits the deepest attention of the legislature; with ease it may be used to train man into a demon of mischief to himself and all around him, or into an agent of unlimited benevolence.

Third, – For the establishment of seminaries over the United Kingdoms; to be conveniently placed, and of sufficient extent to receive all those who require instruction.

Fourth, – For supplying the requisite expenditure for the building and support of those seminaries.

Fifth, – For their arrangement on the plan, which, for the manner of instruction, upon a due comparison of the various modes now in practice, or which may be devised, shall appear to be the best.

Sixth, – For the appointment of proper masters to each of the schools. And,

Last, – The matter of instruction, both for body and mind, in these seminaries, should be substantially beneficial to the individuals, and to the state. For this is, or ought to be, the sole motive for the establishment of national seminaries.

These are the outlines of the provisions necessary to prepare the most powerful instrument of good that has ever yet been placed in the hands of man.

The last national improvement which remains to be proposed, in the present state of the public mind, is, that another legislative act should be passed, for the purpose of obtaining regular and accurate information relative to the value of and demand for labour, over the United Kingdoms. This information is necessary, preparatory to the adoption of measures which will be proposed, to provide labour for those who may be occasionally unable to procure other employment.

In this act, provision should be made,

First, – To obtain accurate quarterly returns of the state of labour in each county, or smaller district; the returns to be made either by the clergy, justices of the peace, or other more competent persons. These returns should contain,

First, – The average price of manual labour within the district, for the period included in the return.

Second, – The number of those in each district who depend on their daily labour, or the parish, for their support; and who may be at the period of these returns unemployed, and yet able to labour.

Third, – The number of those who, at the period of each return, are but partially employed; and the extent of that partial employment.

Provision should also be made to obtain a statement of the general occupations in which the individuals had been formerly employed, with the best conjectures as to the kind and quantity of work which each may be supposed still capable of performing.

The want of due attention to this highly necessary branch of government, occasions thousands of our fellow subjects to be made wretched; while, from the same cause, the revenues of the empire are annually deteriorated to an enormous amount.

We have stated, because it is easy of proof, that the revenues of all countries are derived, directly or indirectly, from the labour of man; and yet the British Government, which, with all its errors, is among the best devised and most enlightened that have hitherto been established, makes extravagant and unnecessary waste of that labour. It makes this waste too in the midst of its greatest pecuniary difficulties, and when the utmost efforts of every individual in the state are requisite!

This waste of human labour, as it is highly unjust to all, is not only impolitic in a national view, but it is most cruel to the individuals who, in consequence of this waste, are the immediate sufferers.

It would be an Herculean task to trace through all their ramifications the various injurious effects which result from the fundamental errors by which man has been, and is governed; nor is the world yet fully prepared for such development. We shall therefore now merely sketch some of the most direct and palpable of these effects, relative to the oversight of governments in regard to the non-application or mis-application of the labour of the poor and unoccupied.

It has been shown that the governing powers of any country may easily and economically give its subjects just sentiments, and the best habits; and so long as this shall remain unattempted, governments will continue to neglect their most important duties, as well as interests. Such neglect now exists in Britain, where, in lieu of the governing powers making any effort to attain these inestimable benefits for the individuals belonging to the empire, they content themselves with the existence of laws, which must create sentiments and habits highly injurious to the welfare of the individuals and of the state.

Many of these laws, by their never-failing effects, speak in a language which no one can misunderstand; and say to the unprotected and untaught, *Remain in ignorance, and let your labour be directed by that ignorance: for while you can procure what is sufficient to support life by such labour, although that life should be an existence in abject poverty, disease, and misery, we will not trouble ourselves with you, or any of your proceedings: when, however, you can no longer procure work, or obtain the means to support nature, then apply for relief to the parish; and you shall be maintained in idleness.*

And in ignorance and idleness, even in this country, where manual labour is or always might be made valuable, hundreds of thousands of men, women, and children, are daily supported. No one acquainted with human nature will suppose that men, women, and children, can be long maintained in ignorance and idleness, without becoming habituated to crime.[3]

3. It would perhaps prove an interesting calculation, and useful to a government, to estimate how much its finances would be improved by giving proper employment to a million of its subjects, rather than by supporting that million in ignorance, idleness, and crime. Will it exceed the bounds of moderation to say, that a million of the population so employed, under the direction of an intelligent government, might earn to the state ten pounds each annually, or ten millions sterling per annum? Ten millions per year would be obtained by each individual earning less than four shillings per week; and any part of the population of these kingdoms, including within the average the too young and the too old for labour, may be

Why then are there any idle poor in these kingdoms? Solely because so large a part of the population have been permitted to grow up to manhood in gross ignorance; and because, when they are, or easily may be, trained to be willing to labour, useful and productive employment has not been provided for them.

All men may, by judicious and proper laws and training, readily acquire knowledge and habits which will enable them, if they be permitted, to produce far more than they need for their support and enjoyment; and thus any population, in the fertile parts of the earth, may be taught to live in plenty and in happiness, without the checks of vice and misery.

Mr Malthus is however correct, when he says that the population of the world is ever adapting itself to the quantity of food raised for its support; but he has not told us how much more food an intelligent and industrious people will create from the same soil, than will be produced by one ignorant and ill-governed. It is however as one, to infinity.

For man knows not the limit to his power of creating food. How much has this power been latterly increased in these islands! And in them such knowledge is in its infancy. Yet compare even this power of raising food with the efforts of the Bosgemens or other savages, and it will be found perhaps as one, to a thousand.

Food for man may be also considered as a compound of the original elements; of the qualities, combinations, and control of which, chemistry is daily adding to our knowledge; nor is it *yet* for man to say to what this knowledge may lead, or where it may end.

The sea, it may be remarked also, affords an inexhaust-

---

made to earn, under proper arrangements, more than four shillings per week to the state, besides creating an innumerable train of other more beneficial consequences.

ible source of food. It may then be safely asserted, that the population of the world may be allowed naturally to increase for many thousand years; and yet, under a system of government founded on the principles for the truth of which we contend, the whole may continue to live, in abundance and happiness, without one check of vice or of misery; and, under the guidance of these principles, human labour, properly directed, may be made far more than sufficient to enable the population of the world to live in the highest state of human enjoyment.

Shall we then continue to allow misery to predominate, and the labour of man to be most absurdly applied or wasted, when it might be easily directed to remove that misery?

The labour of every man, woman, and child, possessing sufficient bodily strength, may be advantageously employed for the public; and there is not perhaps a stronger evidence of the extreme ignorance and fallacy of the systems which have hitherto governed the world, than that the rich, the active, and the powerful, should, by tacit consent, support the ignorant in idleness and crime, without making the attempt to train them into industrious, intelligent, and valuable members of the community; although the means by which the change could be easily effected have been always at their command!

It is not, however, intended to propose that the British Government should now give direct employment to all its working population: on the contrary, it is confidently expected that a national system for the training and education of the poor, and lower orders, will be so effectual, that ere long they will all find employment sufficient to support themselves, except in cases of a great sudden depression in the demand for, and consequent depreciation in the value of, labour.

To prevent the crime and misery which ever follow these

unfavourable fluctuations in the demand for and value of labour, it ought to be a primary duty of every government that sincerely interests itself in the well-being of its subjects, to provide perpetual employment of real national utility, in which all who apply may be immediately occupied.

In order that those only who could not obtain employment from private individuals should be induced to avail themselves of these national works, the rate of the public labour might be in general fixed at some proportion less than the average rate of private labour in the district in which such public labour should be performed. These rates might be readily ascertained and fixed, by reference to the county or district quarterly returns of the average rate of labour.

This measure, judiciously managed, would have a similar effect on the price of labour, that the sinking fund produces on the Stock Exchange; and, as the price of public labour should never fall below the means of temperate existence, the plan proposed would perpetually tend to prevent an excess of nationally injurious pressure on the most unprotected part of society.

The most obvious, and in the first place the best source, perhaps, of employment, would be the making and repairing of roads. Such employment would be perpetual over the whole kingdom; and it will be found true national economy to keep the public roads at all times in a much higher state of repair than perhaps any of them are at present. If requisite, canals, harbours, docks, ship-building, and materials for the navy, may be afterwards resorted to: it is not, however, supposed that many of the latter resources would be necessary.

A persevering attention, without which indeed not anything beneficial in practice can ever be attained, will soon overcome all the difficulties which may at first appear to obstruct this plan for introducing occasional national employment into the polity of the kingdom.

In times of very limited demand for labour, it is truly lamentable to witness the distress which arises among the industrious for want of regular employment, and their customary wages. In these periods, innumerable applications are made to the Superintendents of extensive manual operations, to obtain any kind of employment by which a subsistence may be procured. Such applications are often made by persons, who, in search of work, have travelled from one extremity of the island to the other!

During these attempts to be useful and honest, in the common acceptation of the terms, the families of such wandering individuals accompany them, or remain at home; in either case, they generally experience sufferings and privations which the gay and splendid will hesitate to believe it possible that human nature could endure.

Yet, after this extended and anxious endeavour to procure employment, the applicant often returns unsuccessful; he cannot, by his most strenuous exertions, procure an honest and independent existence: therefore, with intentions perhaps as good, and a mind as capable of great and benevolent actions as the remainder of his fellow men, he has no other resources left but to starve; apply to his parish for relief, and thus suffer the greatest degradation; or rely on his own native exertions, and, to supply himself and family with bread, resort to what are termed dishonest means.

Some minds thus circumstanced, are so delicately formed, that they will not accept the one, or adopt the other of the two latter modes to sustain life, and in consequence they actually starve. These, however, it is to be hoped, are not very numerous. But the number is undoubtedly great, of those whose health is ruined by bad and insufficient food, clothing, and shelter; who contract lingering diseases, and suffer premature death, the effect of partial starvation. The most ignorant and least enterprising of them apply to the parish for support; soon lose the desire of exertion; become permanently dependent; conscious of their degradation in society; and henceforward, with their offspring, remain a burden and grievous evil to the state; while those among this class who yet possess strength and energy of body and mind, with some undestroyed powers of reasoning, perceive, in part, the glaring errors and injustice of society towards themselves and their fellow sufferers.

Can it then create surprise that feelings like those described should force human nature to endeavour to retaliate?

Multitudes of our fellow men are so goaded by these reflections and circumstances, as to be urged, even while incessantly and closely pursued by legal death, almost without a chance of escape, to resist these laws under which they suffer; and thus the private depredator on society is formed, fostered, and matured.

Shall we then longer withhold national instruction from our fellow men, who, it has been shown, might easily be trained to be industrious, intelligent, virtuous, and valuable members of the state?

True indeed it is, that all the measures now proposed are only a compromise with the errors of the present systems: but as these errors now almost universally exist, and must be overcome solely by the force of reason; and as reason, to effect the most beneficial purposes, makes her advance by slow degrees, and progressively substantiates one truth of high import after another, it will be evident to minds of comprehensive and accurate thought, that by these and similar compromises alone can success be rationally expected in practice. For such compromises bring truth and error before the public; and whenever they are fairly exhibited together, truth must ultimately prevail.

As many of the inconsistencies of the present systems are evident to the most intelligent and well disposed minds, the way for the public admission of the important truths which have now been in part unfolded,[4] seems to be rendered easy; and it is confidently expected that the period is at hand, when man through ignorance shall not much longer inflict unnecessary misery on man: because, the mass of mankind will become enlightened, and clearly discern that by so acting they will inevitably create misery to themselves. For the extensive knowledge of the facts which present themselves on the globe, makes it evident to those whose reasoning faculties have not been entirely paralysed, that all mankind firmly believe, that everybody, except themselves, has been grievously deceived in his fundamental principles; and feel the utmost astonishment that the nations of the world could embrace such gross inconsistencies for divine or political truths. Most persons are now also prepared to understand that these weaknesses are firmly and conscientiously fixed in the minds of millions, who, when born, possessed equal faculties with themselves. And although they plainly discern in others what they deem inconceivable aberrations of the mental powers, yet, in despite of such facts, they are taught to believe *that they themselves could not have been so deceived;* and this impression is made upon the infant mind with the greatest ease, whether it be to create followers of the most ignorant, or of the most enlightened systems.

The inhabitants of the world are therefore abundantly conscious of the inconsistencies contained in those systems in which all have been trained, out of the pale of their own peculiar, and, as they are taught to believe, highly favoured sect: and yet, the number of the largest sect in the world is small, when compared with the remaining sects, which have been instructed to think the notions of that larger division an error of the grossest kind; proceeding alone from the ignorance or deception of their predecessors.

4. As soon as the public mind shall be sufficiently prepared to receive it, the practical detail of this system shall be fully developed.

All that is now requisite, previous to withdrawing the last mental bandage by which, hitherto, the human race has been kept in darkness and misery, is, by calm and patient reasoning to tranquillize the public mind; and thus to prevent the evil effects which otherwise might arise from the too sudden prospect of freely enjoying rational liberty of mind.

To withdraw that bandage without danger, reason must be judiciously applied to lead men of every sect (for all have been in part abused) to reflect, that if untold myriads of beings, formed like themselves, have been so grossly deceived as they believe them to have been, what power in nature was there to prevent *them* from being equally deceived?

Such reflections, steadily pursued by those who are anxious to follow the plain and simple path of reason, will soon make it obvious that the inconsistencies which they behold in all other sects *out of their own pale,* are precisely similar to those which all other sects can readily discover *within that pale.*

It is not however to be imagined, that this free and open exposure of the gross errors in which the existing generation has been instructed should be forthwith palatable to the world; it would be contrary to reason to form any such expectations.

Yet, as evil exists, and as man cannot be rational, nor of course happy, until the cause of it shall be removed; the writer, like a physician who feels the deepest interest in the welfare of his patient, has hitherto administered of this unpalatable restorative the smallest quantity which he deemed sufficient for the purpose: he now waits to see the effects which that may produce: should the application not prove of sufficient strength to remove the mental disorder, he promises that it shall be increased, until sound health to the public mind be firmly and permanently established.

REPORT
TO THE COUNTY OF
LANARK

REPORT

To the County of Lanark, of a Plan for relieving Public Distress and Removing Discontent, by giving permanent, productive Employment to the Poor and Working Classes, under Arrangements which will essentially improve their Character, and ameliorate their Condition, diminish the Expenses of Production and Consumption, and create Markets coextensive with Production. By Robert Owen, 1 May 1820.

The following Report was submitted, at the request of a Committee of Gentlemen of the Upper Ward of Lanarkshire, to a General Meeting of the County, held at Lanark on 1 May 1820, and was ordered to be referred to the consideration of a Committee, composed of the following gentlemen: –

NORMAN LOCKHART, Esq., Convener of the Committee

ROBERT HAMILTON, Esq., Sheriff Depute of Lanarkshire

SIR JAMES STEWART DENHAM of Coltness, Bart

SIR WILLIAM HONYMAN of Armadale, Bart

SIR HENRY STEUART of Allanton, Bart

COLONEL GORDON of Harperfield

HUGH MOSMAN of Auchtyfardle, Esq.

PART I

Introduction

THE evil for which your Reporter has been required to provide a remedy, is the general want of employment at wages sufficient to support the family of a working man beneficially for the community.

After the most earnest consideration of the subject he has been compelled to conclude that such employment cannot be procured through the medium of trade, commerce, or manufactures, or even of agriculture, until the Government and the Legislature, cordially supported by the country, shall previously adopt measures to remove obstacles, which, without their interference, will now permanently keep the working classes in poverty and discontent, and gradually deteriorate all the resources of the empire.

Your Reporter has been impressed with the truth of this conclusion by the following considerations:

1st – That manual labour, properly directed, is the source of all wealth, and of national prosperity.

2nd – That, when properly directed, labour is of far more value to the community than the expense necessary to maintain the labourer in considerable comfort.

3rd – That manual labour, properly directed, may be made to continue of this value in all parts of the world, under any supposable increase of its population, for many centuries to come.

4th – That, under a proper direction of manual labour, Great Britain and its dependencies may be made to support an incalculable increase of population, most advantageously for all its inhabitants.

5th – That when manual labour shall be so directed, it will

be found that population cannot, for many years, be stimulated to advance as rapidly as society might be benefited by its increase.

These considerations, deduced from the first and most obvious principles of the science of political economy, convinced your Reporter that some formidable artificial obstacle intervened to obstruct the natural improvement and progress of society.

It is well known that, during the last half century in particular, Great Britain, beyond any other nation, has progressively increased its powers of production, by a rapid advancement in scientific improvements and arrangements, introduced, more or less, into all the departments of productive industry throughout the empire.

The amount of this new productive power cannot, for want of proper data, be very accurately estimated; but your Reporter has ascertained from facts which none will dispute, that its increase has been enormous; – that, compared with the manual labour of the whole population of Great Britain and Ireland, it is, at least, as *forty to one*, and may be easily made as *a hundred to one*; and that this increase may be extended to other countries; that it is already sufficient to saturate the world with wealth, and that the power of creating wealth may be made to advance perpetually in an accelerating ratio.

It appeared to your Reporter that the natural effect of the aid thus obtained from knowledge and science should be to add to the wealth and happiness of society in proportion as the new power increased and was judiciously directed; and that, in consequence, all parties would thereby be substantially benefited. All know, however, that these beneficial effects do not exist. On the contrary, it must be acknowledged that the working classes, which form so large a proportion of the population, cannot obtain even the comforts which their labour formerly procured for them, and that no party appears to gain, but all to suffer, by their distress.

Having taken this view of the subject, your Reporter was induced to conclude that the want of beneficial employment for the working classes, and the consequent public distress, were owing to the rapid increase of the new productive power, for the advantageous application of which, society had neglected to make the proper arrangements. Could these arrangements be formed, he entertained the most confident expectation that productive employment might again be found for all who required it; and that the national distress, of which all now so loudly complain, might be gradually converted into a much higher degree of prosperity than was attainable prior to the extraordinary accession lately made to the productive powers of society.

Cheered by such a prospect, your Reporter directed his attention to the consideration of the possibility of devising arrangements by means of which the whole population might participate in the benefits derivable from the increase of scientific productive power; and he has the satisfaction to state to the meeting, that he has strong grounds to believe that such arrangements are practicable.

His opinion on this important part of the subject is founded on the following considerations:

1st – It must be admitted that scientific or artificial aid to man increases his productive powers, his natural wants remaining the same; and in proportion as his productive powers increase he becomes less dependent on his physical strength and on the many contingencies connected with it.

2nd – That the direct effect of every addition to scientific, or mechanical and chemical power, is to increase wealth; and it is found, accordingly, that the immediate cause of the present want of employment for the working classes is an excess of production of all kinds of wealth, by which, under the existing arrangements of commerce, all the markets of the world are overstocked.

3rd – That, could markets be found, an incalculable addition might yet be made to the wealth of society, as is most evident from the number of persons who seek employment, and the far greater number who, from ignorance, are inefficiently employed, but still more from the means we possess of increasing, to an unlimited extent, our scientific powers of production.

4th – That the deficiency of employment for the working classes cannot proceed from a want of wealth or capital, or of the means of greatly adding to that which now exists, but from some defect in the mode of distributing this extraordinary addition of new capital throughout society, or, to speak commercially, from the want of a market, or means of exchange, co-extensive with the means of production.

Were effective measures devised to facilitate the distribution of wealth after it was created, your Reporter could have no difficulty in suggesting the means of beneficial occupation for all who are unemployed, and for a considerable increase to their number.

Your Reporter is aware that mankind are naturally averse to the commencement of any material alteration in long-established practices, and that, in many cases, such an innovation, however beneficial its tendency, cannot take place unless forced on society by strong necessity.

It is urgent necessity alone that will effect the changes which our present situation demands; one of which respects the mode of distributing the enormous supply of new wealth or capital which has been lately created, and which may be now indefinitely increased. To the ignorance which prevails on this and other subjects connected with the science of political economy may be attributed the present general stagnation of commerce, and the consequent distress of the country.

Your Reporter, undismayed by any opposition he may excite, is determined to perform his duty, and to use his utmost exertions to induce the Public to take into calm consideration those practical measures which to him appear the only remedy adequate to remove this distress.

One of the measures which he thus ventures to propose,

to let prosperity loose on the country, (if he may be allowed the expression), is *a change in the standard of value.*

It is true that in the civilized parts of the world gold and silver have been long used for this purpose; but these metals have been a mere artificial standard, and they have performed the office very imperfectly and inconveniently.

Their introduction as a standard of value altered the *intrinsic* values of all things into *artificial* values; and, in consequence, they have materially retarded the general improvement of society. So much so, indeed, that, in this sense, it may well be said, 'Money is the root of all evil'. It is fortunate for society that these metals cannot longer perform the task which ignorance assigned to them. The rapid increase of wealth, which extraordinary scientific improvements had been the means of producing in this country prior to 1797, imposed upon the Legislature in that year an overwhelming necessity to declare virtually by Act of Parliament that gold ceased to be the British standard of value. Experience then proved that gold and silver could no longer practically represent the increased wealth created by British industry aided by its scientific improvements.

A temporary expedient was thought of and adopted, and Bank of England paper became the British legal standard of value; – a convincing proof that society may make any artificial substance, whether possessing intrinsic worth or not, a legal standard of value.

It soon appeared, however, that the adoption of this new artificial standard was attended with extreme danger, because it placed the prosperity and well-being of the community at the mercy of a trading company, which, although highly respectable in that capacity, was itself, in a great degree, ignorant of the nature of the mighty machine which it wielded. The Legislature, with almost one voice, demanded that this monopoly of the standard of value should cease. But it was wholly unprepared with a remedy.

The expedient adopted was to make preparations for an attempt to return to the former artificial standard, which, in 1797, was proved by experience to be inadequate to represent the then existing wealth of the British Empire, and which was, of course, still more inadequate to the purpose when that wealth and the means of adding to it had been in the interim increased to an incalculable extent. This impolitic measure involved the Government in the most formidable difficulties, and plunged the country into poverty, discontent, and danger.

Seeing the distress which a slight progress towards the fulfilment of this measure has already occasioned, by the unparalleled depression of agriculture, commerce, and manufactures, and the consequent almost total annihilation of the value of labour, it is to be hoped that the Government and the Legislature, and the enlightened and reasonable part of society, will pause while they are yet only on the brink of the frightful abyss into which they are about to precipitate the prosperity and safety of themselves and the country.

The meeting may now justly ask of the Reporter, what remedy he has to offer, and what standard of value he proposes to substitute for gold and silver?

Before proceeding to this part of the subject he begs to claim the indulgence of the meeting for occupying so much of its time, trusting that the intricacy, difficulty, and importance of the question, added to the daily increasing poverty and distress of the working classes (going on apparently without limitation), and the consequent alarming and dangerous state of the country, will be accepted as some apology for him; and more especially when it is considered that he is not advocating any private interest, but simply stating a case in which the prosperity and wellbeing of all ranks in the community are deeply concerned.

To understand the subject on which your Reporter is now about to enter requires much profound study of the whole circle of political economy. A knowledge of some of its parts, with ignorance of the remainder, will be found to be most injurious to the practical statesman; and it is owing to this cause, perhaps, more than to any other, that the world has been so wretchedly governed; for the object of this science is to direct how the whole faculties of men may be most advantageously applied; whereas those powers have been combined, hitherto, chiefly to retard the improvements of society.

Your Reporter, then, after deeply studying these subjects, practically and theoretically, for a period exceeding thirty years, and during which his practice without a single exception has confirmed the theory which practice first suggested, now ventures to state, as one of the results of this study and experience, THAT THE NATURAL STANDARD OF VALUE IS, ON PRINCIPLE, HUMAN LABOUR, OR THE COMBINED MANUAL AND MENTAL POWERS OF MEN CALLED INTO ACTION.

And that it would be highly beneficial, and has now become absolutely necessary, to reduce this principle into immediate practice.

It will be said, by those who have taken a superficial or mere partial view of the question, that human labour or power is so unequal in individuals, that its average amount cannot be estimated.

Already, however, the average physical power of men as well as of horses (equally varied in the individuals), has been calculated for scientific purposes, and both now serve to measure inanimate powers.

On the same principle the average of human labour or power may be ascertained; and as it forms the essence of all wealth, its value in every article of produce may also be ascertained, and its exchangeable value with all other values fixed accordingly; the whole to be permanent for a given period.

Human labour would thus acquire its natural or intrinsic value, which would increase as science advanced; and this is, in fact, the only really useful object of science.

The demand for human labour would be no longer subject to caprice, nor would the support of human life be made, as at present, a perpetually varying article of commerce, and the working classes made the slaves of an artificial system of wages, more cruel in its effects than any slavery ever practised by society, either barbarous or civilized.

This change in the standard of value would immediately open the most advantageous domestic markets, until the wants of all were amply supplied; nor while this standard continued could any evil arise in future from the want of markets.

It would secure the means for the most unlimited and advantageous intercourse and exchange with other nations, without compromising national interests, and enable all governments to withdraw every existing injurious commercial restriction.

It would render unnecessary and entirely useless the present demoralizing system of bargaining between individuals; and no practice perhaps tends more than this to deteriorate and degrade the human character.

It would speedily remove pauperism and ignorance from society, by furnishing time and means for the adequate instruction of the working classes, who might be rendered of far more commercial value to themselves and to society than they have yet been at any period of the world.

It would supply the means of gradually improving the condition of all ranks, to an extent not yet to be estimated.

And, as it would materially improve human nature, and raise all in the scale of well-being and happiness, none could be injured or oppressed.

These are some of the important advantages which could arise (when due preparation shall be made for the change), from introducing the natural standard of value, and abandoning an artificial one, which can no longer serve the purpose.

It now remains to be considered how this change can be effected without creating temporary confusion.

To accomplish this desirable object, several legislative measures will be necessary.

The first, as an intermediate and temporary one, to put a stop to the increasing pecuniary distress of the working classes, will be to relieve the country from the ruinous effects which have been produced by the various attempts to compel a return to cash payments; a longer perseverance in which is calculated to derange the whole of the existing social system. The attempt will prove as vain as to try to restore a full-grown bird to the shell in which it was hatched, or to make the clothes of an infant cover a giant; for the improvements of society have equally outgrown the late system of cash payments. Should the attempt be persevered in, no more wealth will be created, and much of that which is now considered wealth will be destroyed. A perseverance in such a course will compel the working classes to starve or emigrate, while the present higher orders will be left an easy prey to their enemies and to poverty. No real benefit could arise to any party from a return to cash payments, if such a measure were practicable.

The next step is to adopt such measures as will permit the labouring unoccupied poor to be employed to raise their own subsistence, and as large a surplus for the infant, the aged, and the incapacitated poor, as their labour can be made to yield; the labourer to receive an equitable remuneration for the surplus he may create.

But the industry of the poor, thus applied, will tend still further to overstock the markets of the world with agricultural and manufactured produce, and, in the same proportion to decrease the *nominal or monied prices* of both, and of course add to the public distress.

It is this view of the subject that has induced your Reporter so strongly to urge those who take a lead in the affairs of this populous and distressed country to come forward at this critical juncture to recommend to the Government, and to petition the Legislature, to take into their most serious consideration such means as may be proposed to remove the existing obstructions in the way of the general prosperity of the country.

It is the want of a profitable market that alone checks the successful and otherwise beneficial industry of the working classes.

The markets of the world are created solely by the remuneration allowed for the industry of the working classes, and those markets are more or less extended and profitable in proportion as these classes are well or ill remunerated for their labour.

But the existing arrangements of society will not permit the labourer to be remunerated for his industry, and in consequence all markets fail.

To re-create and extend demand in proportion as the late scientific improvements, and others which are daily advancing to perfection, extend the means of supply, the natural standard of value is required.

It will be found equal to the important task which it has to perform.

It will at once remove the obstruction which has paralysed the industry of the country; and experience will prove that this effect cannot be accomplished by any other expedient.

Your Reporter, having given the foregoing general explanation of the principles which his experience leads him to recommend for adoption to relieve the country from its distress and danger, will now proceed to a development of all the measures necessary to put these principles into practice.

PART II

Outlines of the Plan

———

I⊤ is admitted that under the present system no more hands can be employed advantageously in agriculture or manufactures; and that both interests are on the eve of bankruptcy.

It is also admitted that the prosperity of the country, or rather that which ought to create prosperity, the improvement in mechanical and chemical science, has enabled the population to produce more than the present system permits to be consumed.

In consequence, new arrangements become necessary, by which *consumption* may be made to keep pace with *production,* and the following are recommended:

1st – To cultivate the soil with the spade instead of the plough.

2nd – To make such changes as the spade cultivation requires, to render it easy and profitable to individuals, and beneficial to the country.

3rd – To adopt a standard of value by means of which the exchange of the products of labour may proceed without check or limit, until wealth shall become so abundant that any further increase to it will be considered useless, and will not be desired.

We proceed to give the reasons for recommending these arrangements in preference to all others.

And first, those for preferring the spade to the plough for the universal cultivation of the soil.

Practical cultivators of the soil know, that the most favourable circumstances for promoting the growth of vegetation is a due supply of moisture, and that when this is provided for, a good general crop seldom, if ever, fails.

Water enters so largely into the food of all plants, that if its gradual supply can be secured, the farmer and horticulturist feel assured of a fair return for their labour. Whatever mode of cultivation, therefore, can best effect the object of drawing off from the seed or plant an excess of water, and retaining this surplus as a reservoir from which a gradual supply of moisture may be obtained as required, must possess decided advantages.

It is also known to all practical agriculturists, that to obtain the best crops, the soil ought to be well broken and separated; and that the nearer it is brought to a garden mould, the more perfect is the cultivation.

These facts no one will dispute, nor will any deny that the spade is calculated to prepare a better recipient than the plough for an excess of water in rainy seasons, and to return it to the seed or plant afterwards in a manner most favourable to vegetation.

The spade, whenever there is sufficient soil, opens it to a depth that allows the water to pass freely below the bed of the seed or plant, and to remain there until a long continuance of heat draws it forth again to replenish the crop in the ground when it most requires to be gradually supplied with moisture; and the greater the depth to which the soil is opened, the greater will be the advantage of this important operation. Hence the increased crops after deep ploughing and after trenching, although the latter process may be also in some degree assisted by the new or rested soil which it brings into action; yet both these effects are obtained by the use of the spade.

The action of the plough upon the soil is the reverse of that of the spade in the following important particulars:

Instead of *loosening* the subsoil, it *hardens* it; the heavy smooth surface of the plough, and the frequent trampling of the horses' feet, tend to form a surface on the subsoil, well calculated to prevent the water from penetrating below it; and in many soils, after a few years' ploughing, it is there retained to drown the seed or plant in rainy seasons, and to be speedily evaporated when it would be the most desirable to retain it. Thus the crop is injured, and often destroyed, in dry weather, for the want of that moisture which, under a different system, might have been retained in the subsoil.

It is evident, therefore, that the plough conceals from the eye its own imperfections, and deceives its employers, being in truth a *mere surface implement,* and extremely defective in principle.

The spade, on the contrary, makes a good subsoil, as well as a superior surface, and the longer it is used on the same soil, the more easily will it be worked; and by occasional trenching, where there is sufficient depth of soil, new earth will be brought into action, and the benefits to be derived from a prepared subsoil will be increased.

These facts being incontrovertible, few perhaps will hesitate to admit them.

But it may be said that, 'admitting the statement to be true to the full extent, yet the plough, with a pair of horses and one man, performs so much work in a given time, that, with all its imperfections, it may be a more economical intrument for the purpose required.'

Such has been the almost universal impression for ages past, and, in consequence, the plough has superseded the spade, and is considered to be an improved machine for ordinary cultivation.

All this is plausible, and is sanctioned by the old prejudices of the world; but your Reporter maintains that it is not true that the plough is, or has ever been, in any stage of society, the most economical instrument for the cultivation of the soil. It has been so in appearance only, not in reality.

Cultivated as the soil has been hitherto, the direct expense of preparing it by the plough (in the manner in which the plough prepares it), has been in many cases less per acre than it would have been by the spade. The increased crop which the latter implement would have produced, all other circumstances being the same, does not seem to have been taken into account, or to have been accurately ascertained, except by Mr Falla, of Gateshead, near Newcastle, who, for many years, has had a hundred acres under spade cultivation, chiefly for nursery purposes, and who, by his practical knowledge of the subject, has realized, as your Reporter is informed, a large fortune. He has satisfactorily proved, by the experiments of four successive years, that although the expense of cultivation by the spade exceeds that of the plough per acre, yet the increased value of the crop greatly over-balances the increased expense of cultivation, and that even with 'things as they are' the spade is a much better, and a much more economical instrument with which to cultivate the soil, than the plough.

Why, then, your Reporter may be asked, is not the spade more generally used, and why is there now so much reluctance, on the part of those who cultivate the soil for profit, to its introduction?

A little will explain this.

Hitherto, those who have cultivated the soil for profit have generally been men trained to be tenacious of old established practices, all their ideas have been confined within a very narrow range; they have not been taught to think about anything, till lately, except that which was in the common routine of their daily practice. Their minds were uncultivated; yet, having naturally the use of their senses, they could not fail gradually to acquire by experience a useful knowledge of their domestic animals, of pigs, sheep, cattle, and horses. These they could treat and manage well; but, taught as men have ever yet been instructed, they could acquire no knowledge of themselves, and must have consequently remained ignorant of human nature and of the means by which the powers of *men* could be applied more advantageously to the soil than the powers of *animals*. The system in which man has been hitherto trained, so far as our knowledge of history extends, has kept him in utter ignorance of himself and his fellows; and hence the best and most valuable powers of the human race could not be made available for their own well-being and happiness. And if the most enlightened disciples of this system have been incapable of governing human beings aright, and of giving a beneficial direction to their powers, much less could those be equal to the task, whose knowledge of men was necessarily more confined, as is the case with farmers of the present day. These can better direct the employment of ten horses than ten men; and yet the spade husbandry would require that each horse now in use should be superseded by eight or ten human beings; and, to succeed in the business, an economical direction of their powers, which implies a knowledge of human nature in all respects, ought to be as well understood by those who conduct the spade operations, as the nature and management of horses are by farmers of the present day. For this change the cultivators of the soil are not prepared; and however more profitable the spade husbandry may be proved to be than the plough, they are not yet competent to undertake it. Many *preparatory* changes are necessary.

They must acquire as accurate a knowledge of *human* nature as they now possess of common *animal* nature. Agriculture, instead of being, as heretofore, the occupation of the mere peasant and farmer, with minds as defective in their cultivation as their soils, will then become the delightful employment of a race of men trained in the best habits and dispositions, familiar with the most useful practice in arts and sciences, and with minds fraught with the most valuable information and extensive general knowledge, – capable of forming and conducting combined arrangements in agriculture, trade, commerce, and manufactures, far superior to those which have yet existed in any of these departments, as they have been hitherto disjoined and separately conducted.

It will be readily perceived that this is an advance in civilization and general improvement that is to be effected solely *through the science of the influence of circumstances over human nature, and the knowledge of the means by which those circumstances may be easily controlled.*

Closet theorists and inexperienced persons suppose that to exchange the plough for the spade would be to turn back in the road of improvement, – to give up a superior for an inferior implement of cultivation. Little do they imagine that the introduction of the spade, with the scientific arrangements which it requires, will produce far greater improvements in agriculture, than the steam engine has effected in manufactures. Still less do they imagine that the change from the plough to the spade will prove to be a far more extensive and beneficial innovation than that which the invention of the spinning machine has occasioned, by the introduction of which, instead of the single wheel in a corner of a farm house, we now see thousands of spindles revolving with the noise of a waterfall in buildings palace-like for their cost, magnitude, and appearance.

Yet this extraordinary change is at hand. It will immediately take place; for the interest and well-being of all classes require it. Society cannot longer proceed another step in advance without it; and until it is adopted, civilization must retrograde, and the working classes starve for want of employment.

The introduction of the steam engine and the spinning machine added in an extraordinary manner to the powers of human nature. In their consequences they have in half a century multiplied the productive power, or the means of creating wealth, among the population of these islands, more than twelve-fold, besides giving a great increase to the means of creating wealth in other countries.

The steam engine and spinning machines, with the endless mechanical inventions to which they have given rise, have, however, inflicted evils on society, which now greatly over-balance the benefits which are derived from them. They have created an aggregate of wealth, and placed it in the hands of a few, who, by its aid, continue to absorb the wealth produced by the industry of the many. Thus the mass of the population are become mere slaves to the ignorance and caprice of these monopolists, and are far more truly helpless and wretched than they were before the names of WATT and ARKWRIGHT were known. Yet these celebrated and ingenious men have been the instruments of preparing society for the important beneficial changes which are about to occur.

All now know and feel that the good which these inventions are calculated to impart to the community has not yet been realized. The condition of society, instead of being improved, has been deteriorated, under the new circumstances to which they have given birth; and it is now experiencing a retrogade movement.

'Something', therefore, 'must be done', as the general voice exclaims, to give to our suffering population, and to society at large, the means of deriving from these inventions the advantages which all men of science expect from them.

In recommending the change from the plough to the spade cultivation your Reporter has in view such scientific arrangements, as, he is persuaded, will, on due examination, convince every intelligent mind that they offer the only means by which we can be relieved from our present overwhelming difficulties, or by which Great Britain can be enabled to maintain in future her rank among nations. They are the only effectual remedy for the evils which the steam engine and the spinning machine have, by their mis-direction, created, and are alone capable of giving a real and substantial value to these and other scientific inventions. Of all our splendid improvements in art and science the effect has hitherto been to demoralize society, through the mis-application of the new wealth created.

The arrangements to which your Reporter now calls the attention of the Public, present the certains means of reno-vating the moral character, and of improving, to an un-limited extent, the general condition of the population, and, while they lead to a far more rapid multiplication of wealth than the present system permits to take place, they will effectually preclude all the evils with which wealth is now accompanied.

It is estimated that in Great Britain and Ireland there are now under cultivation upwards of *sixty millions* of acres; and of these, *twenty millions* are arable, and *forty millions* in pasture; – that, under the present system of cultivation by the plough and of pasturing, about *two millions*, at most, of *actual labourers* are employed on the soil, giving immediate support to about *three times* that number, and supplying food for a population of about *eighteen millions*. Sixty *millions* of acres, under a judicious arrangement of spade cultivation, with manufactures as an appendage, might be made to give healthy advantageous employment to *sixty millions* of labourers at the least, and to support, in high comfort a population greatly exceeding *one hundred millions*. But in the present low state of population in these islands not more than *five or six millions* of acres could be properly cultivated by the spade, although all the opera-tive manufacturers were to be chiefly employed in this mode of agriculture. Imperfect, therefore, as the plough is for the cultivation of the soil, it is probable that, in this country, for want of an adequate population, many centuries will elapse before it can be entirely superseded by the spade; yet under the plough system Great Britain and Ireland are even now supposed to be greatly over-peopled.

It follows from this statement, that we possess the means of supplying the labouring poor, however numerous they may be, with permanent beneficial employment for many centuries to come.

The spade husbandry has been proved, by well-devised and accurately conducted experiments, to be a profitable mode of cultivation. It is now become also absolutely neces-sary, to give relief to the working classes, and it may be safely calculated upon as the certain source of future perma-nent occupation for them.

The next consideration which demands our attention is, – what constitutes a proper system of spade husbandry? – or, in other words, *how these new cultivators can be placed on the soil and associated, that their exertions may have the most beneficial result for themselves and the community?*

The leading principle which should direct us in the out-line of this arrangement, and from which there should be no deviation in any of its parts, is the public good, or the general interest of the whole population.

To this end, the following considerations must be com-bined.

1st – Where, in general, can the labourers be best placed for spade cultivation?

2nd – What is the quantity of land which it may be the most advantageous to cultivate *in cumulo* by the spade?

3rd – What number of workmen can be the most beneficially employed together, with a view to all the objects of their labour?

4th – What are the best arrangements under which these men and their families can be well and economically *lodged, fed, clothed, trained, educated, employed,* and *governed*?

5th – What is the best mode of disposing of the surplus pro-duce to be thus created by their labour?

6th – What are the means best calculated to render the conduct and industry of these workmen beneficial to their neighbours, to their country, and to foreign nations?

These are some of the leading objects which naturally arise for our consideration in forming arrangements for the introduction of the spade as a substitute for the plough cultivation.

To substitute the spade for the plough may seem most trivial in the expression; and to inexperienced, and even to learned men, – to my respected friends the Edinburgh Reviewers, for instance, who cannot be supposed to have much useful practical knowledge, – will appear to indicate a change equally simple and unimportant in practice.

It generally happens, however, that when a great calamity overwhelms a country, relief is obtained from practical men, and not from mere theorists, however acute, learned, and eloquent. In the present case, simple as at first appears to be the alteration proposed, yet, when the mind of the practical agriculturist, of the commercial man, of the man of science, of the political economist, of the statesman, and of the philosopher, shall be directed to the subject as its importance demands, the change will be found to be one of the deepest interest to society, involving consequences of much higher concernment to the well-being of mankind than the change from hunting to the pastoral state, or from the pastoral state to the plough cultivation.

The change comes, too, at a crisis most momentous for the safety of the civilized world, to re-unite the most jarring interests which were on the extreme point of severing all the old connexions of society.

It comes, too, at a period when the force of circumstances has trained men, even by the destructive art of war, to understand in part the extraordinary effects which may be produced by well-devised arrangements and extensive combinations.

It has occurred, too, at the first moment when experience

has, in some degree, prepared men to comprehend the superior advantages which each may gain by attending to the great interests of human nature, rather than to the mistaken feeling and policy which rivet the whole attention of the individual to benefit himself, or his party, through any other medium than the public good.

Were the subject now before us to be entered upon with more confined views of its interest, magnitude, and importance, it would fail to be understood, and justice could not be done to it. Yet how few of the celebrated political economists of the day have their minds prepared for this investigation!

Having given the outline of the considerations which show the superiority in principle of the spade over the plough as a scientific and economical instrument of cultivation; – having also described briefly the objects to be attended to in forming economical arrangements for the change proposed: – it now remains that the principle should be generally explained by which an advantageous interchange and exchange may be made of the greatly increased products of labour which will be created by the spade cultivation aided by the improved arrangements now contemplated.

These incalculably increased products will render gold, the old artificial standard of value, far more unfit for the task which is to be performed, than it was in 1797, when it ceased to be the British legal standard of value, or than it is now, when wealth has so much increased.

Your Reporter is of opinion that *the natural standard of human labour*, fixed to represent its natural worth, or power of creating new wealth, will alone be found adequate to the purposes required.

To a mind coming first to this subject, innumerable and apparently insurmountable difficulties will occur; but by the steady application of that fixed and persevering attention which is alone calculated successfully to contend against and overcome difficulties, every obstacle will vanish, and the practice will prove simple and easy.

That which can create new wealth is of course worth the wealth which it creates. Human labour, whenever common justice shall be done to human beings, can now be applied to produce, advantageously for all ranks in society, many times the amount of wealth that is necessary to support the individual in considerable comfort. Of this new wealth, so created, the labourer who produces it is justly entitled to his fair proportion; and the best interests of every community require that the producer should have a fair and fixed proportion of all the wealth which he creates. This can be assigned to him on no other principle than by forming arrangements by which the *natural* standard of value shall become the *practical* standard of value. To make labour the standard of value it is necessary to ascertain the amount of it in all articles to be bought and sold. This is, in fact, already accomplished, and is denoted by what in commerce is technically termed 'the prime cost', or the new value of the whole labour contained in any article of value, – the material contained in or consumed by the manufacture of the article forming a part of the whole labour.

The great object of society is, to obtain wealth, and to enjoy it.

The genuine principle of barter was, to exchange the supposed prime cost of, or value of labour in, one article, against the prime cost of, or amount of labour contained in any other article. This is the only equitable principle of exchange; but, as inventions increased and human desires multiplied, it was found to be inconvenient in practice. Barter was succeeded by commerce, the principle of which is, to produce or procure every article at the *lowest*, and to obtain for it, in exchange, the *highest* amount of labour. To effect this, an artificial standard of value was necessary; and metals were, by common consent among nations, permitted to perform the office.

This principle, in the process of its operation, has been productive of important advantages, and of very great evils; but, like barter, it has been suited to a certain stage of society.

It has stimulated invention; it has given industry and talent to the human character; and has secured the future exertion of those energies which otherwise might have remained dormant and unknown.

But it has made man ignorantly, individually selfish; placed him in opposition to his fellows; engendered fraud and deceit; blindly urged him forward to create, but deprived him of the wisdom to enjoy. In striving to take advantage of others he has over-reached himself. The strong hand of necessity will now force him into the path which conducts to that wisdom in which he has been so long deficient. He will discover the advantages to be derived from uniting in practice the best parts of the principles of barter and commerce, and dismissing those which experience has proved to be inconvenient and injurious.

This substantial improvement in the progress of society may be easily effected by exchanging all articles with each other at their prime cost, or with reference to the amount of labour in each, which can be equitably ascertained, and by permitting the exchange to be made through a convenient medium to represent this value, and which will thus represent a real and unchanging value, and be issued only as substantial wealth increases.

The profit of production will arise, in all cases, from the value of the labour contained in the article produced, and it will be for the interest of society that this profit should be most ample. Its exact amount will depend upon what, by strict examination, shall be proved to be the present real value of a day's labour; calculated with reference to the amount of wealth, in the necessaries and comforts of life, which an average labourer may, by temperate exertions, be now made to produce.

It would require an accurate and extended consideration of the existing state of society to determine the exact value of the unit or day's labour which society ought now to fix as a standard of value: – but a more slight and general view of the subject is sufficient to show, that this unit need not represent a less value than the wealth contained in the necessaries and comforts of life which may now be purchased with five shillings.

The landholder and capitalist would be benefited by this arrangement in the same degree with the labourer; because labour is the foundation of all values, and it is only from labour, liberally remunerated, that high profits can be paid for agricultural and manufactured products.

Depressed as the value of labour now is, there is no proposition in Euclid more true, than that society would be immediately benefited, in a great variety of ways, to an incalculable extent, by making labour the standard of value.

By this expedient all the markets in the world, which are now virtually closed against offering a profit to the producers of wealth, would be opened to an unlimited extent; and in each individual exchange all the parties interested would be sure to receive ample remuneration for their labour.

Before this change can be carried into effect, various preparatory measures will be necessary; the explanatory details of which will naturally succeed the development of those arrangements which your Reporter has to propose, to give all the advantages to the spade cultivation, of which that system of husbandry is susceptible.

PART III

Details of the Plan

THIS part of the Report naturally divides itself under the following heads, each of which shall be considered separately, and the whole, afterwards, in connexion, as forming an improved practical system for the working classes, highly beneficial, in whatever light it may be viewed, to every part of society.

1st – The number of persons who can be associated to give the greatest advantages to themselves and to the community.

2nd – The extent of the land to be cultivated by such association.

3rd – The arrangements for feeding, lodging, and clothing the population, and for training and educating the children.

4th – Those for forming and superintending the establishments.

5th – The disposal of the surplus produce, and the relation which will subsist between the several establishments.

6th – Their connexion with the government of the country and with general society.

The first object, then, of the political economist, in forming these arrangements, must be, to consider well *under what limitation of numbers, individuals should be associated to form the first nucleus or division of society.*

All his future proceedings will be materially influenced by the decision of this point, which is one of the most difficult problems in the science of political economy. It will affect essentially the future character of individuals, and influence the general proceedings of mankind.

It is, in fact, the cornerstone of the whole fabric of human society. The consequences, immediate and remote, which depend upon it, are so numerous and important, that to do justice to this part of the arrangement alone would require a work of many volumes.

To form anything resembling a rational opinion on this subject, the mind must steadily survey the various effects which have arisen from associations which accident has hitherto combined in the history of the human species; and it should have a distinct idea of the results which other associations are capable of producing.

Thus impressed with the magnitude and importance of the subject, after many years of deep and anxious reflection, and viewing it with reference to an improved spade cultivation, and to all the purposes of society, your Reporter ventures to recommend the formation of such arrangements as will unite about 300 men, women, and children, in their natural proportions, as the *minimum*, and about 2,000 as the *maximum*, for the future associations of the cultivators of the soil, who will be employed also in such additional occupations as may be advantageously annexed to it.

In coming to this conclusion your Reporter never lost sight of that only sure guide to the political economist, the principle, *that is the interest of all men, whatever may be their present artificial station in society, that there should be the largest amount of intrinsically valuable produce created, at the least expense of labour, and in a way the most advantageous to the producers and society.*

Whatever fanciful notions may govern the mere closet theorist, who so often leads the public mind astray from its true course, the practical economist will never come to any one conclusion that is inconsistent with the foregoing fundamental principle of his science, well knowing that where there is inconsistency there *must be* error.

It is with reference to this principle that the minimum and maximum above stated (viz. 300 and 2,000), have been fixed upon, as will be more particularly developed under the subsequent heads.

Within this range more advantages can be given to the individuals and to society, than by the association of any greater or lesser number.

But from 800 to 1,200 will be found the most desirable number to form into agricultural villages; and unless some very strong local causes interfere, the permanent arrangements should be adapted to the complete accommodation of that amount of population only.

Villages of this extent, in the neighbourhood of others, of a similar description, at due distances, will be found capable of combining within themselves all the advantages that city and country residence now afford, without any of the numerous inconveniences and evils which necessarily attach to both those modes of society.

But a very erroneous opinion will be formed of the proposed arrangements and the social advantages which they will exhibit, if it should be imagined from what has been said that they will in any respect resemble any of the present agricultural villages of Europe, or the associated communities in America, except in so far as the latter may be founded *on the principle of united labour, expenditure, and property, and equal privileges.*

Recommending, then, from 300 to 2,000, according to the localities of the farm or village, as the number of persons who should compose the associations for the new system of spade husbandry, we now proceed to consider –

2nd – *The extent of land to be cultivated by such association.*

This will depend upon the quality of the soil and other local considerations.

Great Britain and Ireland, however, do not possess a population nearly sufficient to cultivate our *best* soils in the most advantageous manner. It would therefore be nationally impolitic to place these associations upon *inferior* lands, which, in consequence, may be dismissed from present consideration.

Society, ever misled by closet theorists, has committed almost every kind of error in practice, and in no instance perhaps a greater, than in separating the workman from his food, and making his existence depend upon the labour and uncertain supplies of others, as is the case under our present manufacturing system; and it is a vulgar error to suppose that a single individual more can be supported by means of such a system than without it; on the contrary, a whole population engaged in agriculture, with manufactures as an appendage, will, in a given district, support many more, and in a much higher degree of comfort, than the same district could do with its agricultural separate from its manufacturing population.

Improved arrangements for the working classes will, in almost all cases, place the workman in the midst of his food, which it will be as beneficial for him to create as to consume.

Sufficient land, therefore, will be allotted to these cultivators to enable them to raise an abundant supply of food and the necessaries of life for themselves, and as much additional agricultural produce as the public demands may require from such a portion of the population.

Under a well devised arrangement for the working classes they will all procure for themselves the necessaries and comforts of life in so short a time, and so easily and pleasantly, that the occupation will be experienced to be little more than a recreation, sufficient to keep them in the best health and spirits for rational enjoyment of life.

The surplus produce from the soil will be required only for the higher classes, those who live without manual labour, and those whose nice manual operations will not permit them at any time to be employed in agriculture and gardening.

Of the latter, very few, if any, will be necessary, as mechanism may be made to supersede such operations, which are almost always injurious to health.

Under this view of the subject, the quantity of land which it would be the most beneficial for these associations to cultivate, with reference to their own well-being and the interests of society, will probably be from half an acre to an acre and a half for each individual.

An association, therefore, of 1,200 persons, would require from 600 to 1,800 statute acres, according as it may be intended to be more or less agricultural.

Thus, when it should be thought expedient that the chief surplus products should consist in manufactured commodities, the lesser quantity of land would be sufficient; if a large surplus from the produce of the soil were deemed desirable, the greater quantity would be allotted; and when the localities of the situation should render it expedient for the association to create an equal surplus quantity of each, the medium quantity, or 1,200 acres, would be the most suitable.

It follows that land under the proposed system of husbandry would be divided into farms of from 150 to 3,000 acres, but generally perhaps from 800 to 1,500 acres. This division of the land will be found to be productive of incalculable benefits in practice; it will give all the advantages, without any of the disadvantages of small and large farms.

The next head for consideration is –

3rd – *The arrangement for feeding, lodging, and clothing the population, and for training and educating the children.*

It being always most convenient for the workman to reside near to his employment, the site for the dwellings of the cultivators will be chosen as near to the centre of the land, as water, proper levels, dry situation, etc., etc., may admit; and as courts, alleys, lanes, and streets create many unnecessary inconveniences, are injurious to health, and destructive to almost all the natural comforts of human life, they will be excluded, and a disposition of the buildings free from these objections and greatly more economical will be adopted.

As it will afterwards appear that the food for the whole population can be provided better and cheaper under one general arrangement of cooking, and that the children can be better trained and educated together under the eye of their parents than under any other circumstances, a large square, or rather parallelogram, will be found to combine the greatest advantages in its form for the domestic arrangements of the association.

This form, indeed, affords so many advantages for the comfort of human life, that if great ignorance respecting the means necessary to secure good conduct and happiness among the working classes had not prevailed in all ranks, it must long ago have become universal.

It admits of a most simple, easy, convenient, and economical arrangement for all the purposes required.

The four sides of this figure may be adapted to contain all the private apartments or sleeping and sitting rooms for the adult part of the population; general sleeping apartments for the children while under tuition; store-rooms, or warehouses in which to deposit various products; an inn, or house for the accommodation of strangers; an infirmary; etc., etc.

In a line across the centre of the parallelogram, leaving free space for air and light and easy communication, might be erected the church, or places for worship; the schools; kitchen and apartments for eating; all in the most convenient situation for the whole population, and under the best possible public superintendence, without trouble, expense, or inconvenience to any party.

The advantages of this general domestic arrangement can only be known and appreciated by those who have had great experience in the beneficial results of extensive combinations in improving the condition of the working classes, and whose minds, advancing beyond the petty range of individual party interests, have been calmly directed to consider what may now be attained by a well-devised association of human powers for the benefit of all ranks. It is such individuals only who can detect the present total want of foresight in the conduct of society, and its gross misapplication of the most valuable and abundant means of securing prosperity. They can distinctly perceive that the blind are leading the blind from difficulties to dangers, which they feel to increase at every step.

The parallelogram being found to be the best form in which to dispose the dwelling and chief domestic arrangements for the proposed associations of cultivators, it will be useful now to explain the principles on which those arrangements have been formed.

The first in order, and the most necessary, are those respecting food.

It has been, and still is, a received opinion among theorists in political economy, that man can provide better for himself, and more advantageously for the public, when left to his own individual exertions, opposed to and in competition with his fellows, than when aided by any social arrangement which shall unite his interests individually and generally with society.

This principle of individual interest, opposed as it is perpetually to the public good, is considered, by the most celebrated political economists, to be the corner-stone to the social system, and without which, society could not subsist.

Yet when they shall know themselves, and discover the wonderful effects which combination and union can produce, they will acknowledge that the present arrangement of society is the most anti-social, impolitic, and irrational, that can be devised; that under its influence all the superior and valuable qualities of human nature are repressed from infancy, and that the most unnatural means are used to bring out the most injurious propensities; in short, that the utmost pains are taken to make that which by nature is the most delightful compound for producing excellence and happiness, absurd, imbecile, and wretched.

Such is the conduct now pursued by those who are called the best and wisest of the present generation, although there is not one rational object to be gained by it.

From this principle of individual interest have arisen all the divisions of mankind, the endless errors and mischiefs of class, sect, party, and of national antipathies, creating the angry and malevolent passions, and all the crimes and misery with which the human race have been hitherto afflicted.

In short, if there be one closet doctrine more contrary to truth than another, it is the notion that individual interest, as that term is now understood, is a more advantageous principle on which to found the social system, for the benefit of all, or of any, than the principle of union and mutual cooperation.

The former acts like an immense weight to repress the most valuable faculties and dispositions, and to give a wrong direction to all human powers. It is one of those magnificent errors, (if the expression may be allowed), that when enforced in practice brings ten thousand evils in its train. The principle on which these economists proceed, instead of adding to the wealth of nations or of individuals, is itself the sole cause of poverty; and but for its operation wealth would long ago have ceased to be a subject of contention in any part of the world. If, it may be asked, experience has proved that union, combination and extensive arrangement among mankind, are a thousand times more powerful to destroy, than the efforts of an unconnected multitude, where each acts individually for himself, – would not a similar increased effect be produced by union, combination, and extensive arrangement, to *create and conserve?* Why should not the result be the same in the one case as in the other? But it is well known that a combination of men and of interests can effect that which it would be futile to attempt, and impossible to accomplish, by individual exertions and separate interests. Then why, it may be inquired, have men so long acted individually, and in opposition to each other? This is an important question, and merits the most serious attention.

Men have not yet been trained in principles that will permit them *to act in union*, except to defend themselves or to destroy others. For self-preservation they were early compelled to unite for these purposes in war. A necessity, however, equally powerful will now compel men to be trained to act together to *create and conserve*, that, in like manner, they may preserve life in peace. Fortunately for mankind the system of individual opposing interests has now reached the extreme point of error and inconsistency; – in the midst of the most ample means to create wealth, all are in poverty, or in imminent danger from the effects of poverty upon others.

The reflecting part of mankind have admitted, in theory, that the characters of men are formed chiefly by the circumstances in which they are placed; yet the science of the influence of circumstances, which is the most important of all the sciences, remains unknown for the great practical business of life. When it shall be fully developed it will be discovered that to unite the mental faculties of men for the attainment of pacific and civil objects will be a far more easy task than it has been to combine their physical powers to carry on extensive war-like preparations.

The discovery of the distance and movements of the heavenly bodies, – of the time-piece, – of a vessel to navigate the most distant parts of the ocean, – of the steam-engine, which performs under the easy control of one man the labour of many thousands, – and of the press, by which knowledge and improvement may be speedily given to the most ignorant in all parts of the earth, – these have, indeed, been discoveries of high import to mankind; but, important as these and others have been in their effects on the condition of human society, their combined benefits in practice will fall short of those which will be speedily attained by the new intellectual power which men will acquire through the knowledge of 'the science of the influence of circumstances over the whole conduct, character, and proceedings of the human race'. By this latter discovery more will be accomplished in one year, for the well-being of human nature, including, without any exceptions, all ranks and descriptions of men, than has ever yet been effected in one or in many centuries. Strange as this language may seem to those whose minds have not yet had a glimpse of the real state in which society now is, it will prove to be not more strange than true.

Are not the mental energies of the world at this moment in a state of high effervescence? – Is not society at a stand, incompetent to proceed in its present course? – And do not all men cry out that 'something must be done'? – That 'something', to produce the effect desired, must be a complete renovation of the whole social compact; one not forced on prematurely, by confusion and violence; not one to be brought about by the futile measures of the Radicals, Whigs, or Tories, of Britain, – the Liberals or Royalists of France, – the Illuminati of Germany, or the mere party proceedings of any little local portion of human beings, trained as they have hitherto been in almost every kind of error, and without any true knowledge of themselves.

No! The change sought for must be preceded by the clear development of a great and universal principle which shall unite in one all the petty jarring interests, by which, till now, human nature has been made a most inveterate enemy to itself.

No! Extensive, – nay, rather, universal, – as the rearrangement of society must be, to relieve it from the difficulties with which it is now overwhelmed, it will be effected in peace and quietness, with the goodwill and hearty concurrence of all parties, and of every people. It will necessarily commence by common consent, on account of its advantage, almost simultaneously among all civilized nations; and, once begun, will daily advance with an accelerating ratio, unopposed, and bearing down before it the existing systems of the world. The only astonishment then will be that such systems could so long have existed.

Under the new arrangements which will succeed them, no complaints of any kind will be heard in society. The causes of the evils that exist will become evident to every one, as well as the natural means of easily withdrawing those causes. These, by common consent, will be removed, and the evils, of course, will permanently cease, soon to be known only by description. Should any of the causes of evil be irremovable by the new powers which men are about to acquire, they will then know that they are necessary and unavoidable evils; and childish unavailing complaints will cease to be made. But your Reporter has yet failed to discover any which do not proceed from the errors of the existing system, or which, under the contemplated arrangements are not easily removable.

Of the natural effects of this language and these sentiments upon mankind in general, your Reporter is, perhaps, as fully aware as any individual can be; but he knows that the full development of these truths is absolutely necessary to prepare the public to receive and understand the practical details which he is about to explain, and to comprehend those enlarged measures for the amelioriation of society, which the distress of the times, arising from the errors of the present arrangements, now renders unavoidable. He is not now, however, addressing the common public, but those whose minds have had all the benefit of the knowledge

which society at present affords; and it is from such individuals that he hopes to derive the assistance requisite to
effect the practical good which he has devoted all the powers
and faculties of his mind to obtain for his fellow-creatures.

Your Reporter has stated that this happy change will
be effected through the knowledge which will be derived
from the science of the influence of circumstances over
human nature.

Through this science, new mental powers will be created,
which will place all those circumstances that determine
the misery or happiness of men under the immediate control and direction of the present population of the world,
and will entirely supersede all necessity for *the present truly
irrational system of individual rewards and punishments:*
– a system which has ever been opposed to the most obvious
dictates of common sense and of humanity, and which will
be no longer permitted than while men continue unenlightened and barbarous.

The first rays of knowledge will show, to the meanest
capacity, that all the tendencies of this system are to degrade
men below the ordinary state of animals, and to render
them more miserable and irrational.

The science of the influence of circumstances over human
nature will dispel this ignorance, and will prove how much
more easily men may be trained by other means to become,
without exception, active, kind, and intelligent, – devoid
of those unpleasant and irrational feelings which for ages
have tormented the whole human race.

This science may be truly called one whereby ignorance,
poverty, crime, and misery, may be prevented; and will
indeed open a new era to the human race; one in which real
happiness will commence, and perpetually go on increasing
through every succeeding generation.

And although the characters of all have been formed
under the existing circumstances, which are together un-

favourable to their habits, dispositions, mental acquirements, and happiness, – yet, by the attainment of this new science, those of the present day will be enabled to place themselves, and more especially the rising generation, under circumstances so agreeable to human nature, and so well adapted to all the acknowledged ends of human life, that those objects of anxious desire so ardently sought for through past ages will be secured to everyone with the certainty of a mathematical procedure.

Improbable as this statement must seem to those who have necessarily been formed, by existing circumstances, into the creatures of the place in which they happen to live; which circumstances, to speak correctly, and with the sincerity and honesty which the subject now demands, could not form them into anything but mere local animals; still, even they must be conscious that the time is not long passed when their forefathers would have deemed it far more improbable that the light cloudy mist which they saw arise from boiling water could be so applied, by human agency, that under the easy control of one of themselves it should be made to execute the labour of thousands. Yet, by the aid of mechanical and chemical science, this and many other supposed impossibilities have been made familiar certainties. In like manner, fearful as men may now be to allow themselves to hope that the accumulated evils of ages are not permanent in their nature, probably many now live who will see the science introduced, that, in their days, will rapidly diminish, and, in the latter days of their children, will entirely remove these evils.

It is now time to return to the consideration of the preparatory means by which these important results are to be accomplished.

Your Reporter now uses the term 'preparatory', because the present state of society, *governed by circumstances,* is so different, in its several parts and entire combination, from that which will arise when society shall be taught to *govern circumstances*, that some temporary intermediate arrangements, to serve as a step whereby we may advance from the one to the other, will be necessary.

The long experience which he has had in the practice of the science now about to be introduced has convinced him of the utility, nay, of the absolute necessity, of forming arrangements for a temporary intermediate stage of existence, in which we, who have acquired the wretched habits of the old system, may be permitted, without inconvenience, gradually to part with them, and exchange them for those requisite for the new and improved state of society. Thus will the means be prepared, by which, silently and without contest, all the local errors and prejudices which have kept men and nations strangers to each other and to themselves, will be removed. The habits, dispositions, notions, and consequent feelings, engendered by old society, will be thus allowed, without disturbance of any kind, to die a natural death; but as the character, conduct, and enjoyment of individuals formed under the new system will speedily become living examples of the vast superiority of the one state over the other, the natural death of old society and all that appertains to it, although gradual, will not be lingering. Simple inspection, when both can be seen together, will produce motives sufficiently strong to carry the new arrangements as speedily into execution as practice will admit. The change, even in those who are now the most tenacious supporters of 'things as they are', though left entirely to the influence of their own inclinations, will be so rapid, that they will wonder at themselves.

This intermediate change is the one, the details of which your Reporter has in part explained, and to which he now again begs to direct your attention.

Under the present system there is the most minute division of mental power and manual labour in the individuals

of the working classes; private interests are placed perpetually at variance with the public good; and in every
nation men are purposely trained from infancy to suppose
that their well-being is incompatible with the progress
and prosperity of other nations. Such are the means by
which old society seeks to obtain the desired objects of life.
The details now to be submitted have been devised upon
principles which will lead to an opposite practice; to the
combination of extensive mental and manual powers in the
individuals of the working classes; to a complete identity
of private and public interest; and to the training of nations
to comprehend that their power and happiness cannot
attain their full and natural development but through an
equal increase of the power and happiness of all other states.
These, therefore, are the real points at variance between
that which *is* and that which *ought to be.*

It is upon these principles that arrangements are now
proposed for the new agricultural villages, by which the food
of the inhabitants may be prepared in one establishment,
where they will eat together as one family.

Various objections have been urged against this practice;
but they have come from those only, who, whatever may be
their pretensions in other respects, are mere children in
the knowledge of the principles and economy of social
life.

By such arrangements the members of these new
associations may be supplied with food at far less expense
and with much more comfort than by any individual or
family arrangements; and when the parties have been once
trained and accustomed, as they easily may be, to the former
mode, they will never afterwards feel any inclination to
return to the latter.

If a saving in the quantity of food, – the obtaining of a
superior quality of prepared provisions from the same
materials, – and the operation of preparing them being

effected in much less time, with far less fuel, and with greater ease, comfort, and health, to all the parties employed, – be advantages, these will be obtained in a remarkable manner by the new arrangements proposed.

And if to partake of viands so prepared, served up with every regard to comfort, in clean, spacious, well-lighted, and pleasantly-ventilated apartments, and in the society of well-dressed, well-trained, well-educated, and well-informed associates, possessing the most benevolent dispositions and desirable habits, can give zest and proper enjoyment to meals, then will the inhabitants of the proposed villages experience all this in an eminent degree.

When the new arrangements shall become familiar to the parties, this superior mode of living may be enjoyed at far less expense and with much less trouble than are necessary to procure such meals as the poor are now compelled to eat, surrounded by every object of discomfort and disgust, in the cellars and garrets of the most unhealthy courts, alleys, and lanes, in London, Dublin, and Edinburgh, or Glasgow, Manchester, Leeds, and Birmingham.

Striking, however, as the contrast is in this description, and although the actual practice will far exceed what words can convey, yet there are many closet theorists and inexperienced persons, probably, who still contend for individual arrangements and interests, in preference to that which they cannot comprehend.

These individuals must be left to be convinced by the facts themselves.

We now proceed to describe the interior accommodations of the private lodging-houses, which will occupy three sides of the parallelogram.

As it is of essential importance that there should be abundance of space within the line of the private dwellings, the parallelogram, in all cases, whether the association is intended to be near the maximum or the minimum in

numbers, should be of large dimensions; and to accommodate a greater or less population, the private dwellings
should be of one, two, three, or four stories, and the interior
arrangements formed accordingly.

These will be very simple.

No kitchen will be necessary, as the public arrangements
for cooking will supersede the necessity for any.

The apartments will be always well-ventilated, and, when
necessary, heated or cooled on the improved principles
lately introduced in the Derby Infirmary.

The expense and trouble, to say nothing of the superior
health and comforts which these improvements will give,
will be very greatly less than attach to the present practice.

To heat, cool, and ventilate their apartments, the parties
will have no further trouble than to open or shut two
slides, or valves, in each room, the atmosphere of which, by
this simple contrivance, may always be kept temperate
and pure.

One stove of proper dimensions, judiciously placed, will
supply the apartments of several dwellings, with little
trouble and at a very little expense, when the buildings are
originally adapted for this arrangement.

Thus will all the inconveniences and expense of separate
fires and fire-places, and their appendages, be avoided, as
well as the trouble and disagreeable effects of mending fires
and removing ashes, etc., etc.

Good sleeping apartments looking over the gardens in
the country, and sitting-rooms of proper dimensions
fronting the square, will afford as much lodging-accom-
modation, as, with the other public arrangements, can be
useful to, or desired by, these associated cultivators.

Food and lodging being thus provided for, the next consideration regards dress.

This, too, is a subject, the utility and disadvantages of
which seem to be little understood by the Public generally;

and, in consequence, the most ridiculous and absurd notions and practices have prevailed respecting it.

Most persons take it for granted, without thinking on the subject, that to be warm and healthy it is necessary to cover the body with thick clothing and to exclude the air as much as possible; and first appearances favour this conclusion. Facts, however, prove, that under the same circumstances, those who from infancy have been the most lightly clad, and who, by their form of dress, have been the most exposed to the atmosphere, are much stronger, more active, in better general health, warmer in cold weather, and far less incommoded by heat, than those who from constant habit have been dressed in such description of clothing as excludes the air from their bodies. The more the air is excluded by clothing, although at first the wearer feels warmer by each additional covering he puts on, yet in a few weeks, or months at most, the less capable he becomes of bearing cold than before.

The Romans and the Highlanders of Scotland appear to be the only two nations who adopted a national dress on account of its utility, without however neglecting to render it highly becoming and ornamental. The form of the dress of these nations was calculated first to give strength and manly beauty to the figure, and afterwards to display it to advantage. The time, expense, thought, and labour, now employed to create a variety of dress, the effects of which are to deteriorate the physical powers, and to render the human figure an object of pity and commiseration, are a certain proof of the low state of intellect among all classes in society. The whole of this gross misapplication of the human faculties serves no one useful or rational purpose. On the contrary, it essentially weakens all the physical and mental powers, and is, in all respects, highly pernicious to society.

All other circumstances remaining the same, sexual delicacy and virtue will be found much higher in nations among whom the person, *from its infancy*, is the most exposed, than among those people who exclude from sight every part of the body except the eyes.

Although your Reporter is satisfied that the principle now stated is derived from the unchanging laws of nature, and is true to the utmost extent to which it can be carried; yet mankind must be trained in different habits, dispositions, and sentiments, before they can be permitted to act rationally on this, or almost any other law of nature.

The intermediate stage of society which your Reporter now recommends, admits, however, of judicious practical approximations towards the observance of these laws.

In the present case he recommends that the male children of the new villagers should be clothed in a dress somewhat resembling the Roman and Highland garb, in order that the limbs may be free from ligatures, and the air may circulate over every part of the body, and that they may be trained to become strong, active, well-limbed, and healthy.

And the female should have a well-chosen dress to secure similar important advantages.

The inhabitants of these villages, under the arrangements which your Reporter has in view, may be better dressed, for all the acknowledged purposes of dress, at much less than the one-hundredth part of the labour, inconvenience, and expense, that are now required to clothe the same number of persons in the middle ranks of life; while the form and material of the new dress will be acknowledged to be superior to any of the old.

If your Reporter should be told that all this waste of thought, time, labour, and capital is useful, inasmuch as it affords employment for the working classes; he replies, that no waste of any of these valuable means can be of the slightest benefit to any class; and that it would be far better, if

243

superior occupations cannot be found for human beings, to resort to a Noble Lord's expedient, and direct them to make holes in the earth and fill them up again, repeating the operation without limit, rather than suffer a very large proportion of the working classes to be immured all their lives in unhealthy atmospheres, and toil at wretched employments, merely to render their fellow-creatures weak and absurd, both in body and mind.

The new villages having adopted the best form and material of dress, permanent arrangements will be made to produce it with little trouble or expense to any party; and all further considerations respecting it will give them neither care, thought, nor trouble, for many years, or perhaps centuries.

The advantages of this part of the Plan will prove to be so great in practice that fashions will exist but for a very short period, and then only among the most weak and silly part of the creation.

Your Reporter has now to enter upon the most interesting portion of this division of the subject, and, he may add, the most important part of the economy of human life, with reference to the science of the influence of circumstances over the well-being and happiness of mankind, and to the full power and control which men may now acquire over those circumstances, and by which they may direct them to produce among the human race, with ease and certainty, either universal good or evil.

No one can mistake the application of these terms to the training and education of the children.

Since men began to think and write, much has been thought and written on this subject; and yet all that has been thought and written has failed to make the subject understood, or to disclose the principles on which we should proceed. Even now, the minds of the most enlightened are scarcely prepared to begin to think rationally respecting it.

The circumstances of the times, however, require that a substantial advance should now be made in this part of the economy of human life.

Before any rational plan can be devised for the proper training and education of children, it should be distinctly known what capabilities and qualities infants and children possess, or, in fact, what they really are by nature.

If this knowledge is to be attained, as all human knowledge has been acquired, through the evidence of our senses, then is it evident that infants receive from a source and power over which they have no control, all the natural qualities they possess, and that from birth they are naturally subjected to impressions derived from the circumstances around them; which impressions, combined with their natural qualities (whatever fanciful speculative men may say to the contrary), do truly determine the character of the individual through every period of life.

The knowledge thus acquired will give to men the same kind of control over the combination of the natural powers and faculties of infants, as they now possess over the formation of animals: and although, from the nature of the subject, it must be slow in its progress and limited in extent, yet the time is not perhaps far distant when it may be applied to an important rational purpose, that is, to improve the breed of men, more than men have yet improved the breed of domestic animals.

But, whatever knowledge may be attained to enable man to improve the breed of his progeny at birth, facts exist in endless profusion to prove to every mind capable of reflection, that men may now possess a most extensive control over those circumstances which affect the infant after birth; and that, as far as such circumstances can influence the human character, the day has arrived when the existing generation may so far control them, that the rising generations may become in character, without any individual exceptions, whatever men can now desire them to be, that is not contrary to human nature.

It is with reference to this important consideration that your Reporter, in the forming of these new arrangements, has taken so much pains to exclude every circumstance that could make an evil impression on the infants and children of this new generation.

And he is prepared, when others can follow him, so to combine new circumstances, that real vice, or that conduct which creates evil and misery in society, shall be utterly unknown in these villages, to whatever number they may extend.

Proceeding on these principles, your Reporter recommends arrangements by which the children shall be trained together as though they were literally all of one family.

For this purpose two schools will be required within the interior of the square, with spacious play and exercise grounds.

The schools may be conveniently placed in the line of buildings to be erected across the centre of the parallelograms, in connexion with the church and places of worship.

The first school will be for the infants from two to six years of age. The second for children from six to twelve.

It may be stated, without fear of contradiction from any party who is master of the subject, that the whole success of these arrangements will depend upon the manner in which the infants and children shall be trained and educated in these schools. Men are, and ever will be, what they are and shall be made in infancy and childhood. The apparent exceptions to this law are the effects of the same causes, combined with subsequent impressions, arising from the new circumstances in which the individuals showing these exceptions have been placed.

One of the most general sources of error and of evil to the

world is the notion *that infants, children, and men, are agents governed by a will formed by themselves and fashioned after their own choice.*

It is, however, as evident as any fact can be made to man, that he does not possess the smallest control over the formation of any of his own faculties or powers, or over the peculiar and ever-varying manner in which those powers and faculties, physical and mental, are combined in each individual.

Such being the case, it follows that human nature up to this period has been misunderstood, vilified, and savagely ill-treated; and that, in consequence, the language and conduct of mankind respecting it form a compound of all that is inconsistent and incongruous and most injurious to themselves, from the greatest to the least. All at this moment suffer grievously in consequence of this fundamental error.

To those who possess any knowledge on this subject it is known, that 'man is the creature of circumstances', and that he really is, at every moment of his existence, precisely what the circumstances in which he has been placed, combined with his natural qualities, make him.

Does it then, your Reporter would ask, exhibit any sign of real wisdom to train him as if he were a being who created himself, formed his individual will, and was the author of his own inclinations and propensities?

Surely if men ever become wise – if they ever acquire knowledge enough to know themselves and enjoy a happy existence, it must be from discovering that they are not subjects for praise or blame, reward or punishment; but are beings capable, by proper treatment, of receiving unlimited improvement and knowledge; and, in consequence, of experiencing such uninterrupted enjoyment through this life as will best prepare them for an after-existence.

This view of human nature rests upon facts which no one can disprove. Your Reporter now challenges all those who, from imagined interest, or from the notions which they have been taught to suppose true, are disposed to question its solidity, to point out one of his deductions on this subject which does not immediately follow from a self-evident truth. He is satisfied that the united wisdom of old society will fail in the attempt.

Why, then, may your Reporter be permitted to ask, should any parties tenaciously defend these notions? Are they, although false, in any manner beneficial to man? Does any party, or does a single individual, derive any real advantage from them?

Could your Reporter devise the means effectually to dispel the impressions so powerfully made on the human mind through early life, by the locality of the circumstances of birth and education, he would be enabled thoroughly to convince those who now suppose themselves the chief gainers by the present popular belief on those points and the order of things which proceeds from such belief, that they are themselves *essential* sufferers in consequence, – that they are deceived and deceive others greatly to their own cost. Superior knowledge of the subject will one day convince all that every human being, of every rank or station in life, has suffered and is now suffering a useless and grievous yoke by reason of these fallacies of the imagination.

Your Reporter is well aware that for ages past the great mass of mankind have been so placed as to be compelled to believe that all derived incalculable benefits from them. Yet there is no truth more certain than that these same individuals might have been placed under circumstances which would have enabled them not only to discover the falsehood of these notions, but to see distinctly the innumerable positive evils which they alone have inflicted upon society. While these fallacies of the brain shall be taught and believed by any portion of mankind, *in them* charity and benevolence, in their true sense, can never exist. Such men have imbibed notions that must make them, whatever be their language, haters and opposers of those who contend for the truth in opposition to their errors; nor can men so taught bear to be told that they have been made the mere dupes of the most useless and mischievous fantasies. Their errors, having been generated by circumstances over which they had no control, and for which, consequently, they cannot be blameable, are to be removed only by other circumstances sufficiently powerful to counteract the effects of the former.

From what has been said it is obvious that to produce such a total change among men as the one now contemplated by your Reporter will require the arrangement of new circumstances, that, in each part, and in their entire combinations, shall be so consistent with the known laws of nature, that the most acute mind shall fail to discover the slightest deviation from them.

It is upon these grounds that your Reporter, in educating the rising generation within his influence, has long adopted principles different from those which are usually acted upon.

He considers all children as beings whose dispositions, habits, and sentiments are to be formed *for* them; that these can be well-formed only by excluding all notions of reward, punishment, and emulation; and that, if their characters are not such as they ought to be, the error proceeds from their instructors and the other circumstances which surround them. He knows that principles as certain as those upon which the science of mathematics is founded may be applied to the forming of any given general character, and that by the influence of other circumstances, not a few individuals only, but the whole population of the world, may in a few years be rendered a very far superior race of beings to any now upon the earth, or which has been made known to us by history.

The children in these new schools should be therefore

trained systematically to acquire useful knowledge through the means of sensible signs, by which their powers of reflection and judgement may be habituated to draw accurate conclusions from the facts presented to them. This mode of instruction is founded in nature, and will supersede the present defective and tiresome system of book learning, which is ill-calculated to give either pleasure or instruction to the minds of children. When arrangements founded on these principles shall be judiciously formed and applied to practice, children will, with ease and delight to themselves, acquire more real knowledge in a day, than they have yet attained under the old system in many months. They will not only thus acquire valuable knowledge, but the best habits and dispositions will be at the same time imperceptibly created in every one; and they will be trained to fill every office and to perform every duty that the well-being of their associates and the establishments can require. It is only by education, rightly understood, that communities of men can ever be well governed, and by means of such education every object of human society will be attained with the least labour and the most satisfaction.

It is obvious that training and education must be viewed as intimately connected with the employments of the association. The latter, indeed, will form an essential part of education under these arrangements. Each association, generally speaking, should create for itself a full supply of the usual necessaries, conveniences, and comforts of life.

The dwelling-houses and domestic arrangements being placed as near the centre of the land to be cultivated as circumstances will permit, it is concluded that the most convenient situation for the gardens will be adjoining the houses on the outside of the square; that these should be bounded by the principal roads; and that beyond them, at a sufficient distance to be covered by a plantation, should be placed the workshops and manufactory.

All will take their turn at *some one or more* of the occupations in this department, aided by every improvement that science can afford, alternately with employment in agriculture and gardening.

It has been a popular opinion to recommend a minute division of labour and a division of interests. It will presently appear, however, that this minute division of labour and division of interests are only other terms for poverty, ignorance, waste of every kind, universal opposition throughout society, crime, misery, and great bodily and mental imbecility.

To avoid these evils, which, while they continue, must keep mankind in a most degraded state, each child will receive a general education, early in life, that will fit him for the proper purposes of society, make him the most useful to it, and the most capable of enjoying it.

Before he is twelve years old he may with ease be trained to acquire a correct view of the outline of all the knowledge which men have yet attained.

By this means he will early learn what he is in relation to past ages, to the period in which he lives, to the circumstances in which he is placed, to the individuals around him, and to future events. *He will then only have any pretensions to the name of a rational being.*

His physical powers may be equally enlarged, in a manner as beneficial to himself as to those around him. As his strength increases he will be initiated in the practice of all the leading operations of his community, by which his services, at all times and under all circumstances, will afford a great gain to society beyond the expense of his subsistence; while at the same time he will be in the continual possession of more substantial comforts and real enjoyments than have ever yet appertained to any class in society.

The new wealth which one individual, by comparatively light and always healthy employment, may create under the arrangements now proposed, is indeed incalculable. They would give him giant powers compared with those which the working class or any other now possesses. There would at once be an end of all mere animal machines, who could only follow a plough, or turn a sod, or make some insignificant part of some insignificant manufacture or frivolous article which society could better spare than possess. Instead of the unhealthy pointer of a pin, – header of a nail, – piecer of a thread – or clodhopper, senselessly gazing at the soil or around him, without understanding or rational reflection, there would spring up a working class full of activity and useful knowledge, with habits, information, manners, and dispositions, that would place the lowest in the scale many degrees above the best of any class which has yet been formed by the circumstances of past or present society.

Such are a few only of the advantages which a rational mode of training and education, combined with the other parts of this system, would give to all the individuals within the action of its influence.

The next object of attention is –

4th – *The formation and superintendence of these establishments.*

These new farming and general working arrangements may be formed by one or any number of landed proprietors or large capitalists; by established companies having large funds to expend for benevolent and public objects; by parishes and counties, to relieve themselves from paupers and poor's rates; and by associations of the middle and working classes of farmers, mechanics, and tradesmen, to relieve themselves from the evils of the present system.

As land, capital, and labour, may be applied *to far greater pecuniary advantage* under the proposed arrangements than under any other at present known to the public, all parties will readily unite in carrying them into execution as soon as they shall be so plainly developed in principle as to be generally understood, and as parties who possess sufficient knowledge of the practical details to direct them advantageously can be found or trained to superintend them.

The chief difficulty lies in the latter part of the business. The principles may be made plain to every capacity. They are simple principles of nature, in strict unison with all we see or know from facts to be true. But the practice of everything new, however trifling, requires time and experience to perfect it. It cannot be expected that arrangements which comprehend the whole business of life, and reduce to practice the entire science of political economy, can at once be combined and executed in the best manner. Many errors will be at first committed; and, as in every other attempt by human means to unite a great variety of parts to produce one grand general result, many partial failures may be anticipated.

In all probability in the first experiment many of the parts will be out of due proportion to the whole; and experience will suggest a thousand improvements. No union of minds previously to actual practice can correctly adjust such a multiplicity of movements as will be combined in this new machine, which is to perform so many important offices for society.

A machine it truly is, that will simplify and facilitate, in a very remarkable manner, all the operations of human life, and multiply rational and permanently desirable enjoyments to an extent that cannot be yet calmly contemplated by ordinary minds.

If the invention of various machines has multiplied the power of labour, in several instances, to the apparent advantage of particular individuals, while it has deteriorated the condition of many others, THIS is an invention which will at once multiply the physical and mental powers of the whole society to an incalculable extent, without injuring anyone by its introduction or its most rapid diffusion.

Surely when the power of this extraordinary machine shall be estimated, and the amount of the work shall be ascertained which it will perform for society, some exertions may be made to acquire a knowledge of its practice.

The same class of minds that can be trained to direct any of the usual complicated businesses of life, may be with ease rendered competent to take a part in the management and superintendence of these new establishments.

The principal difficulty will be to set the first establishment in motion; and much care and circumspection will be requisite in bringing each part into action at the proper time, and with the guards and checks which a change from one set of habits to another renders necessary.

Yet, the principles being understood, a man of fair ordinary capacity would superintend such arrangements with more ease than most large commercial or manufacturing establishments are now conducted.

In these there is a continual opposition of various interests and feelings, and extensive principles of counteraction, among the parties themselves, and between the parties and the public.

On the contrary, in the new arrangements each part will give facility to all the others, and unity of interest and design will be seen and felt in every one of the operations. The mental, manual, and scientific movements will all harmonize, and produce with ease results which must appear inexplicable to those who remain ignorant of the principles which governs the proceedings.

In the first instance men must be sought who, in addition to a practical knowledge of gardening, agriculture, manufactures, the ordinary trades, etc., etc., can comprehend the principles on which these associations are formed, and, comprehending them, can feel an interest and a pleasure in putting them into execution. Such individuals may be found; for there is nothing new in the separate parts of the proposed practice – the arrangement alone can be considered new.

When one establishment shall have been formed, there will be no great difficulty in providing superintendents for many other establishments. All the children will be trained to be equal to the care of any of the departments, more particularly as there will be no counteraction between those who direct and those who perform the various operations.

Let the business be at once set about in good earnest, and the obstacles which now seem so formidable will speedily disappear.

The peculiar mode of governing these establishments will depend on the parties who form them.

Those founded by landowners and capitalists, public companies, parishes, or counties, will be under the direction of the individuals whom these powers may appoint to superintend them, and will of course be subject to the rules and regulations laid down by their founders.

Those formed by the middle and working classes, upon a complete reciprocity of interests, should be governed by themselves, upon principles that will *prevent* divisions, opposition of interests, jealousies, or any of the common and vulgar passions which a contention for power is certain to generate. Their affairs should be conducted by a committee, composed of all the members of the association between certain ages – for instance, of those between thirty-five and forty-five, or between forty and fifty. Perhaps the former will unite more of the activity of youth with the experience of age than the latter; but it is of little moment which period of life may be fixed upon. In a short time the ease with which these associations will proceed in all their operations will be such as to render the business of governing a mere recreation; and as the parties who govern will in a few years again become the governed, they must always be conscious that at a future period they will experience the good or evil effects of the measures of their administration.

By this equitable and natural arrangement all the numberless evils of elections and electioneering will be avoided.

As all are to be trained and educated together and without distinction, they will be delightful companions and associates, intimately acquainted with each other's inmost thoughts. There will be no foundation for disguise or deceit of any kind; all will be as open as the hearts and feelings of young children before they are trained (as they necessarily are under the present system), in complicated arts of deception. At the same time their whole conduct will be regulated by a sound and rational discretion and intelligence, such as human beings trained and placed as they have hitherto been will deem it visionary to expect, and impossible to attain, in everyday practice.

The superior advantages which these associations will speedily possess, and the still greater superiority of knowledge which they will readily acquire, will preclude on their parts the smallest desire for what are now called honours and peculiar privileges.

They will have minds so well informed – their power of accurately tracing the cause and effect will be so much increased, that they must clearly perceive that to be raised to one of the privileged orders would be to themselves a serious evil, and to their posterity would certainly occasion an incalculable loss of intellect and enjoyment, equally injurious to themselves and to society.

They will therefore have every motive not to interfere with the honours and privileges of the existing higher orders but to remain well-satisfied with their own station in life.

The only distinction which can be found of the least utility in these associations is that of age or experience. It is the only just and natural distinction; and any other would be inconsistent with the enlarged and superior acquirements of the individuals who would compose these associations. The deference to age or experience will be natural, and readily given; and many advantageous regulations may be formed in consequence, for apportioning the proper employments to the period of life best calculated for them, and diminishing the labour of the individual as age advances beyond the term when the period of governing is concluded.

5th – *The disposal of the surplus produce, and the connexion which will subsist between the several establishments.*

Under the proposed system the facilities of production, the absence of all the counteracting circumstances which so abundantly exist in common society, with the saving of time and waste in all the domestic arrangements, will secure, other circumstances being equal, *a much larger amount of wealth at a greatly reduced expenditure*. The next question is, in what manner is this produce to be disposed of?

Society has been hitherto so constituted that all parties are afraid of being over-reached by others, and, without great care to secure their individual interests, of being deprived of the means of existence. This feeling has created a universal selfishness of the most ignorant nature, for it almost *ensures* the evils which it means to prevent.

These new associations can scarcely be formed before it will be discovered that by the most simple and easy regulations all the natural wants of human nature may be abundantly supplied, and the principle of selfishness (in the sense in which that term is here used) will cease to exist, for want of an adequate motive to produce it.

It will be quite evident to all, that wealth of that kind which will alone be held in any estimation amongst them, may be so easily created to exceed all their wants, that every desire for individual accumulation will be extinguished. To them individual accumulation of wealth will appear as irrational as to bottle up or store water in situations where there is more of this invaluable fluid than all can consume.

With this knowledge, and the feelings which will arise from it, the existing thousand counteractions to the creation of new wealth will also cease, as well as those innumerable motives to deception which now pervade all ranks in society. A principle of equity and justice, openness and fairness, will influence the whole proceedings of these societies. There will, consequently, be no difficulty whatever in the exchange of the products of labour, mental or manual, among themselves. The amount of labour in all products, calculated on the present principle of estimating the prime cost of commodities, will be readily ascertained, and the exchange made accordingly. There will be no inducement to raise or manufacture an inferior article, or to deteriorate, by deceptious practices, any of the necessaries, comforts, or luxuries of life. Everyone will distinctly see it to be the immediate interest of all, that none of these irrational proceedings shall take place; and the best security against their occurrence will be the entire absence of all motives to have recourse to them. As the easy, regular, healthy, rational employment of the individuals forming these societies will create a very large surplus of their own products, beyond what they will have any desire to consume, each may be freely permitted to receive from the general store of the community whatever they may require. This, in practice, will prove to be the greatest economy, and will at once remove all those preconceived insurmountable difficulties that now haunt the minds of those who have been trained in common society, and who necessarily view all things through the distorted medium of their own little circle of local prejudices.

It may be safely predicted that one of these new associations cannot be formed without creating a general desire throughout society to establish others, and that they will rapidly multiply. The same knowledge and principles which unite the interests of the individuals within each establishment, will as effectually lead to the same kind of enlightened union between the different establishments. They will each render to the others the same benefits as are now given, or rather much greater benefits than are now given to each other by the members of the most closely united and affectionate families.

In their original formation they will be established so as to yield the greatest reciprocity of benefits.

The peculiar produce to be raised in each establishment beyond the general supply of the necessaries and comforts of life, which, if possible, will be abundantly created in each, will be adapted to afford the greatest variety of intrinsically valuable objects to exchange with each other; and the particular surplus products which will serve to give energy and pleasure to the industry of the members of each association will be regulated by the nature of the soil and climate and other local capabilities of the situation of each establishment. In all these labour will be the standard of value, and as there will always be a progressive advance in the amount of labour, manual, mental, and scientific, if we suppose population to increase under these arrangements, there will be in the same proportion a perpetually extending market or demand for all the industry of society, whatever may be its extent. Under such arrangements what are technically called 'bad times', can never occur.

These establishments will be provided with granaries and warehouses, which will always contain a supply sufficient to protect the population against the occurrence even of more unfavourable seasons than have ever yet been experienced since agriculture has been general in society. In these granaries and storehouses proper persons will be appointed to receive, examine, deposit, and deliver out again, the wealth of these communities.

Arrangements will be formed to distribute this wealth among the members of the association which created it, and to exchange the surplus for the surplus of the other communities, by general regulations that will render these transactions most simple and easy, to whatever distance these communities may extend.

A paper representative of the value of labour, manufactured on the principle of the new notes of the Bank of England, will serve for every purpose of their domestic commerce or exchanges, and will be issued only for intrinsic value received and in store. It has been mentioned already that all motives to deception will be effectually removed from the minds of the inhabitants of these new villages, and of course forgeries, though not guarded against by this new improvement, would not have any existence among them; and as this representative would be of no use in old society, no injury could come from that quarter.

But these assocations must contribute their fair quota to the exigencies of the state. This consideration leads your Reporter to the next general head, or –

6th – *The connexion of the new establishments with the government of the country and with old society.*

Under this head are to be noticed, the amount and collection of the revenue, and the public or legal duties of the associations in peace and war.

Your Reporter concludes that whatever taxes are paid from land, capital, and labour, under the existing arrangements of society, the same amount for the same proportion of each may be collected with far more ease under those now proposed. The government would of course require its revenue to be paid in the legal circulating medium, to obtain which, the associations would have to dispose of as much of their surplus produce to common society for the legal coin or paper of the realm, as would discharge the demands of government.

In time of peace these associations would give no trouble to government; their internal regulations being founded on principles of prevention, not only with reference to public crimes, but to the private evils and errors which so fatally abound in common society. Courts of law, prisons, and punishments, would not be required. These are requisite only where human nature is greatly misunderstood; where society rests on the demoralizing system of individual competition, rewards, and punishments; – they are necessary only in a stage of existence previous to the discovery of the science of the certain and overwhelming influence of circumstances over the whole character and conduct of mankind. Whatever courts of law, prisons, and punishments have yet effected for society, the influence of other circumstances, which may now be easily introduced, will accomplish infinitely more; for they will effectually prevent the growth of those evils of which our present institutions do not take cognizance till they are already full-formed and in baneful activity. In time of peace, therefore, these associations will save much charge and trouble to government.

In reference to war also, they will be equally beneficial. Bodily exercises, adapted to improve the dispositions and increase the health and strength of the individual, will form part of the training and education of the children. In these exercises they may be instructed to acquire facility in the execution of combined movements, a habit which is calculated to produce regularity and order in time of peace, as well as to aid defensive and offensive operations in war. The children, therefore, at an early age, will acquire, *through their amusements,* those habits which will render them capable of becoming, in a short time, at any future period of life, the best defenders of their country, if necessity should again arise to defend it; since they would in all probability, be far more to be depended upon than those whose physical, intellectual, and moral training had been less carefully conducted. In furnishing their quotas for the militia or common army they would probably adopt the pecuniary alternative; by which means they would form a reserve, that, in proportion to their numbers, would be a great security for the nation's safety. They would prefer this alternative, to avoid the demoralizing effects of recruiting.

But the knowledge of the science of the influence of circumstances over mankind will speedily enable all nations to discover, not only the evils of war, but the folly of it. Of all modes of conduct adopted by mankind to obtain advantages in the present stage of society, this is the most certain to defeat its object. It is, in truth, a system of direct demoralization and of destruction; while it is the highest interest of all individuals and of all countries to *remoralize and conserve*. Men surely cannot with truth be termed rational beings until they shall discover and put in practice the principles which shall enable them to conduct their affairs without war. The arrangements we are considering would speedily show how easily these principles and practices may be introduced into general society.

From what has been stated it is evident that these associations would not subject the government to the same proportion of trouble and expense that an equal population would do in old society; on the contrary, they would relieve the government of the whole burthen; and by the certain and decisive influence of these arrangements upon the character and conduct of the parties, would materially add to the political strength, power, and resources of the country into which they shall be introduced.

Your Reporter having now explained as much of the separate details of the measures which he recommends, to give permanent beneficial employment to the poor, and, consequently, relief to all classes, as this mode of communication in its present stage will admit, now proceeds to take a general view of these parts thus combined into an entire whole; as a practical system purposely devised, from the beginning to the end, to ameliorate materially the condition of human life.

He concludes that the subject thus developed is new both to theorists and to practical men. The former, being ignorant of the means by which extensive arrangements, when founded on correct principles, can be easily carried into execution, will at once, with their usual decision when any new measures at variance with their own theories are proposed, pronounce the whole to be impracticable and undeserving of notice. The others, accustomed to view everything within the limits of some particular pursuit, – of agriculture, or trade, or commerce, or manufactures, or some of the professions, – have their minds so warped in consequence, that they are for the most part incapable of comprehending any general measures in which their peculiar trade or calling constitutes but a small part of the whole. With them the particular art or employment in which each is engaged becomes so magnified to the individual, that, like Aaron's rod, it swallows up all the others; and thus the most petty minds only are formed. This lamentable compression of the human intellect is the certain and necessary consequence of the present division of labour, and of the existing general arrangements of society.

So far, however, from the measures now proposed being impracticable, a longer continuance of the existing arrangements of society will speedily appear to be so; one and all now reiterate the cry that *something must be done*.

Your Reporter begs leave to ask if this 'something', to be effectual for the general relief of all classes, is expected to come from the mere agriculturist, or the tradesman, or the manufacturer, or the merchant, or the lawyer, or the physician, or the divine, or the literary man; – or from radicals, whigs, or tories; – or from any particular religious sect? Have we not before us, as upon an accurately drawn map, most distinctly defined, all the ideas and the utmost bounds within which this exclusive devotion to particular sects, parties, or pursuits, necessarily confines each mind? Can we reasonably expect anything resembling a rational 'something', to relieve the widely extending distress of society, from the microscopic views which the most enlarged of these circles afford? Or, rather, does it not argue the most childish weakness to entertain such futile expectations? It can never be that the universal division of men's pursuits can create any cordial union of interests among mankind. It can never be that a notion which necessarily separates, in a greater or less degree, every human being from his fellows, can ever be productive of practical benefit to society. This notion, as far as our knowledge extends, has ever been forced on the mind of every child, up to this period. Peace, good will, charity, and benevolence, have been preached for centuries past – nay, for thousands of years, yet they nowhere exist; on the contrary, qualities the reverse of these have at all times constituted the character and influenced the conduct of individuals and of notions, and must continue to do so *while the system of individual rewards, punishments, and competition, is permitted to constitute the basis of human society.*

The conduct of mankind may, not unaptly, be compared to that of an individual who, possessing an excellent soil for the purpose, desired to raise grapes, but was ignorant of the plant. Having imbibed a notion, which had taken deep root in his mind, that the thorn was the vine, he planted the former, watered, and cultivated it; but it produced only prickles. He again planted the thorn, varying his mode of cultivation, yet the result was still the same. A third time he planted it, applying now abundance of manure, and bestowing increased care on its cultivation; but, in return, his thorns only produced him prickles stronger and sharper than before. Thus baffled, he blamed the sterility of the ground, and became convinced that human agency alone could never raise grapes from such a soil; – but he had no other. He therefore sought for supernatural assistance, and prayed that the soil might be fertilized.

His hopes being now revived, he again planted the thorn, applied himself with redoubled industry to its culture, and anxiously watched the hourly growth of his plants. He varied their training in every conceivable manner; some he bent in one direction, and some in another; he exposed some to the full light of day, and others he hid in the shade; some were continually watered, and their growth encouraged by richly manured soil. The harvest, looked for with so much interest, at length arrived, but it was again prickles of varied forms and dimensions; and his most sanguine hopes were disappointed.

He now turned his thoughts to other supernatural powers, and from each change he anticipated at least some approximation of the prickle towards the grape. Seeing, however, after every trial, that the thorns which he planted yielded him no fruit, he felt his utmost hope and expectation exhausted. He concluded that the power which created the soil had ordained that it should produce only prickles, and that the grape would one day or other, and in some way or other, be an after production from the seed of the thorn.

Thus, with a perpetual longing for the grape, and with a soil admirably adapted for the cultivation of vines that would produce the most delicious fruit with a thousandth part of the anxiety, expense, and trouble which he had bestowed upon the thorn, he now in a dissatisfied mood endeavoured to calm his feelings, and, if possible, to console himself for the want of present enjoyment, with the contemplation of that distant better fortune which he hoped awaited him.

This is an accurate picture of what human life has hitherto been. Possessing, in human nature, a soil capable of yielding abundantly the product which man most desires, we have, in our ignorance, planted the thorn instead of the vine. The evil principle which has been instilled into all minds from infancy, 'that the character is formed *by* the individual', has produced, and so long as it shall continue to be cherished will ever produce, the same unwelcome harvest of evil passions, – hatred, revenge, and all uncharitableness, and the innumerable crimes and miseries to which they have given birth; for these are the certain and necessary effects of the institutions which have arisen among mankind in consequence of the universally received and long coerced belief in this erroneous principle.

'That the character is formed *for* and not *by* the individual', is a truth to which every fact connected with man's history bears testimony, and of which the evidence of our senses affords us daily and hourly proof. It is also a truth which, when its practical application shall be fully understood, will be of inestimable value to mankind. Let us not, therefore, continue to act as if the reverse of this proposition were true. Let us cease to do violence to human nature; and, having at length discovered the vine, or the good principle, let us henceforward substitute it for the thorn. The knowledge of this principle will necessarily lead to the gradual and peaceful introduction of other institutions and improved arrangements, which will preclude all the existing evils, and permanently secure the well-being and happiness of mankind.

The system, the separate parts of which have been explained in this Report, will lead to this improved condition of society by the least circuitous route that the present degraded state of the human mind and character will admit. But to understand the nature and objects of these several parts the whole attention and powers of the mind must be called into action.

Can the use or value of a time-piece be ascertained from a

knowledge only of the spring, or of some of the separate wheels, or even of all its parts with the exception of one essential to its movements?

If, then, a knowledge of the whole is absolutely requisite before a simple piece of mechanism to mark time can be comprehended, surely it is far more necessary that a system which promises to impart the greatest benefits ever yet offered to mankind should be so thoroughly examined, in its several parts and entire combination, as to be well understood, before any party ventures to decide whether or not it is competent to produce the effects intended.

The result of such an examination will show, *that each part has been devised with reference to a simple general principle*; and that there is a necessary connexion between the several parts, which cannot be disturbed without destroying the use and value of this new mental and physical combination.

It may be further opposed, as every other very great beneficial change in society has been: but what avail the puny efforts which the united ignorance of the world can now make to resist its introduction in this and other countries, when it may be easily proved, by experiment, to be fraught with the highest benefits to every individual of the human race? Even the strong natural prejudices in favour of all old established customs will contend against it but for a time.

There does not exist an individual who, when he shall understand the nature and purport of this system, will anticipate from it the slightest degree of injury to himself, – or rather, who will not perceive that he must derive immediate and incalculable advantages from its introduction. Circumstances far beyond the knowledge or control of those whose minds are confined within the narrow prejudices of class, sect, party, or country, now render this change inevitable; silence will not retard its progress, and opposition will give increased celerity to its movements.

What, then, to sum up the whole in a few words, does your Reporter now propose to his fellow-creatures?

After a life spent in the investigation of the causes of the evils with which society is afflicted, and of the means of removing them, – and being now in possession of facts demonstrating the practicability and the efficacy of the arrangements now exhibited, which have been the fruit of that investigation, aided by a long course of actual experiments, – he offers to exchange their poverty for wealth, their ignorance for knowledge, their anger for kindness, their divisions for union. He offers to effect this change without subjecting a single individual even to temporary inconvenience. No one shall suffer by it for an hour; all shall be essentially benefited within a short period from its introduction; and yet not any part of the existing system shall be prematurely disturbed.

His practical operations will commence with those who are now a burthen to the country for want of employment. He will enable these persons to support themselves and families, and pay the interest of the capital requisite to put their labour in activity. From the effects which will be thus produced on the character and circumstances of this oppressed class, the public will soon see and acknowledge that he has promised far less than will be realized; and when, by these arrangements, the vicious, the idle, and the pauper, shall be made virtuous, industrious, and independent, those who shall be still the lowest in the scale of old society may place themselves under the new arrangements, when they have evidence before them that these offer greater advantages than the old.

Upon this principle the change from the old system to the new will be checked in its progress whenever the latter ceases to afford decided inducements to embrace it; for long established habits and prejudices will continue to have a powerful influence over those who have been trained in them. The change, then, beyond the beneficial employment of those who now cannot obtain work, will proceed solely from proof, in practice, of the very great superiority of the new arrangements over the old. Unlike, therefore, all former great changes, this may be effected without a single evil or inconvenience. It calls for no sacrifice of principle or property to any individual in any rank or condition; through every step of its progress it effects unmixed good only.

Acting on principles merely *approximating* to those of the new system, and at the same time powerfully counteracted by innumerable errors of the old system, he has succeeded in giving to a population originally of the most wretched description, and placed under the most unfavourable circumstances, such habits, feelings, and dispositions, as enable them to enjoy more happiness than is to be found among any other population of the same extent in any part of the world; a degree of happiness, indeed, which it is utterly impossible for the old system to create among any class of persons placed under the most favourable circumstances.

Seeing, therefore, on the one hand, the sufferings which are now experienced, and the increasing discontent which prevails, especially among the most numerous and most useful class of our population, and, on the other, the relief and the extensive benefits which are offered to society on the authority of facts open to inspection, – can the public any longer with decency decline investigation? Can those who profess a sincere desire to improve the condition of the poor and working classes longer refuse to examine a proposal, which, on the most rational grounds, promises them ample relief, accompanied with unmixed good to every other part of society?

Your Reporter solicits no favour from any party; he belongs to none. He merely calls upon those who are the most competent to the task, honestly, as men valuing their own interests and the interests of society, to investigate, without favour or affection, a 'Plan (derived from thirty years' study and practical experience), for relieving public distress and removing discontent, by giving permanent productive employment to the poor and working classes, under arrangements which will essentially improve their character and ameliorate their condition, diminish the expenses of production and consumption, and create markets coextensive with production'.

MORE ABOUT PENGUINS
AND PELICANS

Penguinews, which appears every month, contains details of all the new books issued by Penguins as they are published. From time to time it is supplemented by *Penguins in Print*, which is a complete list of all books published by Penguins which are in print. (There are well over three thousand of these.)

A specimen copy of *Penguinews* will be sent to you free on request, and you can become a subscriber for the price of the postage – 4s. for a year's issues (including the complete lists). Just write to Dept EP, Penguin Books Ltd, Harmondsworth, Middlesex, enclosing a cheque or postal order, and your name will be added to the mailing list.

Some other Pelican classics are listed overleaf.

Note: *Penguinews* and *Penguins in Print* are not available in the U.S.A. or Canada.

Pelican Classics

PAINE: RIGHTS OF MAN

Edited by Henry Collins

Paine's *Rights of Man* (1791/2) enshrines the radical attitude
to politics in its purest form. The causes he champions in this
great classic of democracy – popular rights, national independence, economic growth, revolutionary war, and even social
security – are familiar themes of today, and many of Paine's
teeming ideas have only lately been put into practice.

Also in the Pelican Classics

Bukharin and Preobrazhensky : The ABC of Communism
Edited by E. H. Carr

Burke : Reflections on the Revolution in France
Edited by Conor Cruise O'Brien

Clausewitz: On War
Edited by Anatol Rapoport

Darwin : The Origin of Species
Edited by J. W. Burrow

Halifax : Complete Works
Edited by J. P. Kenyon

Hobbes : Leviathan
Edited by C. B. Macpherson

Hume : A Treatise of Human Nature
Edited by Ernest C. Mossner

J. F. Cooper : The American Democrat
Edited by George Dekker and Larry Johnston

Spencer : The Man Versus the State
Edited by Donald Macrae

Adam Smith: The Wealth of Nations
Edited by Andrew Skinner

Hume : The History of Great Britain (Vol. 1)
Edited by Duncan Forbes